TELEVISION
CRITICISM

*To Paul, spouse, partner, and friend, whose
creativity and scholarship I admire.*

*I also dedicate this book to my granddaughter
Elizabeth Helen Stupp, who brings me so much joy.*

*Finally, I wish to include my two dogs, Argus and
Coco, in this dedication because they lay at
my feet while I wrote this book, patiently
waiting until I finished so we could go
outside and play.*

TELEVISION CRITICISM

VICTORIA O'DONNELL
MONTANA STATE UNIVERSITY

SAGE Publications
Los Angeles • London • New Delhi • Singapore

For information:

Sage Publications, Inc.
2455 Teller Road
Thousand Oaks,
California 91320
E-mail: order@sagepub.com

Sage Publications India Pvt. Ltd.
B 1/I 1 Mohan Cooperative
    Industrial Area
Mathura Road, New Delhi 110 044
India

Sage Publications Ltd.
1 Oliver's Yard
55 City Road
London EC1Y 1SP
United Kingdom

Sage Publications Asia-Pacific Pvt. Ltd.
33 Pekin Street #02-01
Far East Square
Singapore 048763

Printed in the United States of America

Library of Congress Cataloging-in-Publication Data

O'Donnell, Victoria.
Television criticism / Victoria O'Donnell.
    p. cm.
Includes bibliographical references and index.
ISBN-13: 978-1-4129-4166-2 (cloth)
ISBN-13: 978-1-4129-4167-9 (pbk.)
    1. Television criticism. 2. Television criticism—United States. I. Title.

PN1992.8.C7O33 2007
791.45—dc22

                                                        2006032000

Printed on acid-free paper

09   10   11   10   9   8   7   6   5   4   3   2

Acquiring Editor:	Todd R. Armstrong
Editorial Assistant:	Katie Grim
Production Editor:	Sarah K. Quesenberry
Marketing Associate:	Amberlyn M. Erzinger
Copy Editor:	Bill Bowers
Proofreader:	Kevin Gleason
Indexer:	Ellen Slavitz
Typesetter:	C&M Digitals (P) Ltd.
Cover Designer:	Edgar Abarca

Contents

Introduction   xiii

PART I: ORIENTATION

Chapter 1. The Work of the Critic   **3**
   Introduction   3
   The Ends of Criticism   4
   Journalistic Television Criticism   4
   The Critical Stance   6
   Criticism and Culture   8
   Narrative and Contextual Reality   9
   Critical Categories and Critical Choices   13
   The Business of Television   15
   The Familiar and the Unfamiliar in Television   16
   Critical Orientation   17
   Summary   18
   Exercises   19
   Suggested Readings   20

Chapter 2. Demystifying the Business of Television   **21**
   Introduction   21
   The Role of Advertising, Ratings, and Schedules   22
      Advertising   22
      Ratings   22
      Categories of Ratings   24
      Ratings and the Cost of Advertising   25
      The Sweeps   26
      Why Television Shows Get Renewed or Canceled   27
      Shortcomings of the Nielsen Rating System   28
      Ratings in the Summer   28

The Strategies of Television Advertising   29
Product Promotion Within Television Programs   30
Product Placement   30
Scheduling and Advertising   32
Noncommercial Channels   34
The Production of a Television Show   34
Production Houses   34
Pilots and the "Pitch"   35
The Production Team   37
The Producer   37
Writers   38
The Writer's Treatment   40
Directors   41
Casting   42
Putting a Show Into Production   43
Summary   45
Exercises   46
Suggested Readings   48

PART II: FORMAL ASPECTS OF TELEVISION

Chapter 3. Television Style   **51**
Introduction   51
Length of Shot and Framing   52
Multi-Camera Production   54
Reaction Shots   54
Lighting   55
Production on Film Versus Digital Video   56
Style, Reception, and Digital Video Practices   57
Modes of Presentation   59
Television Sound and Editing   60
Production Styles   61
Art Direction   62
The Split Screen   64
Directors   65
Actors   66
Summary   66
Exercises   67
Suggested Readings   68

Chapter 4. Television, the Nation's Storyteller   **69**
Introduction   69
Storytelling and the Human Condition   70

The Nature of Narrative   73
Narrative Theories   74
 Aristotle's Narrative Theory   74
 Propp's Narrative Theory   75
 Barthes's Narrative Theory   75
Narrative Structure   77
Intertextuality   79
Characters   80
Archetypes   83
Myth   85
Structural Analysis of Myth   88
Close Analysis of Narrative Structure   92
Summary   92
Exercises   93
Suggested Readings   94

Chapter 5. Television Genres   **95**
Introduction   95
Television Genre, Production, and Scheduling   97
The Rules for Classifying Genres   97
Genre and Television Criticism   99
Comedy   100
 Situation Comedy   100
 Animated Situation Comedy   110
 Variety Comedy   112
Talk Shows   112
 Nighttime Talk Shows   112
 Daytime Talk Shows   113
 Information Talk Shows   114
News   114
 National and World News   115
 Local News   115
 News-Talk   116
 24-Hour News   117
Magazine Shows   117
 News-Talk-Entertainment   117
 Investigative or Public Affairs   118
 Celebrity News   119
Drama   119
 Crime Shows (Detective, Police, FBI,
  and Forensic Science)   120
 Workplace Drama   121

Family Drama   123
Hybrid Drama   123
Teleplays and Telefilms   124
Docudrama   125
Soap Opera   125
Science Fiction   127
Reality Shows   127
Sports   128
Children's Television   129
Game Shows   129
Other Genres   130
Summary   131
Exercises   132
Suggested Readings   133

**PART III: THEORETICAL APPROACHES
TO TELEVISION CRITICISM**

Chapter 6. Rhetoric and Culture   137
Introduction   137
Rhetoric   138
Classical Rhetoric   140
Rhetoric Over the Ages   141
Intentionality   142
The Symbolic Nature of Rhetoric   142
The Rhetoric of Kenneth Burke   143
Television Rhetoric   145
Rhetoric and Values   147
Cultural Studies   149
British Cultural Studies   151
Power, Ideology, and Hegemony   152
Hall's Encoding/Decoding Model   154
The Codes of Television Production   156
Decoding and Pleasure   158
Summary   159
Exercises   161
Suggested Readings in Rhetoric   162
Suggested Readings in Cultural Studies   162

Chapter 7. Representation and Its Audience   163
Introduction   163
What Is Representation?   164

Television Representation   165
Interpreting Representation   165
Reception of Televisual Images   166
Symbols   168
The Illusion of Reality   168
The Need for Images   169
Representation of the "Other"   170
Advice for Television Critics   174
Representation and Collective Memory   176
Summary   177
Exercises   178
Suggested Readings   180

Chapter 8. Postmodernism   **181**
Introduction   181
The Emergence of New Technologies   182
Postmodernism Defined   183
Postmodern Television   185
MTV   188
  MTV's Influences   *190*
Postmodern Theories   191
Summary   194
Exercises   195
Suggested Readings   196

PART IV: CRITICAL APPLICATIONS

Chapter 9. Guidelines for Television Criticism   **199**
Introduction   199
Critical Orientation   200
Story and Genre   201
Organization   203
  Opening Segment   204
  The Structure of the Program   205
Demographics   205
Context   206
The Look of the Program and Its Codes   207
Analysis   209
Judgment   211
Writing Television Criticism   212
Summary   213

Chapter 10. Sample Criticism of a Television Program:
    CSI: Crime Scene Investigation   **215**
        Introduction   215
        Thesis   215
        Purpose   216
        Description of CSI   216
        Description of the Episode   217
        Production Information   217
        Questions for Analysis   219
        Analysis and Interpretation   221
                Visual Style   221
                Visual Credits   222
                Story and Substance   224
                Hermeneutic Code   226
                Representation   229
                Viewer Involvement   230
        Summary   230
        Suggested Readings   231

References   233

Index   247

About the Author   261

Acknowledgments

Sara Miller McCune, former president of Sage Publications, encouraged me to write this book a long time ago. Margaret Seawell, former editor at Sage Publications, patiently waited for me to finish it. Todd Armstrong, current editor at Sage, saw me through the book's completion with many helpful suggestions. Professors Barbara Baker of Central Missouri State University and Peter Lev of Towson State University offered many valuable recommendations in their reviews of my manuscript. Sarah Quesenberry, production editor at Sage Publications, has been a jewel. She received and assembled the parts of this book, kept me up to date on its progress, was always timely in responding to my questions, and she generously acquired the photos for this book. Bill Bowers was the copyeditor. I wish to express my sincere gratitude to all of you.

This book could not have been written without the hundreds of students who took my film and television criticism classes and who wrote graduate theses and dissertations about film and television under my direction. They were a joy to teach and to join in discussions about films and television programs. It pleases me so much that many of them still stay in touch with me.

I also wish to thank my friends Patricia Hill, camera operator for *M*A*S*H, Cheers, Frasier, Caroline in the City,* and *The New Adventures of Old Christine,* and Jeff Meyer, director for *Coach, Everybody Loves Raymond* and *Yes, Dear,* for introducing me to their writers, directors, and producers and for letting me sit in on television program run-throughs and taping. They also provided very useful information about the television business. I am also grateful to the directors at the Museum of Television and Radio, who allowed me to spend many hours in both their locations, New York City and Beverly Hills, viewing tapes of their television seminars with professionals.

I have dedicated this book to Paul Monaco, but I also wish to acknowledge his valuable contribution to it. He coauthored Chapter 3, "Television Style," which reflects his professional experiences as a film and video creator and educator.

Introduction

Television presents the new American Dream.

—Ron Howard on *Today*,
24 March 1999

Years ago, when my youngest son came home from a day at the Montessori kindergarten, he watched late-afternoon television shows. I discussed this with his teacher who said not to worry. "He does stimulating activities in school, so when he comes home, he just wants to relax by watching television," she said. Of course, we all use television to relax. We laugh at the comedies and watch crimes get solved. Even shows that would not seem to be relaxing, such as the grisly *CSI: Crime Scene Investigation*, comfort us because we see good triumphing over evil. We can enjoy vicarious experiences by watching reality shows, see how other people live on the talk shows, find out what is news, check the weather, and keep up with sports on the news shows and channels, stay informed through public affairs programs, and get new recipes on the food channels. When a national or world crisis occurs, we are more likely to turn on the television. A survey conducted by the Pew Internet and American Life Project and *Federal Computer Week* magazine one year after the September 11, 2001 attacks on the World Trade Center in New York City found that 57 percent of Americans said they would go to their television sets to get information first (AP, 2003, p. A7). Another survey conducted four days after 9/11 found that Americans watched an average of 8.1 hours of television coverage of the disaster (Vedantam, 2001). Television is not only a very important part of our life, it has the power to change our lives. Haynes Johnson, a Pulitzer Prize–winning journalist for *The Washington Post*, said in a speech at the Annenberg School of the University of Pennsylvania in 1993:

From the fall of the Soviet Union to Tiananmen Square, the umbilical cord of television, those electronic impulses, actually moved and changed history. It was no one person who led it. It was no Genghis Khan, no Caesar, no Roman Legion, but television that really propelled all those events. ("Haynes Johnson delivers the Annenberg lecture", 1994, p. 5)

Most of you who read this book have never known a life without television. Television sets are turned on for several hours in more than one room in our homes, and they are turned on all day long in malls, fitness clubs, university student unions, bars, restaurants, airports, schools, department stores, and appliance stores. We can receive television on our cellular phones, wristwatches, and computers. Television producers envision shooting more close-ups to accommodate smaller screens. The Fox network developed "mobisodes," customized mini-programs for cell phones to promote television series (McDowell & Ressner, 2006). Video images are featured in rock concerts and fashion shows. Banks have television sets turned on for customers waiting in line to see a teller; hotels put television sets in bathrooms and elevators; dentists are using high-tech headsets that let patients tune to a channel while having their teeth drilled; doctors have the Better Health Network playing in waiting rooms; veterinarians have Animal Planet turned on for clients in the waiting rooms; and many public schools start the day with Channel One, a teen news network with an abundance of athletic shoe and food commercials. Television sets in airports have a special "drown-out" volume control. If people sitting near the set are talking, the volume automatically rises. Paul Farhi wrote in *The Washington Post,* "Like an invisible gas, television's flickering light . . . has seeped into nooks and crannies that once were blissfully TV-free" (Farhi, 1997, p. 21).

In 1971, when there were three broadcast networks and cable and satellite television were less widespread, the average American household had the set on for slightly more than six hours a day (Farhi, 1997). With multiple television sets in households and hundreds of channels to choose from, different family members may be watching preferred programs individually rather than together. The more choices we have, the more likely we are to diverge in our preferences.

Cable television and satellite transmission deliver hundreds of channels to viewers. Remote control devices make rapid channel switching, known as "surfing" or "grazing," a norm for many viewers whose desire for television images cannot be satisfied by one channel at a time. Some television sets have second windows to allow a viewer to watch a drama while keeping one eye on the football game. High-definition television (HDTV) provides images so sharp that watching the television screen is like looking out a window and is capable of showing four different channels on equal-sized windows on one screen. The Internet enables us not only to watch television news and features, but also, with devices like Slingbox, to watch our favorite television programs or sports events on our laptop computers and cell phones. In addition, the public watches more movies than ever before on rented and purchased DVDs.

Technological advancement has perpetuated the mass production of television images. Historian Asa Briggs said that this basic technological revolution is comparable to the Industrial Revolution and to other times of radical change in human history ". . . that involved the mind as well as the body" (Haigh, Gerbner, & Byrne, 1981, p. 208). With the information highways of the 21st century and audiovisual innovations for computers, Briggs's analogy seems even more compelling today than when he wrote it in 1981. Let us stop to consider what concerned Briggs when he wrote: "In a world of pictures, we have not learned the simple ABCs of interpretation and criticism" (Haigh, Gerbner, & Byrne, 1981, p. 208).

Television images are mediated by television production techniques, by the medium itself, and by the constraints of programming decisions. As Nick Browne said, "Television must be studied in terms of the institution that provides it, the advertising that drives it, and the audience that consumes it" (Browne, 1994, p. 69). Pay-per-view and DVD and video rentals give us the opportunity to watch recent and older television series and films. DVD recorders, VCRs, and DVRs allow us to record our favorite programs when we are not at home and to avoid the commercials when we watch recorded programs. These devices have changed the way people watch television—formerly, most people were passive *viewers,* but now they have become active *users* (Bellamy & Walker, 1996). Because people can encounter a variety of programs, watch more than one program at a time, and avoid content they do not want to see, such as commercials, advertisers have been encouraged to try adaptation and corrective strategies to assure their clients that their products are seen. For example, there has been an increase in the 15-second spot, based on the assumption that a shorter commercial would not allow the viewer enough time to zap it. Another strategy incorporated into the shorter spot attempts to simulate grazing or surfing by placing plentiful images and rapid editing of the commercials. Product placement (common in motion pictures), infomercials, and integration of the product and program are other strategies. The cast of *Friends* appeared in a series of Diet Coke ads written by the program's writing staff. As television changes, so does advertising.

The word "television" literally means seeing at a distance. As Joshua Meyrowitz (1985) reminded us, we respond to media images as if we were seeing something firsthand. Physical presence no longer seems required for firsthand experience. The obsessively repeated images of the two airplanes flying into the Twin Towers of the World Trade Center, the explosion of the space shuttle *Challenger,* and the videotaped beatings of Rodney King and Reginald Denny in Los Angeles are examples that provoked "firsthand" reactions from a shocked public in a manner similar to the firsthand reactions of a shocked and grieving public to the assassination of President John F. Kennedy on November 22, 1963. Each of these instances was not fictional, yet they were mediated with camera work and editing decisions as fictional representation is on television.

Yet the quantity of television programs and varying opportunities in the ways we watch them does not make us better viewers. With more to choose from, it would seem that we could use some help in order to become more discriminating viewers. This book has been written to help you become a serious watcher of television, for as Alexander Nehamas (1990) wrote in *The South Atlantic Quarterly*: "Television rewards serious watching." A serious television watcher with critical acumen recognizes that criticism employs theoretical and critical standards, and that television is a business that employs talented professionals, who also take television seriously.

Figure 1 represents my model of the elements of television that critics should consider.

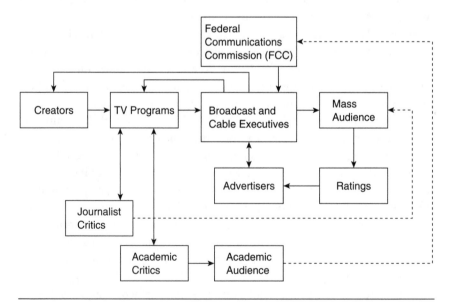

Figure 1   O'Donnell Model of the Elements of Television

The United States Federal Communications Commission (FCC)—created by an act of Congress on June 19, 1934—regulates broadcasting. The **FCC** has the authority to fine television stations for violating decency standards. It has been cracking down on television for decency violations since Janet Jackson bared her breast during the Super Bowl halftime show in 2004. The obscenity and indecency standards apply to over-the-air broadcasters, but not to cable and satellite programming. Sanctions have been leveled against Fox, NBC, and CBS stations or affiliates for violations. This is controversial because it is not altogether clear how much protection television enjoys from the Constitution's First Amendment, which guarantees free speech (Federal Communications Commission, 2006).

The **creators** are the writers, producers, artistic directors, directors, costumers, actors, editors, camera operators, sound and music directors, animators, and special effects staff who develop the **television programs**, the finished products. Their creative work and the ways in which a television show is initiated and produced are discussed in Chapter 2, "Demystifying the Business of Television" and in Chapter 3, "Television Style." The producers pitch their programs to the **broadcast and cable channel executives**. The broadcast and cable channel executives are the administrators of the television networks and cable companies, both at the national and local levels. They are very powerful and determine what goes on and stays on the air and on what days and at which times a program is aired. **Advertising** pays for the broadcast channels, while viewer subscriptions support cable and satellite programming. The **mass audience** is numbered in the millions and is measured by **ratings**, which, in turn, determine whether a program is successful or not. This is discussed in Chapter 2. **Journalist critics** write for newspapers and the Internet. They tend to give plot summaries and discuss the pros and cons of story, visual style, and acting. **Academic critics**, which is what you will become, write for an **academic audience** utilizing the theoretical and critical standards discussed in this book. Chapter 1, "The Work of the Critic," discusses the nature of criticism, both journalistic and academic. It offers a critical orientation that will help you determine what and how you will criticize.

This book is divided into four parts: Part I orients you to the work of the critic and the business of television. Part II is about the formal aspects of television, its style, its position as the nation's storyteller, and the classification system known as television genre. Part III will introduce you to the major theoretical approaches to television criticism, rhetoric, cultural studies, representation, and postmodernism. Part IV includes the critical applications, with guidelines for television criticism and a sample criticism of a television show, *CSI: Crime Scene Investigation*.

PART I

Orientation

1

The Work of the Critic

Oh, gentle lady, do not put me to't. For I am nothing if not critical.

—William Shakespeare, Iago to
Desdemona, *Othello*, Act 2, Scene I

Introduction

What is the advantage of knowing how to perform television criticism if you are not going to be a professional television critic? The advantage to you as a television viewer is that you will not only be able to make **informed judgment** about the television programs you watch, but also you will better understand your reaction and the reactions of others who share the experience of watching. Critical acuity enables you to move from casual enjoyment of a television program to a fuller and richer understanding. A viewer who does not possess critical viewing skills may enjoy watching a television program and experience various responses to it, such as laughter, relief, fright, shock, tension, or relaxation. These are fundamental sensations that people may get from watching television, and, for the most part, viewers who are not critics remain at this level. Critical awareness, however, enables you to move to a higher level that illuminates production practices and enhances your understanding of culture, human nature, and interpretation.

Students studying television production with ambitions to write, direct, edit, produce, and/or become camera operators will find knowledge of television criticism necessary and useful as well. Television criticism is about the evaluation of content, its context, organization, story and characterization, style, genre, and audience desire. Knowledge of these concepts is the foundation of successful production.

The Ends of Criticism

Just as critics of books evaluate works of fiction and nonfiction by holding them to established standards, television critics utilize methodology and theory to comprehend, analyze, interpret, and evaluate television programs. As a critic, you can gain greater understanding and appreciation about television programming, as well as about your own culture and the social forces within it. You may also be able to demystify the meaning of a television program and create new perceptions for other viewers by communicating the criticism to them. As a critic, you become a "transformer" capable of generating new understanding and new awareness in the minds of other television viewers. Your comprehension of the importance of producing, writing, directing, camera work, sound, sets, costumes, and other production values opens up your understanding and appreciation of the aesthetic pleasures of good television and provides specific reasons for the displeasure caused by what some regard as poor television. As a critic, you will engage with the essential organization of television programs, context, time-space manipulation, the use of images and language, conventions and variations of genre, narrative patterns, character development, and the episodic nature of television. You will also examine social and cultural values, ideology, possible meanings, codes, and the representation of gender, race, sexuality, age, ethnicity, employment, and nationality. As a critic, you must also understand the nature of the business of television and the viewing audience, its expectations, desires, participation, and satisfaction. Criticism also goes beyond understanding of the program itself and asks what conceptual or theoretical implications have resulted.

Journalistic Television Criticism

Journalists began writing television criticism in 1946, when Jack Gould of *The New York Times* and John Crosby of the *New York Herald Tribune* began reviewing television program content. From that time and into the 1950s, television critics had to wait to see the programs when they were aired in order to write about them because television was broadcast live. After more television programs were made on film, beginning with *I Love*

Lucy, critics could preview the shows and have their columns published before the shows were on the air. The critics' reviews were influential because television executives and producers monitored their evaluations of programs; thus the importance of professional television criticism increased. Yet, the programs that the critics praised—e.g., *Studio One,* which broadcast modern plays and adaptations of Shakespeare, and *Playhouse 90,* a televised anthology of 90-minute original and adapted plays—were often not as well liked by the public, which appeared to prefer the classic sitcoms, such as *The Honeymooners* with Jackie Gleason, Art Carney, Audrey Meadows, and Joyce Randolph and *I Love Lucy* with Lucille Ball and Desi Arnaz. In later years, print television criticism became less important as an influence on program decision making, although government agency personnel read television criticism in trade publications in order to examine responses to possible government policies.

Today there is a plethora of television criticism in newspapers, magazines, and on the World Wide Web. The TV Barn Web site (http://blogs.kansas city.com/tvbarn/) includes the Crixlist, links to the professional critics from A to Z. Major newspapers, such as *The New York Times* and *Los Angeles Times,* employ several television critics. The "criticisms" typically range from mere listings of current programs and their broadcast times to descriptive vignettes of upcoming programs. However, critics such as Tom Shales of *The Washington Post,* Robert Bianco of *USA Today,* and Howard Rosenberg of the *Los Angeles Times* write about television's style and taste and "prod TV's creators and distributors to reflect on larger aesthetic and social implications of their lucrative, but ephemeral, occupations" (Brown in Newcomb, 1997). As James A. Brown explains in Newcomb's *Encyclopedia of Television,* journalistic television criticism is part of the publisher's larger purpose to gain readers for the newspaper or magazine, thus it

> . . . puts a premium on relevance, clarity, brevity, cleverness, and attractive style. The TV column is meant to attract readers primarily by entertaining them, while also informing them about how the system works . . . The critic serves as a guide, offering standards of criteria for judgment along with factual data, so readers can make up their own minds . . . The critic-reviewer's role grows in usefulness as video channels proliferate; viewers inundated by dozens of cable and over-air channels can ensure optimum use of leisure viewing time by following critics' tips about what is worth tuning in and what to avoid. (Brown in Newcomb, 1997, p. 1643)

Brown lists the criteria for good journalistic television criticism as "sensitivity and reasoned judgment, a renaissance knowledge coupled with exposure to a broad range of art, culture, technology, business, law, economics, ethics, and social studies all fused with an incisive writing style causing commentary to leap off the page into the reader's consciousness" (Brown in Newcomb, 1997, pp. 1643–1644). These criteria would serve the academic television critic well, but they are general and have no specific reference to standards of judgment and methodology.

The Critical Stance

The word "criticism" tends to have a negative connotation because we often associate it with finding something wrong with objects and people. If a person finds fault with something or someone, we are likely to say, "He or she is too critical." If your parents do not like your hairstyle or the way you dress, you might say, "Don't criticize me so much."

Yet we define criticism differently when we check the newspaper or a Web site to find out what a television or film critic wrote about a television show or film before deciding what to watch. In this context, the critic usually writes about the quality of a television show or film—the story, the acting, the visual and sound aspects, and special effects. A critic may praise or pan a television program or film, thus telling the reader what is good and/or bad about it. For several years, I wrote film criticism in the local newspaper for the Bozeman Film Festival. If I thought a film had good qualities, I would urge my readers to be sure to see it. Sometimes filmgoers would disagree with my judgment, telling me, "I did not like the film." Others would thank me for alerting them about a film they might not otherwise have gone to see had they not read my review. This illustrates two points: (1) criticism is subjective; and (2) criticism can be persuasive.

1. *Criticism is subjective:* We bring to criticism our life experiences, our beliefs, attitudes, and values. Thus we observe the critical object through our own perceptual filters. Perception is the process of extracting information from the world outside us as well as from within ourselves. Each individual has a perceptual field that is unique to that person and shaped by many influences, and this field forms the filters through which we perceive (O'Donnell & Kable, 1982). Our perceptions are based on our values, beliefs, attitudes, and experiences. Thus, as a critic, you are likely to have a perspective that includes biases and past experiences. You are also apt to select certain parts of a program to criticize. Thus, in addition to being subjective, criticism is also partial. Because most dramas and comedies on television are episodic, it is not likely that you would take on an entire season of a series to criticize unless you were writing a doctoral dissertation or a

book about a series. The usual selection is a single episode, although you are advised to be aware of the other episodes in a series. A television program is not a reality that can be examined or proven in a completely objective manner. Therefore, you should not be concerned with finding the single correct interpretation, for there may be many possible ones. There may be a dominant meaning inscribed within the script, but different viewers can give alternative or multiple meanings to the same script. A television performance is potentially open to alternative interpretations. However, a competent critic who applies systematic analysis based on sound principles is not only more likely to evaluate fairly but also to illuminate. Readers of good criticism may have their appreciation of the critical object enhanced and thus may be moved to watch it.

2. *Criticism can be persuasive*: A television critic often functions as an advocate on behalf of a program or even a network, urging viewers to tune in to it. Further, a critic may construct a persuasive argument, offering good reasons and evidence to support the evaluation of a program. Criticism is capable not only of affecting our choices to watch a television program, but, more important, it can alter our perceptions, enabling us to see and hear more details, to anticipate certain moments, to ponder certain questions, and to recognize special qualities. Most students who take film and television criticism courses tell me that they see so much more than they did before taking the course and, furthermore, they are eager to talk about what they see. On the other hand, their friends, who have not studied critical methodologies, report that they do not like to watch films or television with their critic friends because they interpret too much and then talk about it during the screening.

Since television is so pervasive and—along with the Internet—is the most significant form of communication in the world, it is important to be sensitive to and understand what is communicated. Television is a cultural mirror, but it is also a two-way mirror in that it not only reflects our culture but also illuminates and influences how we see ourselves and others. Social science researchers have produced hundreds of studies regarding the influence of television on viewers. Whether viewers' behavior and/or attitudes are changed is not the primary concern of the television critic; however, the critic is an important observer of the content of television programs who can help us understand why such influence may occur.

Cultivation studies claim that people view the world as more violent than it actually is, causing them to be fearful, insecure, and dependent on authority as the result of seeing violence on television. The researchers concluded after their long-range study of heavy television viewing that "one correlate of television viewing is a heightened and unequal sense of danger and risk in a mean and selfish world" (Gerbner, Gross, Signorellli, Morgan, & Jackson-Beeck, 1979, p. 191). A television critic can note that, while the depiction of actual physical violence may be declining in current television programming, characters dealing with the consequences of violence seem to be a more recent trend on shows such as *Law & Order, Law & Order SVU, Law & Order Criminal Intent, NYPD Blue, CSI: Crime Scene Investigation, CSI: Miami, CSI: New York,* and *Numb3rs.*

Fashions, body image, and hairstyles are also copied from actors on television. Critics can note that imitations occur from show to show or appear in magazines and other publications. Subtle attitudes toward gender, race, and occupation as represented on television may or may not shape or reshape viewers' perceptions of reality, but you as a critic can observe changes in television programming itself. Cultural studies researchers use audience-response studies, wherein viewers are interviewed in depth, to determine how television programs affect viewers (Morley, 1988). Television situation comedies, such as *The Cosby Show* and *Will & Grace,* may have made programs with African Americans or gays in leading roles more acceptable to the viewing public, but probably did not resolve the actual tensions experienced by the general public concerning racial issues or homosexuality (Dow, 2001). Television viewers tend to make what they watch fit their own lives and experiences; therefore, the television critic can note other aspects of these programs. For example, according to John Marcus, writer for *The Cosby Show,* Bill Cosby insisted that the parents on the show be smarter than their children and that the characters' behavior be true to real-life behavior. The viewers would therefore comfortably identify with Cosby as a parent but not necessarily with his race. Since audience identification with television characters is a major key to audience enjoyment, approval or disapproval of controversial issues may not be the most important factor.

Criticism and Culture

Television programs reflect a society's values, norms, and practices as well as its fads, interests, and trends. Because of this your awareness and understanding of your own society give you insight into the meanings generated in television's fictional stories, coverage of real-life stories, and other types of programming. Here you must use your own interpretative resources to make inferences about social relationships and configurations of value. Television programming, its structure, timing, and commercialism appropriate the structure and priorities of society, the distribution of goods and power, values and motives for behavior, and systems of reward and punishment. Its focus is tempocentric; that is, the time we live in is the most important time. Although television programs reflect the nation's cultural pluralism and may present a multiplicity of meanings, television programming, in general, reflects majority preferences because its commerce needs to appeal to the largest possible target audience. One can even say that television not only reflects culture, but that it also creates culture. As David Marc pointed out:

> Culture today is produced and distributed by a very few corporations, which, through their many divisions and subsidiaries, make decisions about what culture all members of society will consume, from the top of the social ladder to the bottom . . . The success of the system is dependent on its ability to persuade the public to collaborate with it in the creation of a social product. (Marc, 1995, pp. 53 & 56)

While the networks such as ABC, CBS, Fox, and NBC try to appeal to viewers between 18 and 49 years old, cable stations such as MTV, Lifetime, Fox Reality, Food Network, Disney, Discovery, Animal Planet, and Sci-Fi appeal to very specific interests. This is known as "brand identity" because specific channels appeal to target audiences. For example, Lifetime appeals to adult women with stories featuring heroines and villainesses and their relationships, while FX has introduced charismatic but deeply flawed men in various professions (plastic surgery, firefighting, police work). This specificity, too, may be a reflection of culture in that it suggests that we live in an era of individualized culture, what Walt Whitman characterized as an America of "contradictory multitudes." We have so many choices—and we have television sets in different rooms as well as television reception on computers and telephones—that each member of a family can watch selected channels according to individual interests.

Because television programming is a reasonably good mirror of American culture, television criticism can go beyond description and evaluation of a television program or series to a level of deeper cultural diagnosis.

Narrative and Contextual Reality

Several television programs represent actual news events in fictional stories. In this way, television echoes real-life drama and reinforces its credibility by presenting familiar and true-to-life stories that appeal to viewers' interests. When the fictional Tony Soprano had legal troubles on an episode of *The Sopranos,* his cohorts compared his problems with the legal woes of the real-life Joseph "Big Joey" Massino, the Mafia mob boss accused of murder in New York. Three other programs, two of which were season finales in 2001, had stories about school shootings, reflecting the real-life horror of school violence and students being gunned down by their classmates or outsiders. *ER*'s May 17, 2001 finale was about the doctors and nurses trying to save gunshot victims after an angry father shot them at a foster care facility. *Third Watch*'s May 21st finale had police and paramedics rushing to the scene of a high school massacre. *Law & Order*'s next-to-last episode in the 2000–2001 season on May 16 was about a school shooting in which four high school students were killed and eight were seriously wounded, but the shooter did not turn the gun on himself. Instead, the police had to track down the likely suspects. After questioning two innocent suspects, the detectives found the killer, a 16-year-old son of wealthy parents. The boy, who had been teased by his classmates, said the shooting was his revenge. The prosecutors insisted on trying him as an adult, which raised another sensitive issue from real-life news stories. Both sides of the question (whether or not to try a 16-year-old as an adult) were represented on the show. The boy's parents naturally opposed it, but the prosecuting attorneys were not in complete agreement either; thus audience members were left to choose their own positions on the issue. One of the prosecutors, Abby Carmichael (Angie Harmon), took a rigid stance in favor of trying the shooter as an adult and was incensed that he got away with the crime. The other prosecutor, Jack McCoy (Sam Waterston), was more indecisive on the issue. Each of these positions represents the true-to-life controversy wherein some teen offenders are tried as adults and some are not. Because the police had obtained their information from the school psychologist, it was deemed privileged information and therefore inadmissible. Also, because the police failed to get a court order to search the boy's home, the charges against the boy were dismissed. When the prosecutors told the parents of the students who were shot that the case had been dismissed on a technicality, the parents were outraged. When one of the parents said that some students knew before the shooting that it was going to happen, the police followed up, locating a boy who had videotaped the incident because he had received a phone call the previous night from another boy, who told him that something bad was going to happen. Subsequently, he brought his video camera to school. Under pressure, he gave up the informant's name, who, when interviewed by the detectives, said that he, like the shooter, had been mercilessly teased. "You don't know what it's like," he said. Finally, the father of the boy who shot the students in the school cafeteria agreed to testify in court, in a new trial, that his son had confessed to him. That was enough for the jury to convict him of second-degree murder and send him to prison. As the bailiff led him out of the courtroom, the boy plaintively called to his father, "Daddy." The program revealed not only the complex legal and psychological issues, but it also vividly portrayed how tragic the consequences of the shooting were for everyone concerned.

Barry Schindel, executive producer and head writer of *Law & Order,* said that the program is

> . . . a show that has a long history of looking at the criminal justice system as it occurs. If we didn't do the show, people would be asking, "Why aren't your characters considering the events of a school shooting?" . . . TV is reflecting what's going on in society. Just when you think you've seen it all, you've seen something else. (Reuters, 2001)

Robert Thompson, director of Syracuse University's Center for Popular Television, said of these stories that reflect the news: "It's gripping and disturbing. Television is kind of the way that the entire collective subconscious of our culture plays out these issues" (Reuters, 2001).

The search for causation in high school violence has revealed that teasing may be a factor. Both *Law & Order SVU* (a spin-off of *Law & Order* about victims of sexual crimes) and *Without a Trace* (a program about missing persons originally inspired by the real-life missing person, Chandra Levy) featured episodes in 2004 about high school students teasing their classmates. *Law & Order SVU* had a story about an overweight girl who is driven to murder one of the popular students because she could not take her classmates' ridicule anymore. An unpopular high school boy who disappeared in an episode of *Without a Trace* had been tied up in a horse stall, stripped, and covered with filth by a group of popular girls who took a picture of him and put it on the Internet. When he was returned to his home, he begged his parents to let him transfer to another school. Both of these programs gave viewers a glimpse into real-life problems.

An episode of *Law & Order SVU* in late fall 2005 dealt with three orphans from Hurricane Katrina (which had hit the southern United States a few months before the show aired) who were kidnapped by a child molester whose possession of anthrax is exposed by a newspaper reporter who goes to jail rather than reveal his source. In just one show, four headlines were put together; certainly this was a bit of overkill.

CSI: Crime Scene Investigation and *CSI: Miami* utilize actual forensic science as the basis for their programs. Because both fictional and real-life crime scene investigators work for the state and must testify in court, they have to produce provable evidence based on scientific procedures. Jerry Bruckheimer, the producer of both shows, said, "On *CSI* I told them to use the correct terminology even if the audience doesn't know it, because even if they don't understand it, they'll know it's real" (Stein, 2003, p. 71). Consultants for the *CSI* shows, which added a third spin-off, *CSI: New York,* in the fall of 2004, include a forensic pathologist and a former crime scene analyst (CSA) as well as science researchers.

After the September 11, 2001 terrorist attacks on the Twin Towers of the World Trade Center in New York City and the Pentagon in Washington, DC, television responded rapidly with shows about fictional terrorists. *The West Wing* aired an episode about the president dealing with a terrorism crisis in a show that was written and shot in the three weeks after the real attack (Hollywood in wartime, 2001). The 2005–2006 television season included several shows (*E-Ring, Numb3rs, 24*) with terrorism as the main focus. The unsettling fear of terrorism in the world has also been represented in several shows about strange deaths and unexplained phenomena (*Invasion, Surface, Threshold*).

Of course, not all cultural context plots are so tragic or serious. Comedy series also draw from real life for their humor. Through comic situations at home or at work, we can recognize our own fallibility and laugh at it. In contextualized situations, we experience the fictional comedy more intensely because it takes place in a real setting. Sometimes the decision to film in an actual setting is driven by production decisions. On March 3, 2004, *Yes, Dear* featured the former governor of California, Gray Davis, in a scene at a Los Angeles Lakers basketball game. Tim Conway, who played the lead actor's visiting father-in-law, got into a scripted argument with Davis in the team owner's special box. Conway made a joke that criticized Davis's handling of the state's budget and threw a glass of water in his face. Davis then chased Conway out of the owner's box, through the bleachers, and onto the floor during halftime—in front of the game's real spectators, who were unaware that a television show was being filmed. Jeff Meyer, the director of that *Yes, Dear* episode, said in a personal interview that the choice to film at an actual game was to have a live basketball audience in the show (O'Donnell, 2004). *Yes, Dear,* like most sitcoms, is normally filmed before live studio audiences in order to enhance the actors' sense of performing. To film the episode at a real basketball game was worth it to the producers of the show even though they needed to obtain complicated permissions from the NBA and the Lakers organization. Later, when Alan Kirschenbaum, *Yes, Dear*'s co-creator and executive producer, returned to his seat in the stands after filming, he overheard the man next to him saying to his friend who had just returned with their drinks: "You won't believe it, Joe, but Tim Conway was just chasing the former governor, Gray Davis, around the court," to which Joe replied: "No way, man!"

Critical Categories and Critical Choices

The narrative of the aforementioned segment of *Law & Order*, the remarks of Schindel and Thompson, and the real-life context behind the program are just a few of the items that a television critic would consider. *Law & Order* is rich with issues, cultural values, legal information, courtroom ritual, psychological subtexts, controversy, family norms, gender, racial, age, and employment representation, and ideological hegemony or dominant cultural beliefs. It also has a distinctive style, a signature look, ensemble acting, realistic sets, and a musical theme. The viewing audience is expected to be an informed, thinking, and feeling audience that actively participates in the program by responding to and grappling with the issues. Critics may choose to deal with one or some of these categories, utilizing theoretical background and methodological analysis to appreciate, understand, and evaluate their observations.

How then do you, as a television critic, differ from other television viewers? You will analyze a television program in order to understand how it works and the choices its creators and producers made. You take television seriously and evaluate its expression of ideas, values, and conflicts, which give you and your readers deeper insight into our culture. You may make

Photo 1.1   Police detectives at the crime scene in the first half of
Law & Order.

Photo 1.2   The prosecuting attorneys discuss the case in the second half of *Law & Order*.

observations about what seems to be lacking in a program—but subsequently, you need to know what possible alternatives there are. As a competent critic, you know that different viewers derive different meanings from the same television program; therefore, you can interpret several possible meanings and their importance to those who might determine them. Further, you will go beyond the program itself and ask what conceptual or theoretical implications may have resulted. Finally, you will communicate to others the results of the critical observations in ways that can enrich their understanding. These critical observations are based on your informed judgment. Different academic television critics do not necessarily agree on what are the best critical methods and theories through which to criticize television, but as Horace Newcomb pointed out in the sixth edition of *Television: The Critical View*, their works are

> . . . good faith attempts to recognize and understand how social life, now dependent on mass media, on popular forms of expression and entertainment, on the far-reaching lines of information afforded by new technologies, can best be taught and understood, learned and used by all citizens. (Newcomb, 2000, p. 6)

In order to do the work of a television critic, you have to (1) choose a television program to criticize; (2) submit yourself to the program and stay alert; (3) determine what questions to ask as you watch the program; and (4) choose or develop a methodology to answer the questions. Thus, your work as a television critic is to **understand** the various elements of a television program from script to performance in order to **analyze**, through **critical methodology**, how the elements make a program what it is; to **interpret** the sundry meanings that the program may have by understanding the nuances of the culture in which it appears and the multiple meanings it may have for different audiences; to pass **judgment** on the quality of the program; and, finally, to **communicate** that judgment to an audience. The chapters that follow will help you decide what questions to ask by presenting both theories and methods for analysis, as well as necessary information regarding the phenomena that make up a television program. It is also essential to understand that television production and distribution is a business dependent on profits.

The Business of Television

Because television production is a business that depends on public support measured by the ratings systems and paid subscriptions to cable channels, the programming norms tend to appeal to what the public prefers. From a business perspective, television programming is a product that is funded by advertising and/or subscription to cable and satellite services and used by the viewing public. The motive of television executives whose networks and cable channels are funded by advertising is simple: to deliver viewers to advertisers and advertising to viewers. Television commercials cause audiences to be the true medium of exchange. What sells products is what supports television programming. Therefore, the product-culture largely determines what cultural models go on the air. Advertising is maintained if viewing levels and profiles support it; it is a matter of supply and demand. In other words, programming is determined by the interests and profits of the institution that produces and backs it. Network decisions also reflect the tastes and political ideologies of the controlling executives and the advertising sponsors. Chris Carter, creator of the successful television series *The X-Files*, told an audience at Montana State University that every script for his show had to be approved by the Fox network executives and "censors." In the second season of the show there was a script about a necrophiliac, a person who likes to have sex with corpses. The script was finally approved when the word "necrophiliac" was changed to "death fetishist." Another script for *The X-Files* that featured a story about incest and inbreeding was originally vetoed, but then, Carter said, it was allowed during "Sweeps Week," the times in February, May, August, and November when ratings companies measure viewing statistics for local television stations in each television market nationwide to set advertising rates (Carter, 2001). This latter example underscores the priority of the need for mass audience support. Television executives and producers try to figure out what it is that audiences desire and then satisfy that desire in order to maintain an audience following. Once the formula of desire/satisfaction is embodied in a television program, the show is then marketed to the consumers, the viewing public. Unhindered by advertising and the FCC,[1] HBO, a cable subscription network, has taken risks by developing programs that depict nudity, violence, and the use of obscene and sexually explicit language. *The Sopranos, Deadwood, Sex and the City, Six Feet Under, Big Love,* and other HBO programs have attracted discriminating audiences and have won many awards. FX, a basic cable channel owned by Fox, has included shows that have violence, sex, foul language, and drug use in popular series such as *The Shield, Rescue Me,* and *Nip/Tuck.*

Knowledge of the critical methodology for analysis of television, together with an understanding of the business of television, enables you to realistically evaluate what you view. A competent television critic also knows his or her own culture and recognizes its representation in a television program.

The Familiar and the Unfamiliar in Television

Technological developments—satellite transmitters, videocassette and DVD recorders, the DVR, cable and digital systems, television on computer screens, the World Wide Web, and the development of possible interrelationships between and among different media—have given viewers an array of choices and enlarged awareness of the world and its people. Television today allows us to view programs from unfamiliar communities and countries, sometimes in other languages, giving us the experience of hearing and seeing different narrative forms and representations of cultural norms other than our own. These exposures and the choices they give us also provide opportunities to compare the familiar with the unfamiliar, and this requires knowledge of the familiar. Critical methodologies enable us to enhance our knowledge of the familiar and equip us to confront the unfamiliar. It is also important to recognize that the institutions of United States television are the dominant television industries in the world, and that American programming has become popular around the globe. While visiting the Tate Gallery in London, I noticed that the woman at the information desk had a picture of George Clooney as the screensaver on her computer. She told me that *ER* is her favorite television show, but that what they see in England is the previous year's season. American programming has, in many cases, been adopted as a model for programming in other countries. A few years ago, my husband and I checked into a small hotel in Milan. The desk clerk was watching Italy's version of *The Dating Game,* a game show in which men and women choose a date by asking questions of several candidates. Except for the language difference, the show was nearly identical to America's *The Dating Game.* Of course, it works both ways. England's *Who Wants to Be a Millionaire* and *Weakest Link* were the prototypes for America's versions of these very popular quiz shows.

This chapter started off with the notion that critical acuity would give you a fuller and richer appreciation for a television program, as well as a better understanding of viewer response to it. Each of the chapters of this book is designed to help you become a critic who not only knows how to evaluate a television program but who also can construct a persuasive argument to support that judgment. To get started, you may be asking some very basic questions, such as, "How do I choose a television program to criticize?" and "How do I know what methods to use to criticize it?" So let us examine some basic critical orientation concepts.

Critical Orientation

First, it is perfectly acceptable to select one of your favorite television programs to criticize. Your familiarity with the show will enable you to select critical questions more easily, and your resulting critique will help you gain a deeper understanding of why you like it. For example, I liked *NYPD Blue,* which had its last season in 2004–2005, and I often watched it for pure enjoyment as opposed to criticizing it. If I were to do a critique of *NYPD Blue,* my job would be somewhat easier because I am familiar with the format and style of the show; I know most of the characters' names and their fictional histories; I have read *True Blue: The Real Stories Behind NYPD Blue* by David Milch, the co-creator of the program, and Detective Bill Clark, a book about the real-life cases that have inspired the writers; and I am able to relate to many of the emotions that are conveyed by the main characters.

Second, you may select a television program that grapples with issues that interest you. The surface issues of *NYPD Blue* are not very familiar to me. I have never lived in an urban environment where gangs, drug dealers, hustlers, muggers, and murderers are common in the streets, and—perhaps because these are unfamiliar—I am curious about them. However, what truly

interests me about *NYPD Blue,* the *CSI* programs, and the three *Law &
Order* shows is how the detectives solve a case, that is, how they use clues and
evidence to construct an argument, not only to name the perpetrator but also
to identify how and why the crime occurred. I also appreciate that the detectives are both female and male with equal abilities. Perhaps there are issues
that you would like to be involved in, and therefore you may select a television program about the law, medicine, children, teenagers, reality, music,
science, animals, sports, or politics. Perhaps you are interested in how television presents information about disease or the environment. You may wish
to observe how certain occupations are portrayed on television or how gender, age, race, and ethnicity are represented. Perhaps you would like to compare and contrast the ways in which the news is presented by different
networks or by different anchors, or you may want to trace the human values that underlie the format and presentation of news stories. You may wish
to examine certain sports coverage or look at the role of celebrities on television talk shows. You may be especially interested in a certain type of television program or a genre, whether it is a miniseries or reality-based television.

Third, you may want to attempt the application of a methodology to see
what you can learn by applying it. You can examine how a narrative is
shaped and structured, examine the conventions of genre, look for the various codes of television and try to extrapolate meaning from them, examine
the characteristics of "families" and family values, look for evidence of the
postmodern phenomena, and/or observe and evaluate the "look" and style of
a television program. The following chapters present ways of observing, analyzing, and evaluating television programs. Chapter 9 consolidates those that
precede it into a set of critical questions to ask of a television program.

Fourth, you may be interested in the making of a television show. Television programs are the result of the work of the creators, the executive producers, producers, writers, directors, actors, set designers, costumers, music
directors, visual and sound editors, camera operators, and other staff, who
may or may not be an independent production company. Their creative
work and the ways in which a television show is initiated and produced is
the subject of Chapter 2, "Demystifying the Business of Television."

Summary

Criticism is the practice of informed judgment through which a person
understands, evaluates, and communicates to others the what, how, and
why something is considered to be of quality. The result can illuminate,
enlighten, and bring about appreciation for that which is criticized. Television criticism can bring about a fuller and richer understanding of people's

reactions to a television program. Because television is ubiquitous in society, it is important to practice sound television criticism. Not only will the television critic gain deeper understanding of the production process, aesthetics, and genre standards, but also the critic can develop insight into cultural contexts and cultural norms inherent in the narrative and action of programs.

Television critics choose a program to criticize, watch the program in an alert state, determine what questions to ask, and choose or develop a methodology to answer the questions. The subsequent analysis and evaluation are then communicated to an audience.

Television criticism is subjective in that it subjects a program to interpretation through the critic's perceptual filters. Television criticism can also be persuasive in that it can alter the perceptions of recipients.

Television production and distribution is a business dependent upon advertising and subscriptions as well as audience support. Television production develops a "look," a visual style that should enhance the narrative as well. Mainstream representations of race, gender, sexuality, age, and occupation reflect societal changes and new norms. Narratives on fiction and nonfiction television reinforce cultural values. Television programs and their scheduling are bound by genres. These aspects, all of which you should be familiar with as a television critic, are explored in each of the parts of this book.

Exercises

1. Think of a time in your life when you received personal and constructive criticism. How did it help you in a positive way? Did it change you in any way?

2. Make a list of what you can gain from being an informed television critic.

3. What does it mean to be a "transformer" when you are a television critic?

4. Read an example of television criticism in a newspaper like *The New York Times,* the *Los Angeles Times, USA Today,* or any other major newspaper, or go to the TV Barn Web site (http://blogs.kansascity.com/tvbarn/) and find the Crixlist to read television criticism online. What does the journalistic television criticism tell you? Do you think it is objective? Does it persuade you to watch a particular show?

5. What does it mean to say that television criticism is subjective? What does it mean to say that television criticism is persuasive?

6. Watch both a fiction and a nonfiction television program of your choice. Analyze your own perceptions of the content. Does this reveal your own biases and past experiences?

7. Have you ever been influenced by someone else to watch a particular television program? If so, did you continue watching the same program?

8. Have you ever been persuaded to adopt a hairstyle, a type of clothing, or an attitude because you observed it in a television program?

9. Can you name the "brand identity" of the television cable station that you watch on a regular basis? How do you regard yourself in terms of that brand?

10. Watch a television show such as *Law & Order, Without a Trace, CSI,* or any of the episodic dramas. Can you identify true-to-life events in the story?

11. How do you, as a television viewer, participate when you watch? Do you fill in the blanks or predict what will happen?

12. Why is it important for a television critic to take television seriously?

13. What does the desire/satisfaction formula mean from a television business perspective?

14. What should you consider when you select a television show to criticize?

Suggested Readings

Marc, David. (1995). *Bonfire of the Humanities: Television, Subliteracy, and Long-Term Memory.* Syracuse, NY: Syracuse University Press.

Nehamas, Alexander. (Winter 1990). Serious watching. *South Atlantic Quarterly,* 89(1), 157–180.

Newcomb, Horace, Ed. (1997). *Encyclopedia of Television* (3 vols.). Chicago: Fitzroy Dearborn.

Newcomb, Horace, Ed. (2000). *Television: The Critical View,* 6th ed. New York: Oxford University Press.

http://blogs.kansascity.com/tvbarn/ See Crixlist for links to journalists who write television criticism.

Note

1. Because access to HBO is by subscription only, it is considered a private contractual agreement between viewers and HBO and not bound by FCC rules.

2

Demystifying the
Business of Television

There's no business like show business.

—song by Irving Berlin

Introduction

This chapter focuses on what you need to know about the business of television. It is divided into two parts that cover essential information about (1) the role of advertising, the influence of ratings, and the making of daily schedules and time slots; and (2) how a television show is produced and the roles of the producers, writers, and directors. The section on writing is longer than the other parts regarding production because an overwhelming majority of people in the television industry regard writing as the most important aspect of production.

Knowledge of each of these areas will help you understand why the final outcome is what it is. Because the creative process that goes into the making of a television program or series is dependent on the business of television production and delivery, restraints, institutional controls, and public tastes—and the subsequent popularity of television programs—the end product may not live up to critical demands. As an effective critic, you will use high standards and will be free to make suggestions for improvement, but you must also recognize the restrictions and limitations of the medium and judge how good or bad a program is accordingly. This chapter is not intended to provide a complete understanding of the television industry, but rather it will enable you to understand enough about the business of television to place it in that context when evaluating a program or series.

The Role of Advertising, Ratings, and Schedules

Advertising

The common wisdom in television is that its primary role is to deliver consumers to advertisers. Advertising income is what pays for television programs that are broadcast on commercial networks. The networks derive 100 percent of their revenues from advertising and product placement. With the exception of premium subscription channels such as HBO and Showtime, cable and satellite television include advertising and develop special programming or promotions and also offer local advertising. In the business of television, the goal is to sell as many commercials as possible and to charge as much as advertisers are willing to pay. In the business of advertising, the goal is to buy time in television programs watched by an audience who fits the demographic characteristics that advertisers market products to and to buy these audiences as efficiently as possible. In other words, television sells audiences to advertisers for billions of dollars.

A good illustration that the television audience is the commodity that networks and individual stations sell to advertisers is the description of the audience in terms of "costs per thousand." In other words, the cost to purchase air time for a commercial is divided by the number of people in thousands. For example, if the cost for a commercial is $300,000 and the audience for a program is 40 million women 18 to 49 years old, then the cost-per-thousand is $300,000 divided by 40,000 = $7.50. The advertiser is spending $7.50 for every 1,000 women 18 to 49 years old who watch the program in which the commercial is placed. How is such a description derived? Audience research provides the estimates of the size and demographics of the audience. Certain audience characteristics desired by advertisers are also incorporated into programming choices and their exposure to audiences (Lometti, 1997).

Ratings

Television revenues are determined by data derived from a quantitative measurement of the size and composition of the audience that are established by ratings and shares measured by a media market research firm known as the A. C. Nielsen Company, which advertises itself as "the television standard." The Nielsen Company measures and compiles statistics on television audiences and sells this data to advertisers, advertising agencies, program syndicators, television networks, local stations, and cable and satellite program and system operators. (The Arbitron Company had been Nielsen's competitor for compiling local television ratings—this company got out of the television business but still does radio ratings.) At one time, a gadget known as the Audimeter or the Nielsen black box was used to send daily reports to a central office, but to acquire audience demographics, Nielsen supplemented it with viewer diaries.

Webster, Phalen, & Lichty define ratings as "a body of data on people's exposure to electronic media" (Webster, Phalen, & Lichty, 2000, p. 10). Ratings are derived from a formula that calculates the percentage of the nationwide audience with television sets who are watching a particular program—in other words, how many people out of the total possible audience are watching at that time. The networks base their advertising rates on the regular weekly data that Nielsen produces, while stations in smaller markets—because they cannot afford Nielsen's research year-round—rely on Sweeps four times a year for all their important ratings numbers. Webster, Phalen, & Lichty describe the ratings as follows: "Ratings are the tools used by advertisers and broadcasters to buy and sell audiences; the report cards that lead programmers to cancel some shows and clone others. Ratings are road maps to patterns of media consumption . . . They are objects of fear and loathing" (Webster, Phalen, & Lichty, 2000, p. 12).

Demographics is the practice of describing groups of people according to gender, age, ethnicity, income, educational level, and other information. Demographics identify target audiences for advertisers and commercial broadcasters. Advertisers believe that pinpointed messages aimed at their best prospects will be most successful; therefore, while age, gender, and occupation are considered important, they are also interested in whether individuals share a certain set of values (Buzzard, 1990). Thus, they may target the Generation X audience—with its perceived emphasis on material goods and action activities—for one ad, and Baby Boomers—who are concerned with health and security—for another. Nielsen devised a Peoplemeter, which uses a programmed box on top of the television set that includes demographic descriptions as well as channel selections. This system now dominates the production of national television ratings (Russell & Lane, 2002).

Ratings are reported in various newspapers and industry magazines. In June 2002, *USA Today* began reporting the Nielsen ratings by total viewers rather than by households. *USA Today* also reports the Nielsen breakdown of prime-time ratings by networks, cable, syndicated channels, and by age groups 18–49.

Categories of Ratings

There are several categories of ratings for television: the Nielsen Television Index (NTI), an estimate of how many people with certain demographic characteristics view each program based on a sample of 4,000 homes; the National Audience Demographics (NAD), a report that provides demographic information on network programs for both household and on a per-person basis; the Nielsen Station Index (NSI), a quarterly measurement of each local television station in each nationwide market; the Designated Market Areas (DMA), diaries in which separate samples of people record their viewing habits; Nielsen Syndicated Service (NSS), a service for syndicated television shows; and the Nielsen Homevideo Index (NHI), a service for cable networks, superstations, and home video. Other special reports are also produced for videocassette and DVD usage, sports programming, and political elections.

On December 26, 2005, Nielsen Media Research began to measure what is recorded on digital video recorders (DVRs), such as TiVo. An estimated 7 percent of the nation's 110 million homes with televisions now have digital video recorders, and that is expected to rise to 25 percent sometime in 2007. A code embedded in a television program can tell when something that has been recorded is actually watched. Nielsen can even tell when people fast-forward through the commercials. Nielsen gives its clients, mostly television networks, advertisers, and ad agencies, a list of how many people watch each program live each week. By recording DVR usage, Nielsen can offer three lists: (1) the number of people who watch a show live; (2) the number who watch it within 24 hours; and (3) the number of people who watch it within a week. The information regarding fast-forwarding through the ads may result in advertisers asking for lower fees if they have evidence of how many commercials are skipped (Bauder, 2005). Nielsen's data can be accessed on its Web site at www.nielsenmedia.com.

Public broadcasters usually do not use commercial advertisements, but they do have sponsors such as ExxonMobil, which supported *Masterpiece Theatre* as the sole corporate sponsor from its 1971 debut until 2004, making it the largest sponsor in public television's history. In 1984, the Federal Communications Commission (FCC) relaxed the rules, allowing about 350 public broadcasting stations to air commercial messages as long as they did not ask for a sale or make price or quality comparisons and were not aired during local, 2.5-minute program breaks. The public broadcasters had requested the right to advertise after their federal funding was cut back by 30 percent, but not all public stations air advertisements (Wells, Burnett, & Moriarty, 2002). Public broadcasting also has pledge drives during which programs are interrupted to appeal to prospective donors. Because they must justify their existence by serving an audience in addition to keeping their sponsors satisfied that they have adequate viewers, many public broadcasting station managers subscribe to Nielsen ratings or use research consultants to analyze their data. The Public Broadcasting Service (PBS) subscribes to national ratings in order to evaluate the appeal of its programming. Ratings help the public broadcasters learn when the largest number of viewers is available for their programs, thus they can make adjustments to their program schedules and their pledge drives (Webster, Phalen, & Lichty, 2000). I served as the "talent" for the some of the pledge drives for Montana Public Television. We found that we got the most pledges on Saturday night, especially during *The Lawrence Welk Show,* even though they were reruns since the show's host, Lawrence Welk, had died many years before.

Ratings and the Cost of Advertising

Ratings are used as references for negotiations for the price of advertising time as well as for the salaries of the actors, the news anchors, and other on-screen personnel, decisions about syndicating programs, and other vital issues. Because ratings determine how much the advertisers pay for commercials, the larger the desired audience, the higher the cost of commercials.

> The desired audience for advertising tends to be 18- to 49-year-old consumers with disposable income—thus television programs are geared to that segment of the population. The lead characters in many television programs tend to be 20–30 years old because the shows are designed to appeal to a younger segment of the population aged 18 to 34, to compensate for an audience that presumably watches little television. Reality programs such as *Survivor* and *Fear Factor* are designed to court young adults whom the advertisers hope will develop strong brand loyalty to their sponsors (Mitchell, 2002). Although older consumers have more spending power, advertisers view them as less flexible in their buying choices and therefore worth fewer advertising dollars (Singhania, 2002).

After a great deal of media hype, 52.2 million people watched the final episode of *Friends* on May 6, 2004, driving up the price of a beer commercial that evening to $2 million (Carter, 2004). Typically the Super Bowl broadcast, because of its huge audience, has the highest-priced commercials. In the year 1984, Apple Computer aired its *1984* commercial, a mini-epic about Big Brother propagandizing on a big screen in front of colorless, automaton humans when suddenly an athletic woman in red shorts, outrunning the "thought police," hurls a sledgehammer at the screen, which explodes in a flash of light. Ridley Scott made this commercial that ended with the announcer saying, "On January 24th, Apple Computer will introduce Macintosh. And you'll see why 1984 won't be like *1984*." The next day, 200,000 consumers went to Apple dealers to view the new Macintosh computer, and 72,000 bought one in the next 100 days. The tremendous success of this ad ushered in a new era for advertising on the Super Bowl. As Jerry Della Femina, Chairman of Della Femina Rothschild Jeary Advertising, wrote in *The Wall Street Journal*, "In my world—advertising—the Super Bowl is judgment day. If politicians have Election Day and Hollywood has the Oscars, advertising has the Super Bowl" (26 January 2001, p. A14). Television commercials for the February 1, 2004 Super Bowl cost $2.3 million for a 30-second spot, and the broadcast reached about 130 million Americans. "People sit back and say, '$2.2 million, $2.3 million,' when can this end?" said Len Short, executive vice president for brand marketing at America Online (AOL), which is spending $10 million on commercials and sponsorship of the Super Bowl halftime show. "It gets to be more of a cultural phenomenon every year ... a great place to launch something" (Associated Press, 2004, p. 4C).

The Sweeps

Ratings Sweeps (the name is taken from the practice of sweeping all local markets four times a year) are the month-long periods in November, February, May, and July during which ratings set the advertising rates for all the other months for local stations. Nielsen introduced these Sweeps periods in the 1960s, and they have been big business ever since. Television programs are promoted, news specials are publicized, blockbuster miniseries and made-for-TV movies are aired, and series finales, often with cliffhanger situations, are shown in May. This is why many reruns are shown the month before the Sweeps because networks wait until the Sweeps months to air new scripts. Competition among channels is keen during the Sweeps with newspapers and electronic trade journals reporting the winners. Ratings are reported first with shares second. The *share* is a mathematical formula that calculates the percentage of the nationwide audience with sets turned on and tuned into a particular program during a given time. This is a measure of the actual possible audience, known as Households Using Television (HUT). Shares enable station and network executives to learn how well their programs are doing compared with their competition. A good example is given in the *Encyclopedia of Television:*

> For example, station WXXX airs *Jeopardy!* At 7 p.m. Sample data estimate that 10,000 or 10 percent of the city's 100,000 TV households are viewing that program. Some 40,000 households are viewing other programs, but another 50,000 are not using their TV sets. Since 10,000 of the 50,000 active viewers (20%) are watching *Jeopardy!*, that program has a share of 20 even though its rating (the percentage of TV households) is only 10. (Newcomb, 1997, vol. 3, p. 1482)

If all households with television sets had people watching television during a given time period, the rating and the share would be equal, but this never happens; thus, the share for a program is always greater than its rating. The gap is greatest during periods of light viewing.

Why Television Shows Get Renewed or Canceled

Ratings and shares are what determine whether programs get canceled or continued. ABC revamped its entire line of shows for the fall 2004 season based on its low ratings in 2003–2004. Lloyd Braun, Chair of ABC Entertainment, explained that there had been a number of reality shows that failed causing a serious backlash among its advertisers (Carter & Rutenberg, 2003). Although it is a rare phenomenon, viewer reaction may sometimes "save" a television program. The first time this occurred was in 1968, when—despite a low number of viewers—NBC renewed *Star Trek* for a third season due to a massive letter-writing campaign that was secretly started by the show's creator, Gene Roddenberry (Cavanaugh, 2006). In 1984, the CBS program *Cagney and Lacey* was canceled because it had finished 55th among 99 prime-time series. Viewer outrage expressed in "an avalanche of mail," favorable press attention, and Tyne Daly's Emmy for her portrayal of one of two policewomen convinced CBS executives to restore the show. Also, according to David Poltrack, who was the vice president for research at CBS, "*Cagney and Lacey* had enthusiastic advertisers, despite the mediocre ratings. Its core audience, women 25 to 54, is the most saleable demographic segment" (Viewer Reaction saves *Cagney and Lacey*, 1984, p. 11C.). *Hill Street Blues* finished 89th in the ratings during its first half season, but its small audience was demographically made up of POMs, an acronym for professionals, operatives and managers, a clearly defined target audience with disposable income, and the show thus escaped cancellation (Marc & Thompson, 1995). CBS canceled *Joan of Arcadia* in May 2005.

Angry fans e-mailed the network, asking executives to reconsider their decision. The show had received critical praise, but it did not have good ratings in its spot on Friday night. Although the show was basically about teenagers, the Friday night audience has a median age of 53.9, out of the range for advertising revenue. David Bauder of Associated Press wrote, "There's a better chance of seeing Los Angeles paralyzed by a July snowstorm than CBS changing its mind" (Bauder, 2005, p. 6).

Shortcomings of the Nielsen Rating System

There have been various complaints about the Nielsen rating system, especially from the networks, according to David Lieberman, who writes for *USA Today*. Lieberman (1996) wrote that among the complaints are: (1) Nielsen does not count the viewers who watch television away from home, for example, in offices, hotel rooms, on college campuses, or in bars; (2) Nielsen undercounts children, who often forget to note their activities in the Nielsen diaries or meters; (3) surveys include too many older and wealthy viewers, which especially exaggerates the viewers of premium cable channels such as HBO and Showtime; (4) Nielsen undercounts minority viewers; and (5) because Nielsen measures local viewing only four times a year, it encourages stations to run contests or sensational programs during Sweeps months to boost their ratings (Lieberman,1996).

In 2004, a congressional task force was appointed to study the issue of minority representation in the Nielsen Peoplemeter system in New York City, Los Angeles, Boston, and Chicago because there have been sharply lower ratings for programs popular in black and Latino homes. Critics believe that these minority groups are undercounted in the Nielsen system (Congress to audit Nielsen system, 2004). Nielsen Media Research countered these charges with an ethnic measurement (see Web site: http://www .nielsenmedia.com/ethnicmeasure).

Ratings in the Summer

Summer television used to be filled with nothing but rerun programs, but that has changed in recent years. To acquire more viewers during the summer months, many new television programs have been developed, but the ratings make little difference in the summer because advertising rates are set for the fall. For example, in the summer of 2004, the quiz show *Jeopardy!* had a record-breaking winner with Ken Jennings, who won 38 games and $1,321,660. His long run boosted *Jeopardy!*'s ratings. According to an Associated Press release, *Jeopardy!* producers were probably annoyed that this happened during the summer when higher ratings don't mean as much financially. Michael Davies, executive producer of *Who Wants to be a Millionaire,* said that when the syndicated *Millionaire* had two big winners on shows taped to air in the summer, he delayed them to the fall (*Jeopardy! Star Jennings gives show a big boost,* 25 July, 2004).

The Strategies of Television Advertising

Typically, the basic formula for ads on television is eight minutes of ads for a half-hour show; however, because air time is so expensive, advertisers often run shorter commercials, resulting in more ads per minute. Marketing communications company Young & Rubicam uses the AQRI rule—"arouse quick related interest" to relate to viewers' lives or experiences (Bellamy & Walker, 1996). In addition to ads for products, promotions for other television shows and films frequent the airwaves during the breaks of a show. Movie studios advertise heavily on Thursday nights to reach young adults before the weekend's new movie releases (The Thursday factor, 2005, p. 10). Advertisers prefer sponsoring shows that put viewers in a mood to buy. *The Day After,* a 1983 made-for-television movie about a nuclear holocaust, posted some of the highest ratings in the history of television. Yet some sponsors were afraid to run ads during the show because its message might make the audience feel bad and would not put the viewers in a mood to buy their products (Stark, 1997).

Advertisers also link actors in popular television shows to their products. The writers and producers of the popular series *Friends* created a mini-episode starring the six actors in character for Diet Coke at a cost of $10 million. This ad was also tied to a contest in which the winner would sit in on a taping of a *Friends* episode (Bellamy & Walker, 1996). A commercial for Mercedes Benz with Dennis Franz of *NYPD Blue* giving a citation to a driver, however, was not aired on NBC or CBS because they felt it promoted a show on rival ABC (Abelman, 1998).

Advertising often functions as entertainment to hook the viewers. In the 1990s, Taster's Choice began running serialized commercials created by the McCann-Erickson ad agency that followed the romantic encounters of a man and woman who shared a fondness for this coffee. The commercials presented a soap opera environment in each episode that ended with ambiguous dialogue to create in the viewers a desire to tune in to see whether these people would become a couple. The commercials were so successful that they were given credit for a 10 percent increase in product sales soon after they were aired. MasterCard had a "priceless" commercial serial in 2004–2005 about a Boston Terrier dog that gets lost in the redwood forest when his family drives away in a camper. Subsequent commercials depicted the friendly dog being picked up by a truck driver, given water by a Native American in the Mojave Desert, and offered a ride on a motorcycle. The suspense built as the dog seemingly made his way home and was finally reunited with his family.

Product Promotion Within Television Programs

The Project for Excellence in Journalism reported a study of the content of the ABC, CBS, and NBC morning shows, calling them "a kind of sophisticated infomercial" because they tended to promote the products of their parent companies. The report said that one third of the content on these morning shows essentially sold something—a book, a compact disk, a movie, or another television program. Twenty-seven percent of the products promoted on *The Early Show* are owned by Viacom, the parent company of CBS; 21 percent of the *Good Morning America* promotions are owned by the Walt Disney Company, which owns ABC; 12 percent of the products promoted on *Today* are owned by General Electric, which owns 80 percent of NBC (Associated Press, 2001). The remaining 20 percent is now owned by Vivendi Universal.

Likewise, game shows announce the brand names of the prizes they offer, such as automobiles, furniture, and appliances, and the names of airlines, hotels, and resorts that serve as prizes. Of course, in the process of covering the action of most athletic contests, televised sports also show the stadium billboards that promote specific products. An increasing number of sports arenas are named for their corporate and business sponsors, thus the sponsors' names are openly mentioned in the television coverage.

Product Placement

Product placement (brand names purposely placed within the context of a program) is another source of income for television programs. Although television product placement is not exactly new, it has become a widespread strategy in the 21st century. Erik Barnouw (1978) pointed out in *Sponsor* that in the 1940s, in the early days of television, there were *sub rosa* sponsors. Writers and directors were told that if they could put a certain brand of potato chips in a televised party scene, a publicity agent would send a $100 check. On a documentary program about skiing, the skiers would end with a social hour and be shown drinking Old Crow whiskey. Product placement has been used in films for a long time. When Reese's Pieces candy was shown in the 1982 film *ET,* sales of the candy increased by 65 percent.

Sometimes brand names of products are part of television's narrative. For example, Tony Soprano of HBO's *The Sopranos* says he prefers Gulden's mustard or says that he will buy a Whitman's Sampler box of candy. For his father-in-law's 75th birthday, he buys him a Beretta shotgun. When Tony wants a beer, he says, "Bring me another Rolling Rock." Steven Antin, producer of the WB show *The Young Americans* signed a deal with Coca-Cola in 2000 for $25 million, promising that the cast would be seen drinking Coca-Cola in every episode (Longworth, 2002). Paula Abdul, Simon Cowell, and Randy Jackson, the judges on *American Idol*, sip Coca-Cola from glasses inscribed with the Coke logo. ABC signed major marketers to embed brands such as Schick and Cingular Wireless into reality shows like *All American Girl*. Segments of the show had examples of women's intuition, and Schick had a women's shaver named Intuition (Elliott, 2003). *Extreme Makeover: Home Edition* refurbishes houses with Sears products. Leslie Moonves, CBS executive, said, "We're making more and more of those deals: the kind of cars they drive in *CSI*; the kind of orange juice they drink in *Two and a Half Men*" (Associated Press, 'Stealth ads' infiltrate TV programming, 2005 p. TW21).

Another form of product placement for television is the digital insertion of brands into selected versions of programs based on viewers' brand preferences. This is a legal practice, but product placement can sometimes be questionable. Christopher Turner, a clinical assistant professor of medicine at the University of Michigan, presenting a paper at the 2002 National Communication Association, pointed out that an episode of the medical drama *Chicago Hope* featured a malnourished, breast-fed baby. Dr. Turner said that the show was sponsored by baby milk products that were not advertised. He also explained that manufacturers of medical devices use television drama to interject claims for the devices. For example, he said that the A-2000 BIS monitor, which records a cardiac patient's EKG and anesthetic depth, is heavily marketed to the medical community. A story line on *Chicago Hope* had an anesthetized patient hear a female doctor make a remark about his anatomy, which he remembered when he woke up. Because of the threat of lawsuits, the offending doctor argued to install a BIS monitor as a solution to make sure that the patient is asleep. However, as Dr. Turner pointed out, the U.S. Food and Drug Administration does not allow BIS to advertise this claim (Turner, 2002).

Because television is available 24 hours every day and because there are hundreds of channels to choose from, the television audience has become increasingly fragmented. With the enormous success of HBO and other cable channels such as MTV, CNN, and ESPN, there has been erosion in the viewership of the broadcasting networks ABC, CBS, NBC, and Fox. There is major competition for audiences, and strategies are planned to acquire them, especially in the 18- to 49-year-old range. One such strategy is "narrowcasting" or reaching for target audiences. CNN and CNN Headline News keep viewers informed of the latest developments in news. Lifetime and Oxygen attempt to attract women viewers by featuring numerous made-for-TV "weepies" and talk shows with emphasis on female issues. The various Fox sports channels and ESPN appeal to sports devotees alongside specific sports channels such as Golf and NFL Network; Animal Planet (APL) engages animal lovers; Court TV attracts people who like to watch trials and reruns of crime shows; the Food Channel interests people who like to cook; and the Sci Fi Channel entertains science fiction and horror fans. Advertising tends to match the interests of the limited audiences that watch these narrowcast channels. Schedules are devised to match programs with the audiences most likely to tune in at certain times.

Scheduling and Advertising

The use of television as an advertising vehicle is determined by demographic characteristics or who is watching at what time. Television programming is divided into parts of the day. Prime time is between 8:00 p.m. and 11:00 p.m. EST on weekdays and 7:00 p.m. to 11:00 p.m. on Sundays. These are the most expensive advertising times because 75 percent of adults are most likely to view situation comedies, drama serials, reality television, and special reports during these hours. Daytime is between 9:00 a.m. and 4:00 p.m. EST. Daytime advertising can reach up to 65 percent of the adult population. Early daytime is between 7:00 a.m. and 9:00 a.m., appealing to working men and women with a wide variety of advertised products. High-profile news programs are given a separate time of day with demographics favoring the older segments of the adult population. Late night programming appeals to younger adults, while weekends favor sports fans. Because more than 60 percent of television households receive all their television via cable or satellite (Donnelly, 1996), advertisers target precisely defined audiences of certain channels and programs and/or place regional or local ads within the programs. When CNN lagged behind Fox News in the ratings, advertisers began to withdraw because the CNN audience was too old and not as affluent (Gomery, 2006).

Schedules are designed to get viewers who tune into a popular program to stay and watch subsequent programs; thus, a new show or one with low ratings is placed after a very popular show such as *CSI* or *Lost*. Network executives from NBC, CBS, ABC, and Fox who appeared on a satellite seminar from the Museum of Television and Radio explained that they create "flow" with their prime-time schedules. The television concept of flow has to do with viewer inertia and staying with a channel into the next program. Raymond Williams also used the term "flow," meaning a planned stream of television programs, from trailers, commercials, and public service announcements to the next program in the schedule. Williams wrote: "We can be 'into' something else before we have summoned the energy to get out of the chair, and many programmes are made with this situation in mind: the grabbing of attention in the early moments; the reiterated promise of exciting things to come, if we stay" (Williams, 1974, p. 94).

Instead of thinking about what time to air a single show, network executives build scheduling blocks from 8:00 to 11:00 p.m. (The Making of a Prime-Time Schedule, 1997). They use the "hammock" strategy of placing a new or less successful program before and sometimes after successful series. The "tent-pole" strategy is the opposite of the hammock technique whereby they schedule a successful program between two less successful programs or a new one. Another technique is to place series of the same or similar genre or that have similar demographic appeals back-to-back (Bellamy & Walker, 1996). The network executives also said it is important to create programs that complement other technologies such as the Internet and Web sites. NBC developed the one-minute mini-movie to air during commercial breaks in two 30-second installments. The opening half was developed to air during one show (*Will & Grace*) and the conclusion during the next show (*Coupling*) (McDowell, 2003).

Most television shows open immediately on the hour or half hour with scenes from the last episode and a strong lead-in, the beginning of the narrative that sets the theme of the show. This is followed by a myriad of commercials—some of which are 10 to 15 seconds long—and other promotions. Unless the viewer has recorded the show on a VCR, DVD, or DVR to allow fast-forwarding through the commercials, that person sits through the commercials in order to be there when the next segment of the show begins. In order to follow the narrative of a show, the viewer is likely exposed to the ads. Credits at the end of the show are often accompanied in a split screen by an epilogue or outtakes from the show to keep the viewer from switching channels. A new strategy for American broadcasting is off-the-hour starting and ending times. Common in cable television, the "off the clock" practice is not popular with the public. The rationale is to keep people from changing the channel to watch another show because the one they are watching has not yet ended or has started early. *ER,* for example, on NBC starts before the hour to keep viewers from switching to *Without a Trace* on CBS (Bobbin, 2005).

Noncommercial Channels

Home Box Office (HBO), part of the AOL Time Warner conglomerate, changed American television by eliminating commercials and repeating its programs several times throughout the week's schedule so viewers have ample opportunities to catch up with missed episodes. Showtime, which originally featured primarily movies, has added series, miniseries, and special programming uninterrupted by commercials to its schedule. HBO and Showtime do not have to attract an audience for advertisers. Although the audience for premium channels may be relatively small at any given time— compared to the mass audience that the networks must have to keep their ratings high—shows on premium channels are very popular and successful at winning awards such as the Emmy and Golden Globe. Because HBO usually produces 13 episodes per season of shows like *The Sopranos,* compared with 22 for the networks, the creators have more time, artistic freedom, and bigger budgets. Shows are shot on film with cinematic visual techniques such as moving cameras, cinematic shot-counterpoints, long takes, and sophisticated nighttime photography. They are often shot on location and have high production values. HBO also allocates huge budgets for marketing and promoting its products (Akass & McCabe, 2004). HBO is not censored in the way that broadcast networks are because it does not go over the public airways. Shows like *The Sopranos* have much profanity, violence, and nudity but also excellent acting and direction. HBO scheduled series like *Rome, Deadwood, Sex and the City, The Sopranos, Six Feet Under,* and *Big Love* to have their first shows of the week on Sunday evenings with the new seasons beginning in the spring, summer, or early in the new year. In addition to feature-length films, HBO features original programming, its signature focus. Because of the popularity of original programming, HBO has developed more series per season.

The Production of a Television Show

Production Houses

Television shows are created, developed, and produced by professional production houses, most of which are located on the West Coast. The networks also have their own production houses, for example, NBC Productions and CBS Productions. The networks also produce their own news and sports programs. The networks prefer to own the shows that they air because they can eventually make huge profits by selling reruns of the shows they produced into the syndication market (Grover, 1997). Film giants such as Universal, Paramount, Disney, and Warner Brothers are production studios with big budgets where many television shows are made. Warner Brothers actually made *Friends* for NBC instead of for its own WB network. The Walt Disney Company is the parent company of the ABC network. Actors and stars also may have their own production houses. For example, David Letterman has Worldwide Pants, which not only produces *The Late Show with David Letterman,* but also *The Late Late Show with Craig Ferguson,* and *Everybody Loves Raymond.* There are also a variety of independent production houses that produce only one or two shows, for example, Charles, Charles, and Burrows, which was famous for *Cheers.*

Pilots and the "Pitch"

If a creator has the funds or financial backing to make a pilot, a complete pilot or a 20-minute sample of one might be made in a production house and then offered to a network or cable organization. Since it costs approximately $1 million to produce a pilot for a half-hour show and almost $2 million for a one-hour show, most creators of television shows will first "pitch" an idea to the network or cable group. A pitch is a description of the concept of a prospective show or series; it is a brief story line presented to a network executive. Pitches are usually made by experienced writers because new writers are seldom given the opportunity.

> John Marcus, the head writer for *Taxi* and *The Cosby Show,* said in a seminar at the Museum of Television and Radio in 1996: "Executives have poker faces and skeptical attitudes . . . Pitching doesn't invoke your skills as a writer but your skills as a salesman." David Mich, a writer for *Saturday Night Live,* who also participated in the seminar, added: "Executives do things like try on designer jeans during a pitch, or they sleep" ("From Pitch to Polish: The Collaborative Process," 1996).

The executives ask questions of the pitch, for example, what is the motivation for the story; what propels the script; what is the nature of the lead character? The executive also asks specific questions about locale and possible actors and will make suggestions as well. There are many stories about famous pitches. For example, Warner Brothers Television President Peter Roth told of the pitch for the hit show *Without a Trace,* the show about the FBI's work to find missing persons: "The pitch for *Without a Trace* was a magazine thrown on my desk with the headline WHERE IS CHANDRA LEVY? (Chandra Levy was a congressional intern in Washington, DC who went missing in April 2001. Her body was found 13 months later in a park in the District of Columbia.) The one-line pitch was 'Whoever finds her'" (Stein, 2003, p. 72).

Because television executives prefer to build on the successes of previous series, resemblance to other shows is often a factor in the pitch. Todd Gitlin, author of *Inside Prime Time,* coined the term, "hybrid pitch," which he described as a writer-producer trying to sell a new television series to network executives by telling them that the prospective show is brand new and there has never been one like it before and then saying that it is a blend of two familiar hit shows from the past. Gene Roddenberry, creator of *Star Trek,* pitched his show to NBC as *Wagon Train* to the stars (Meehan, 2005). *Battlestar Galactica* was pitched as an "absolutely, new break-through show that would ably merge the *Star Trek* and *Bonanza* franchises" (Kubey, 2004, p. 9).

If the executives respond positively to the pitch, they will ask for an outline or a script, and—if the subsequent reaction is also positive—they will commission a pilot to be made at the network's expense. Pilots are usually made in March or April. In late spring, pilots are screened before focus groups, small groups of people whose comments after a screening are compiled and interpreted by a market researcher. Computer programs also enable the members of a focus group to record their likes and dislikes while they watch the pilot. Focus groups are designed to obtain perceptions of people from demographic clusters such as age, occupation, income, lifestyle, and product purchases. Because television is so competitive, data from focus groups have become increasingly important. As the season progresses, maintenance research (the retesting of regular television programs with focus groups) is conducted to measure the appeal of story lines, characters, and other factors. Many pilots never actually get on television; however, if a pilot is considered a probable winner, the network or cable company will contract with the producer for a certain number of episodes, usually five or six, sometimes 10 or 11 (a half season); or sometimes 22 (a full season). The gold standard is 88 episodes or four seasons. The network's top executives announce their decisions about which new series to order and announce them to advertisers and the public in mid-May. It is in May that the broadcast networks (ABC, CBS, NBC, Fox, WB, and UPN, along with cable networks such as MTV and USA) will try to sell 75 percent of their commercial time for the upcoming season. In July, the pilots are screened by members of the Television Critics Association for publicity purposes. Production for the specified number of episodes also begins in July.

The Production Team

Once a series is signed on for the upcoming season, the producer of the series puts together a team of coproducers, writers, actors, directors, assistant directors, editors, and technical crew members.

The Producer

The producer, who is usually the senior writer, along with other writers, develops the series for the season, and oversees the creation and production of episodes, each at a different stage of development. In an article about Brian Grazer, producer of 24 and other television shows for 25 years, Mimi Avins wrote that "a producer often incubates ideas, then finds a creative team to understand and execute his vision" (Avins, 2005, p. F10). Television is a producer's medium, as Horace Newcomb and Robert S. Alley (1983) noted in the title of their book, *The Producer's Medium*, because they found that producers were the primary figures in television. When asked, "What does a producer do?" Lee Rich, founder of Lorimar and producer of *Dallas, Falcon Crest,* and *Knot's Landing,* answered:

> A producer does exactly what it sounds like. Somebody had to put all the pieces together. Somebody else may come up with the idea and then turn it over to somebody who will do it and put it all together. A guy who is making sure it gets done, the pages are shot, and the whole thing is done on a day-to-day basis. (Kubey, 2004, p. 104)

There are many types of producers for a television series. The executive producers are the creators and senior writers who are also known as the "show runners" because they oversee the television programming, tackling everything from negotiating with network executives to counseling actors to defining the creative vision of a series—and much more. For example, Barbara Hall (*Judging Amy*), Stephen Bochco (*NYPD Blue*), and David E. Kelley (*The Practice*) are show runners. Co-executive producers, producers, associate producers, and consulting producers also may be directors, writers, lead actors, and consultants. The line producer (or on-the-line producer) is the detail person who oversees the show from its concept to its production. The line producer supervises the budget, oversees the construction of the sets, and keeps the costs in line. A former line producer at CBS told me that his job was saying "no" to most requests. *CSI: Crime Scene Investigation,* the CBS series that held the number one place in the ratings during most of the 2003–2005 seasons, has four executive producers who are also writers, the lead actor, and the head director, four co-executive producers, 10 producers, three line producers, three associate producers, three consulting producers, and two supervising producers. Some of the same people hold more than one position. Information about and the names of a television program's personnel can be obtained from the program's Web site.

Writers

Writers are considered the most important personnel for a television program, whether it is a series, a soap opera, a news program, a movie-of-the-week, or a special. Sid Caesar, famous for the comedy shows *The Show of Shows* and *Caesar's Hour* in the 1950s, was asked about the importance of writing. His answer, an old line from vaudeville, "If it's not on the page, it ain't on the stage" is echoed by many performers of the 21st century. Caesar, whose writers for the 39 shows that he did each year included Mel Brooks, Neil Simon, Woody Allen, and Larry Gelbart, said, "Writing is the most important thing" (Kubey, 2004, p. 30).

The creator/executive producer is the senior writer in charge of the story line throughout the season, but there is a staff of eight to 10 writers for every episode. Some senior writer/producers such as David E. Kelley (*Ally McBeal*) and Aaron Sorkin (*The West Wing*) wrote every script, but most senior writers develop the concept and the season story line then turn the writing for each episode over to a team of writers. Some of these writers are freelancers who write no more than two or three scripts a year, but in order to have their scripts read, they must have agents. There are also specialty writers who get called in to "punch up" a script, particularly for situation comedies.

As writers on the regular staff gain seniority, they are given the title of producer. Eventually, many create their own shows, as did Dick Wolf, creator of *Law & Order, Law & Order SVU,* and *Law & Order: Criminal Intent.* Wolf started out as a writer for *Hill Street Blues* in 1985, moved up to coproducer of *Miami Vice* from 1986–1988, and began creating his own shows, which were not outstandingly successful until he came up with *Law & Order.* Barbara Hall, the first woman staff writer on *M*A*S*H,* wrote for *Moonlighting, Family Ties,* and *Newhart* and was a producer for *Northern Exposure* and *Chicago Hope. Judging Amy* was not her creation (Amy Brennerman's mother was a judge, and the actress conceived the series), but Hall's script for the pilot gave so much impetus to the series that she was made executive producer and show runner. Likewise, Steven Bochco wrote for *Columbo, McMillan and Wife,* and *Banacek* before he became a producer at Universal.

He then joined MTM Enterprises and created *Hill Street Blues*. Many writers start out in their twenties and thirties, and tend to be very well educated with backgrounds in English literature and acting in college.

The standard procedure for television series writers is to meet in a room to discuss the script for the upcoming episode. They talk about plot lines that may be taken from their own experiences and from news stories. Phil Rosenthal and Jeremy Stevens, writers for *Everybody Loves Raymond*, explained that they

> would come together every morning and sit around and just catch up with each other in terms of what's new or pressing . . . We realized fairly quickly that the main source of our stories is our lives and that a lot of the humor was going to come out of the gravel of our lives. (Fernandez, 2005, p. E7)

Rosenthal's wife, actress Monica Horan, said that his exact words to her appear in the scripts, for example, when Raymond says to his television wife Debra, "You're my girl," Horan said, "that is what Phil says to me" (Fernandez, 11 May 2005, p. E7). One of the writers for *Threshold* has a blog online (Berg, 2005) where she talked about how ideas for the show are derived. She said that the executive and co-executive producers had seen an old Vincent Price horror film that caused them to suggest a story line about an alien invasion as a harbinger of the end of the world. The writer then prepared an outline for approval by the network and later started writing the first draft before going into the room with the other writers (Berg, 2005). Dick Wolf said that the main source for story ideas for *Law & Order* is the front page of the *New York Post* (Unger, 1997) and law reviews (Creating Prime-Time Drama: Law and Order, 1997); Christopher Lloyd, Peter Casey, and David Lee, former executive producers for *Frasier,* said they and the other writers discuss what happened to them the previous weekend or a story from the back of the newspaper, select the funniest incident, and talk it into a treatment (The creative process, 1997).

Animated shows have become increasingly popular on television, none more so than the long-running show *The Simpsons*. Matt Groening, the creator, explained that all the writers get together in a rented hotel suite at the beginning of the season. There they spend a day or two throwing out ideas while a secretary records what they say and makes notes for them. In subsequent meetings, the story ideas are fleshed out, and other writers write the scripts. Groening said that the scripts get "written, rewritten, rewritten again" (Kubey, 2004, p. 144). When Kubey asked how he learned to tell a story in 22 minutes, Groening said he learned as a staff writer for James Brooks:

It's been the greatest learning experience in my life. I've learned more about structure, storytelling, and pacing. Everything is a writing problem to be solved, so even though these cartoons were very simple in dialogue it was a matter of learning how to tell a story and keep people interested . . . We do storyboards about 120 pages long and our scripts vary from 40–60 pages. Once that is approved, the animation is filmed. There are 80 animators and it takes six months to do a single show. (Kubey, 2004, pp. 142 & 145)

Dramatic television programs that appear on PBS, for example *American Playhouse,* or the *Hallmark Hall of Fame* are basically movies made for television. *American Playhouse* producers do not pitch their stories. They bring in the best writers they can find who tell stories, or they work with short stories or novels and find writers to adapt them for television. The philosophy of this kind of drama is to emphasize the writer and tell a story in as interesting a way as possible. They put their scripts through many drafts with suggestions from all of the production staff to "explore the world of the script and the characters and what they might do" (American Playhouse, 1992).

The Writer's Treatment

A *treatment* is an overview of the plot with details of the chronological rundown of the scenes of the prospective script with information about the setting, plot, and characters, and may include a few examples of dialogue and a few key camera shots. The Writers Guild of America suggests 10–15 pages of a treatment for a half-hour show; 15–25 pages for a one-hour show; 25–40 pages for 90 minutes; and 40–60 pages for a two-hour show (Hilliard, 1991).

CSI executive producers/writers Ann Donahue, Carol Mendolsohn, and Anthony Zuiker read a lot of science and interview paramedics and crime scene analysts for their story ideas. Zuiker, the series creator, discussed the complexities of the writing process on the national, weekly public radio series, *The Infinite Mind:*

"The first thing we do is somebody will walk into the room with a kernel of an idea. It may be a piece of technology. It may be a small story line. It may be a character arc and we sort of go from there. We have six—six or seven writers in the room at one time. We'll all be in a room with a bunch of grease boards and grease pens and we'll begin to talk it out pre the research stage, and we'll talk about an opening teaser, a through-line. We'll break down several beats [scenes] of Act 1, 2, 3 and 4. We'll talk about the act outs, the spins and turns.

"After we talk about all of the process of the beats we'll have for the episode, we'll go to outline stage where the appropriate writers who are assigned will jot down every beat of the episode. Then they'll go commence to writing . . ."

"It's just like an outline, and once they write the first draft, it'll come in. We'll give notes. We'll get notes from the network, from our peers, from the actors, and then we'll get notes from the director and we'll accommodate some notes based on production . . . If we need a black bottom pool vs. a white bottom pool, we'll make that adjustment. If we found a two-story house vs. a one-story house, we'll make that adjustment to reflect in the dialogue, and then every single day of shooting, we'll do small dialogue tweaks and execution tweaks until the last roll of film is run. And then we'll get to the editing room and watch the director's cut, then the producer's cut, and then the network, you know, final master, and we'll continue to do writing and ad libs and loop lines until it airs that day . . . We have to make sure that when we execute our stories that they're all forensically driven, and by using 'CSI' shots and snap-zooms, we really show the audience the intense micro. That's the one thing we keep in mind. Another thing we keep in mind is we want to make sure that it—we're always telling a great mystery with twists and turns 'cause our show really isn't so much a whodunnit but rather a howdunnit."

"The challenge to writing is to be able to underwrite and to be able to write 30 percent of the dialogues so the audiences can fill in 70 percent of the subtext. We hope that we challenge people cerebrally as they watch the show, as they're able to sort of tap into the minds of our characters and what they're thinking and what are their attitudes and deal with death in a very personal level and deal with a crime that could happen on their neighborhood block."

"There's no rhyme or reason. Basically we just sit back and say, 'What is interesting and engaging to us? What excites us?' And we're hopeful that America will follow and they have" (Television and the Mind, 2002).

SOURCE: Reprinted with permission of Lichtenstein Creative Media, Inc.

Directors

Most television series have multiple directors, sometimes a different one for each episode. *CSI* had 21 directors in three seasons, although Danny Cannon, who is considered to be the head director as well as an executive producer, directed 15 episodes. The director sits in the room with the writers and gets the final script before the actors (unless an actor is also a producer). The director then blocks the rehearsal and the camera shots. During the taping, the director usually stays in the control room communicating with the camera operators through a microphone or via the assistant director. The assistant director often prepares the camera shots. For live television, the director sits in front of multiple monitors, selecting the best shots with great speed. Larry Auerbach, the director for *One Life to Live,* said: "Each director has a unique approach to the material, to the way he shoots it, puts it together, but you also have a producer who sits in the control room when you are doing your dress [rehearsal] and provides a third eye" (Kubey, 1990, p. 118). Directors rely on their instincts and experience to set the tone of a television show.

Casting

The network executives have the last word on casting. Warren Littlefield, the president of NBC entertainment in 1994, said, "Casting is everything" (Kolbert, 1994, p. C13). After the final script with well-defined characters is completed, the casting director sends a "breakdown," a description of the characters complete with production details, to agents, who send photos and résumés suggesting possible actors for the parts. When *Friends* casting director Ellie Kanner sent out her breakdown, she received 1,000 glossy photos for the six regular characters on the show. She chose 75 to come in to audition for the producers and director. Those who looked promising were called back to read in front of Warner Brothers executives. Before actors audition for the network, the production studio negotiates what they will be paid if they get the part. Contracts for the actors commit them to staying for several years if the series lasts that long. The network executives, and not the producers, generally make the final casting decisions. Leslie Moonves, who was the president of Warner Brothers Television in 1994, said: "My concern can't solely be the best actor. I'm looking for people who are attractive. That's part of the crass commercialism the studios and the networks have to look at. I have to think, 'Am I going to have a *TV Guide* cover in six months, and what's that going to look like?' " (Kolbert, 1994, p. C18).

According to Joshua Brand, executive producer of *Northern Exposure,* the networks' first choice for an actor is always someone who has acted in a successful television show. He said that the network chief, Brandon Tartikoff, did not like Michael J. Fox for *Family Ties,* but in that case the producers prevailed (The Future, 1993). John Wells, executive producer of *ER,* explained the exception to the rule in the case of his series:

> Under ordinary circumstances there is a certain amount of pressure to use recognizable names or faces when casting shows. The networks provide extensive lists of suggested performers to choose from—not for any cynical reason, just for the obvious business reason that nobody's going to watch your show unless they know somebody to watch it for. *ER* was different. We felt so confident

that people would watch the show because of Michael Crichton's and Steven Spielberg's involvement that we were able to start casting the show without the usual pressures. We had the freedom to cast the best actors for the parts. (Pourroy, 1995, pp. 8–9)

Many television dramas and situation comedies have ensemble acting. Barbara Miller, head of casting for Warner Brothers, described the casting problems: "Ensemble casting is particularly difficult because you really have to balance it out. It's not as if you find one person for the lead and then assign the rest of the parts, the parts for ER were pretty equal all the way around" (Pourroy, 1995, p. 13). Extras also have to be cast. For example, ER's assistant director in charge of casting and directing the extras works with Central Casting to find the many extras who appear as patients and their families, ambulance drivers, orderlies, and housekeeping personnel in the hospital.

Putting a Show Into Production

When production begins for a new season in July, 22–24 episodes have to be made. There may be six or eight scripts ready to go at the beginning, but once a series is underway, there are about eight days between conception of a script and the taping or filming of the finished product. This means very long work days that may last for 16–20 hours as the production staff races to complete a show for broadcast. Although procedures vary for different series, the following is the usual procedure:

After the writers have their initial meeting in the room and agree on the treatment, one of the writers makes a 10-page outline that is scrutinized by the other writers before either the single writer or some of the writers complete a draft script of about 40–48 pages for a half-hour episode. To allow for commercials and other messages during the broadcast, 22 minutes is the standard for a script for a 30-minute program; 44 minutes is the standard for a 60-minute program. Sometimes half the writers write the script, and the other half punch it up. Once a script is written, the actors and producers have a table reading. They sit around the table, and the actors read the script for the writers, producers, director, and perhaps a few network representatives. Sometimes fans will be included to listen. The actors give some input about what works for their characters and what does not. The writers then make notes about what does not work and revise the script, often late into the same night. If they have not been present at the table reading, representatives from the network also read the script and suggest changes. After the script is revised, the actors, the director, and the camera operators have a run-through rehearsal where they block the movement and read the lines aloud with scripts in hand. All the producers watch the run-through from the front row of the studio. At the end of each scene, the actors walk up to the front row and discuss the script with the director and producers. Lines and words from the script get changed, and sometimes entire scenes are revised or dropped. As new pages get written, different colored sheets of paper are inserted into the script to mark the changes. The final production of the show for most situation comedies is in front of a live audience. Scenes are taped and retaped when there are bloopers or last-minute changes have to be made. (I am indebted to my friend Patricia Hill, camera operator, for allowing me to sit behind the producers and directors in run-throughs and filming of various episodes of *Frasier* and *Caroline in the City* at Paramount Television Studios.) The taping may take four to six hours before everyone is satisfied. The tape goes to the editors, and the show is aired about a month later.

Complicated production for a series such as *ER* has a longer production schedule: seven days of preparation, eight days of filming, and five days of postproduction editing and sound mixing. *The Sopranos* takes 8 days to prepare, 15 to film, and several more days to edit and mix the sound. Preproduction of the next episode overlaps with the production phase of another episode, and that overlaps with the postproduction phase of the previous show.

Soap opera production is different because instead of 22–24 episodes, 260 must be written and produced. Agnes Nixon, long-time writer for *The Guiding Light, One Life to Live,* and *All My Children,* explained that she and the other writers determine a long-range story projection for six to eight or 10 months that gets updated as needed. The projection is sent to the network for approval. Six weeks prior to taping, each episode is plotted in outline form, act-by-act, scene-by-scene, and that goes out to the network for approval. Once approved, the outlines go to the associate writers who write and edit the scripts. The directors get the scripts three weeks in advance, but the actors get them the night before taping. They have teleprompters, but most soap opera actors memorize their lines very quickly. They rehearse, block, and perform an episode all on the same day.

Nixon discussed network censorship when she told about wanting to do a show on uterine cancer. The sponsor, Procter & Gamble, balked, but finally told her she could do the show if she did not use the words "cancer," "uterus," and "hysterectomy." She did the show without the words and managed to get her message across. Proof of this was the many letters she received from women who said the information in the show prompted them to get medical checkups.

Nixon discussed the unwritten subtext, a very important concept in television acting:

> Subtext is a word that's in almost every scene of every outline. Subtext is what she is feeling and not saying. Sometimes, I'll start out with subtext, and it will be even more important than what she is saying, and we want to make sure that the viewer understands that though Erica is putting on a great front, she's really terrified inside . . . This affects the camera work. Sometimes the camera will not be on the person who's speaking. What the camera shows, the audience sees. The camera says to the viewer, "Look how Erica, who is saying nothing, is reacting." (Kubey, 2004, pp. 72–77)

Sets range from a single sound stage to complicated sets and locations. Shows like *CSI, NYPD Blue,* and *ER*—supposedly set in Las Vegas, New York City, and Chicago, respectively—are filmed in Los Angeles studios with sets that look like the cities where they are supposed to take place. The staff, crew, and actors go to those cities every three or four months to do exterior shots for authenticity. If the writers want outdoor shots in their scripts, they often have to change the scripts and wait until the next trip to the city. (More information on sets and art design can be found in Chapter 3, "Television Style")

After the show is "wrapped," it is sent to postproduction for editing, sound mixing, and other changes. Despite all the care that goes into producing a television show, it is normal for them to change before they air. If the network executives do not like the way the show is going, they may scratch the first few episodes, bring in new producers, and completely reshoot the show. New versions are written with new or changed characters; actors may get dropped or added; locations may be changed. Sometimes actors who were killed off the previous year come back to life, as Buffy did on *Buffy the Vampire Slayer.* The head of Studios USA Television, Ken Solomon, said that they do not wait until the November Sweeps to make changes, because ". . . the audience very likely by then will have tuned in and tuned out" (Auto pilot, it's not, as fall season nears, 1998, p. D3).

Summary

Television is a business that relies on audience viewership. The process of making television shows inevitably involves disappointment. Roughly eight out of ten new television shows fail. Concepts, characters, and scripts that seemed promising often do not work in production. Research audiences that form focus groups may not warm up to them. Yet sometimes there are pleasant surprises, and shows that had low expectations turn out to be quite successful in execution. Scott Siegler, a former development executive for Warner Brothers, explained why it is so hard to predict what will please audiences:

> Because it's a mass audience . . . You can work off precedents about what's worked on television before. You can work off whatever smattering of sociological information you gleaned from whatever sources. You can let your personal judgments enter into it to some extent . . . You can ask whether this is something that people in Georgia or Nebraska will appreciate because they'll be able to translate it into their understanding. But you never really know. And there are so many variables in programming that even when you've reached a pretty general consensus about a genre not working or a kind of attitude not working, you can never be quite sure that that rule applies." (Gitlin, 1983, pp. 22–23)

Rino Scanzoni, chief investment officer for ad buyer Mediaedge:cia, looked at it from the perspective of advertising and spin-off shows: "It's a struggle for TV networks to create 'watercooler' hits that can command ad rates of half a million bucks for 30 seconds. That's why TV viewers are seeing more spin-offs of current hits such as CBS' new *CSI: New York*. Once viewers buy into a series, there's a real appetite for new shows" (McCarthy, 2004, p. 6B).

The love-hate relationship between the creators of television shows and the networks was comically expressed by Ellen DeGeneres, who hosted the 2001 Emmy Awards on CBS on November 4: "They can't take away our creativity, our joy. Only television executives can do that."

The television critic needs to be aware of the many economic constraints that influence television production. Television is a business and has to make a profit. However, writers, directors, actors, and even producers want their products to be of high quality, for they are creative and talented people. As a television critic, you recognize how much depends upon the mass audience and its preferences. Therefore, knowledge of the television business as well as how television style is created (the subject of Chapter 3) enhances understanding of why television is the way it is.

Exercises

1. Find the television ratings in *USA Today* or on the Nielsen Web site www.nielsenmedia.com. (The Nielsen homepage is http://www.nielsen .com. It has a link to www.nielsenmedia.com.) Check the ratings and shares for the current week on (1) broadcast television; (2) cable; (3) syndication; (4) among African Americans; and (5) among Hispanics. Note how Nielsen includes DVR recording.

2. During a Sweeps Week (November, February, May, and July), examine the television schedule to determine how the programs are different at that time.

3. Find a television program that has been canceled. Go back to the ratings to see where it was ranked.

4. Watch a television commercial and describe its AQRI (arouse quick related interest).

5. Watch a half-hour or one-hour television program, paying attention to all the commercials. See if you can guess the show's demographics from the commercials.

6. Watch a half-hour or one-hour television program and note all the products that are placed within it.

7. How many products get free air time on a morning news or game show?

8. Watch a show on local cable television. See how many commercials are targeted to precisely defined audiences.

9. Analyze the flow of broadcast programs from 8:00 p.m. to 11:00 p.m. and describe the building blocks. Where is a less successful program placed?

10. Look for broadcast programs that are scheduled "off the clock," and note what programs on other networks are in competition with them. If you watch the beginning or end of a show that is off the clock, will you miss the opening or closing of a competing program?

11. Select a series on HBO: (1) find how many times the episode is repeated during the week; and (2) find how many episodes are scheduled for a single season.

12. At the end of a television show, watch the credits and find the name of the production house that produced it.

13. Select a very successful television series, then name newer shows that resemble it.

14. Go to a television series Web site and look at the roles and names of the personnel (producers, directors, writers, and so on).

15. Pay close attention to the writing of a television show. How much do you, as a member of the audience, fill in what is not spoken in the dialogue?

16. Examine the unwritten subtext of a television program. How do the camera work and the acting communicate the subtext?

17. If at all possible, visit a television studio to observe the taping of a television program or a live production. Discuss what you observed and what you learned.

Suggested Readings

Gitlin, Todd. (1983). *Inside Prime Time*. New York: Pantheon Books.

Kubey, Robert. (2004). *Creating Television: Conversations with the People Behind 50 Years of American TV*. Mahwah, NJ: Lawrence Erlbaum.

Marc, David & Thompson, Robert J. (1995). *Prime Time, Prime Movers*. Syracuse, NY: Syracuse University Press.

Newcomb, Horace & Alley, Robert S. (1983). *The Producer's Medium: Conversations with Creators of American TV*. New York: Oxford University Press.

Webster, James G., Phalen, Patricia F., & Lichty, Lawrence W. (2000). *Ratings Analysis: The Theory and Practice of Audience Research*, (2nd ed.). Mahwah, NJ: Lawrence Erlbaum.

www.nielsenmedia.com

PART II

Formal Aspects of Television

3

Television Style

The ventures of dreamland are thine for a day.

—Silas Weir Mitchell, "Dreamland"

Introduction

When we watch television, we seldom think about how it is produced, yet it is television style created by production techniques that allows us to enjoy the programs we watch. When we watch the reality show *Survivor,* we see a group of 16 men and women who appear to be stranded on an island that is miles from camp, coping with little or no convenient resources and dangerous elements. Yet, there are as many as 20 camera people, directors, producers, and others there with them. If the 16 people who play the survivor game were really alone on the island, there would be no television show about them. Because they are the invisible entities behind the show, the production professionals are not noticed by the viewers at all. As a television critic, you do not have to know the technical requirements of producing a television show, but it is useful to remember that what we see on the screen is the product of many talented people who work in the television industry. Knowing something about production techniques may help the critic talk about what is seen and heard and how it came about.

The following discussion of television style was written for this book in collaboration with Paul Monaco, film and television producer, director, editor, writer, and professor of cinema and video. He writes from an experience of professional academic and media production of 20 years.

Length of Shot and Framing

Motion picture production developed distinctive stylistic approaches during the 50 years of making movies prior to the advent of broadcast television immediately after the Second World War. Often spoken of as "film language," the stylistic choices for directors and editors may be summarized briefly. The first 30 years of filmmaking consisted of silent movies, produced without synchronous sound, so the fundamental film aesthetic developed with a strong emphasis on visual communication. As such, there are several elements of film language that were established very early in the 20th century. Visually, all shots that appear on the screen, for both movies and television, may be described as long, medium, or close. A long shot includes an entire human figure from the bottom of the feet to the top of the head, creating a full picture. A medium shot is framed on a human figure at or near the waist, so that the torso and head fill the picture, while the legs and feet are below the lower frame line and out of the picture. A close-up shows only the head. There are a variety of shots that are gradients between these long, medium, and close shots that use intermediate framing, such as the medium long shot, the medium close shot, or the extreme close-up.

What we see on television can always be thought of and described as being a long shot, a medium shot, or a close-up shot, with variants of distance from camera to subject. All types of material seen on television, and all genres of TV production, use these shots. Compared to motion picture production, strong tendencies exist in television toward medium shots. Medium shots are prominently used for news commentators, for interviewers, for talk shows, and for sports commentators when they are on air. Most live and live-on-tape production in these genres favors the medium shot. Medium shots, moreover, are favored in the production of fictional dramas and comedies produced for television. The medium shot lends itself to what is considered the most natural framing for conversation. The heart of a great deal of writing for television drama and comedy is talk.

The genres of news, talk, information programming, and commentary in particular remind us that, although television production derives in part from the traditions of motion pictures, television also derives—and some would argue more strongly—from the traditions of broadcast radio. Talk is

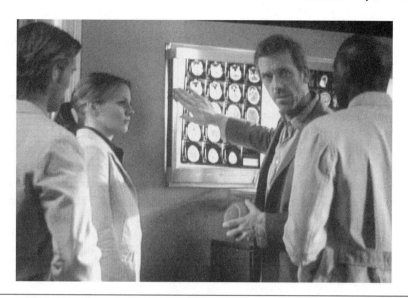

Photo 3.1   A medium shot on *House.*

very important on television. Television is every bit as much an audio medium as it is a visual medium.

Over time, the typical style of television production developed a reliance on a medium shot that is actually framed tighter than one that is described as cutting a figure at the waist. That standard framing of a shot for television is best described as an "elbows" shot. TV directors and camera operators commonly use the term "elbows." Any reference to elbows frames a shot of a figure so that the lower edge of the screen is at roughly the middle point of his or her arms. A great deal of television production uses this framing. Dramas, situation comedies, and soap operas nearly always do, but the commonality of this framing to production for television spreads more widely as well.

To say that any particular shot or a frame line is standard or dominant in television production still must be understood to mean that other shots are used as well. Long shots are not as common in television production as they are in motion pictures, but they exist in all genres of television. They often serve to draw the viewer's engagement out of a comedy or a drama emotionally. Hence, they are frequently used for transitions into and out of scenes. In sports programming, by contrast, long shots are absolutely vital to portraying the action of the game, which can only be shown with a long, wide-angle shot.

Multi-Camera Production

Live and live-on-tape production for television is normally multi-camera production, meaning several cameras are in use simultaneously. Four-camera production schemes have been common in television historically for the production of both dramatic and comedy programming. Such multi-camera production schemes allow for a good deal of coverage and are particularly useful in the confined interior settings common to much of dramatic and comedy production for television. Multi-camera production in these circumstances is considered especially amenable to episodic programming. The characters and locations are familiar and repetitious from week to week. Traditionally, television favored such production as economical and effective.

Reaction Shots

Early in the development of motion picture production, filmmakers discovered the power of the reaction shot, in which a facial expression or the gesture of a person who is not talking in a scene is revealed. This capacity to fill the screen with the reaction of a figure in a scene to another character's action became more sophisticated in feature film production after the coming of synchronous sound to the movies in 1927. Production for mainstream Hollywood feature films standardized the reverse angle shot, so that an editor could choose to show a single shot on either the speaker or the listener in a conversation. This ability, to cut to a reaction shot, is definitive of one of the primary aesthetic devices available to any filmmaker. Television has made coverage on reactions even more pronounced and prominent than in the movies. Part of this is because production for television usually is more intimate than the visual coverage provided in movies made for exhibition in theaters on the big screen. Live coverage in specific television genres—such as the talk show, quiz show, public affairs programming featuring experts with differing opinions, and sports broadcasting—lends itself so well to revealing the reactions of people being interviewed, pondering a question, arguing, or responding to a play in a game.

In television comedy and drama, reaction shots have taken on increasing importance as production styles have evolved over the half century since the 1950s. Situation comedies are models of using reaction shots to emphasize the humor of a line. Because successful television is episodic, regular viewers are familiar with the characters and their relationships in a particular show. This familiarity facilitates the viewer's understanding and appreciation of these sorts of reactions. The same is true for episodic drama, and nowhere is this more evident than in the daily daytime television soap operas. Prime-time drama relies heavily on reaction shots to convey realization, discovery, and a character's coming to terms with troubling or devastating feelings or events. *Without a Trace, ER, Grey's Anatomy, House, 24,* and the *CSI* series are typical of exceptionally popular dramatic programs in which coverage on shots of a character's reaction to other characters and the episode's story line are vital to the style.

Multi-camera production of live talk shows, quiz shows, and sporting events, of course, lends itself to the coverage of reactions. This is true for comedy and dramatic production as well, but television production with a single camera also utilizes reaction shots. Although several directors guide the making of different episodes of *The Sopranos,* for example, every episode is heavy on reaction shots, and their importance to the development of the story line and the revealing of a character's feelings is vital. This style of utilizing reaction shots so much meshes with the fact that the characters in the series—most prominently Tony Soprano and his wife Carmela—are strong and well-established for the viewers.

Lighting

"If you can't light it, you can't film or tape it." This simplistic maxim is the heart of all motion picture and television production. Once any figure or object is adequately lit so that it can be seen, a vast array of aesthetic and stylistic choices confronts the maker of film or television. The look of television production tends toward balanced lighting that avoids extremes of light and shadow and treats all figures in a scene equally. The source of light in such traditional television production has been treated as comparatively inconsequential. Lights in a television production studio hang from a grid above the action, and these lights are set to produce a common look so that generally all portions of the space are lit similarly. This mode of lighting is very different from what is used historically in single-camera film production. The use of single camera in motion picture production requires much more time because there are far more setups. Motion picture lighting, since the early 1970s, has used lower light and permitted greater latitude in allowing light and shadow to push or pull toward greater extremes of brightness or darkness. There has even been a stylistic tendency in motion picture production toward the use of "available light," with minimal addition of lighting in certain locations. In this sense, television productions have almost always been "better" lit than movies because production for television uses more standardized and brighter lighting as a rule.

Manipulation of the lighting strongly affects the tone of a scene, and the emotional mood that is conveyed by that scene to viewers. Television production, however, historically has been very modest in the use of lighting to influence tone and mood. Such a use of lighting is far more a convention of modern motion picture production that even in dramatic features produced for theatrical release tends toward favoring low light, accepting what is called natural, available light for scenes, and permitting the wide use of extremes of brightness and darkness, light and shadow, to create mood and emotional responses. While television production has steered away from extreme and artistic lighting schemes, the aesthetic choices about lighting are still essential to production.

Because the producers wanted more intimacy between the characters for the second season of the television series *House* and to give the audience the impression that they were witnessing reality, Roy Wagner, the cinematographer, had the number of lights pulled down, and the line producer, Gerrit van der Meer, redesigned the sets. They put ceilings on all interior sets, including hallways, offices, the lobby, waiting room, and operating rooms. The ceilings enclose the spaces, and fluorescent fixtures built into the sets are the only source of light with beams of light that can be controlled. As Wagner said, "That's important because the eye automatically goes to the brightest light in the frame. We want the audience looking at the actors" (How Roy Wagner reveals, 2005, p. 2). The new lighting setup gave the directors the freedom to shoot in any direction, including looking up toward ceilings. It also trimmed the budget and the time it takes to light the scenes.

Production on Film Versus Digital Video

For a great many years, people in the television industry talked about entertainment shows for television being "taped," but many of the episodic dramas and comedies on TV were actually filmed. The use of celluloid film produces a "look" in which colors are more deeply saturated, detail is more precise, and the foregrounding of figures and objects is sharp. It was only in the late 1990s that any appreciable number of major episodic dramas and comedies made for network television began to be produced using digital video cameras rather than film and film cameras. The production crews did not necessarily welcome this change, and a number of long-running shows continued using film. For example, the production of *Frasier* continued to use film instead of digital video production through its final season in the spring of 2003.

The industry-wide changeover to digital cameras and production had almost nothing to do with aesthetic choices or with production style. Like many producers' decisions, it was driven by economics. Film had two areas of extra cost that digital video production did not have. First, the use of film required larger camera crews, so that a four-camera production normally required a minimum of 12 camera professionals, three on each camera. Second, the costs of film stock and the processing of film were thought to be considerably higher than the cost of taping—even using the highest-end and most expensive digital cameras. Not surprisingly, for a while professional production personnel debated the use of the new digital technologies in the camera department. As for the preferred look in terms of color saturation, light and shadow, and detail, most professionals preferred the look of film. Many craftspeople in the industry also argued that the economic arguments for conversion to digital video production were misleading and/or mistaken. This argument advanced the notion that the hourly rental of time for digital editing was so expensive that conversion to digital production might save little or no money.

Gradually, digital cameras prevailed. The definitive influence in the final choice of digital cameras over motion picture cameras and the use of film in production for television was that digital postproduction (for editing and sound) swept away the technologies and practices of motion picture editing and double-track system sound. Motion picture and television craftspeople are famously capable of adapting to technological changes and the use of new equipment. What constituted a digital revolution in television production from the late 1990s into the early 21st century was absorbed and mastered quickly and well. Viewers did not notice when, and if, their favorite entertainment shows changed from production in film to production with digital cameras. Although the shift from traditional editing and sound technologies and practices to digital ones affected the professional workplace in television considerably, what the viewers see and hear in their homes was not necessarily changed in any perceptible way.

Style, Reception, and Digital Video Practices

Among the ironies and complexities of television style is that all the formal characteristics of picture and sound finally may depend less on what went into the television production and more on the equipment on which you view it. Ostensibly, the goal of improving what the viewer sees and hears at home is behind the conversion from analog television to high-definition digital television in the United States that was mandated in the Telecommunications Act, passed by the U.S. Congress in 1996. This conversion is to be completed nationwide by the end of the first decade of the 21st century, although meeting that goal has proven costly and suffered several delays.

Proponents of the conversion to high-definition television believe that the costs and difficulties will prove to be worth it because viewers will see a considerably sharper and clearer picture, the sound quality will be vastly improved, and the elongation of the screen's width will deliver programming in a vastly more impressive pictorial frame. Critics argue that the mandated conversion serves only the interests of the two Japanese companies, Sony and Panavision, who invested heavily in HDTV but found that potential viewers showed little interest in it on an open market. Thereupon these two companies had to turn to America's national politicians to force its adoption. Supporters claim that high definition promises a much more rewarding aesthetic experience for viewers. Critics assert that there is no evidence that a wider picture and sharper sound are necessarily what television viewers are seeking in the experience of watching TV.

While digital production on tape has grown quickly and steadily, there are some notable holdouts in areas of production in which film is still largely preferred for image capture; put simply, the picture on film still always looks better and more nuanced visually. Once captured on celluloid with the film look, such footage must then be transferred to a digital tape format for editing. High-end commercials for many products promoted nationwide, for example, still are often shot on film. Here the preference for the film look in glossy national advertising campaigns prevails.

Moreover, while the introduction of HDTV in the first several years of the 21st century promotes the utilization of 24-p and digital video camera use for dramatic and comedy production, at the same time there is a shift away from multi-camera production to single-camera production. While the use of digital cameras saves production money at one end by replacing more expensive equipment, the choice to follow single-camera production practices increases the length of all productions and their costs. Single-camera production is a technique developed in, and associated with, the movies. The preference for it, however, may be questionable when the production in question is for television. In the late 1990s, the shift to single-camera production techniques found HBO at its vanguard. Signature HBO successes like *The Sopranos, Sex and the City,* and *Six Feet Under* were single-camera productions, and there is little doubt that these successes influenced other productions to tend toward single-camera direction and production.

To the question: "Can the average viewer recognize when he or she is seeing a single-camera production or a multi-camera production on television?" the general answer is no. Studio productions, such as talk shows and newscasts, nearly always are multi-camera productions even though they are shot entirely with digital video cameras. Multi-camera techniques lend themselves to quick cutting from shot to shot, audience coverage including an array of immediate audience reactions shots, and the ability to pull out wide on a shot in a blink of the eye. Single-camera techniques permit directors and actors more time to work through the material of a scene because there are more camera setups, and because a number of takes are required to provide adequate coverage of any scene. The single-camera technique tends to slow the dramatic action and development, and provides coverage so that a character's reactions tend to be given greater attention. Nonetheless, single-camera production had come into vogue during the first decade of the 21st century, although no specific aesthetic intention was connected to that development.

Modes of Presentation

Historically, most television production for drama and comedy has aimed at a mode of presentation like that of classic Hollywood film. Movements and focusing of the camera lens were intended to be unobtrusive. Editing generally followed patterns of continuity and the editing formulas for achieving that appearance. Disruption in the flow of the story was minimized in favor of clear and distinct break points. Television production in principle has had to follow strict points of division in order to accommodate breaks for commercials. Again, HBO, a cable network without commercial sponsorship of specific program segments, led the way toward a new form of narrative integrity and wholeness in its typical dramatic and comedy production. Here, again, however, television style is diverse and multifaceted.

Sports coverage presents an example of production decisions that are determined by the discrete nature of the game or competition itself. News coverage on television has a strong tendency toward a stylistic emphasis on immediacy, underscored by handheld camera work and a visual involvement in the developing action of any scene. With handheld camera movements, the viewer's eye follows the movements, irregularities, and pacing of the camera's lens. Handheld camera styles draw the viewer to the image, make emphatic the viewer's identification with the point of view of the camera, and thus are assumed to visually engage the viewer's emotions more. Some reality programming, such as the early reality show *Cops*, abides by this style. Such an approach to camera work emphasizes engagement, handheld techniques, and the following of action. Reaction footage is minimized in the final cutting, and may not have been filmed at all because the attention of the camera work is the action as it happens in front of the police officers. *NYPD Blue*, the former weekly drama about police detectives in New York City, was a show that tended to establish a visual style based on handheld camera work and abrupt camera movements, including swish pans where the camera lurched in one direction or the other, but usually left to right, creating a particular "look" that became characteristic for creating transitions within a sequence. Cinematographer Roy Wagner, who employs a blend of handheld, Steadicam (a camera strapped to the body of the camera person), and dolly (a camera mounted on moving wheels) shots on the series *House,* said: "When the story becomes chaotic and out of control, we'll handhold the camera to create visual tension, so the audience subliminally feels a sense of urgency" (How Roy Wagner reveals, 2005, p. 3). From this reality style of handheld camera work, television news, live coverage, and other forms of informational programming display a strong affinity for the use of editing wipes and the blending of pictures.

Television Sound and Editing

There is very little silence on TV. The production style for all genres and types of programming requires a sound design that is dense and unrelenting. A common term for this practice in the industry calls such sound in a production "wall-to-wall." Talk predominates on television, hearkening back to the medium's traditions which are derived from radio. Even when there is relatively less talk, music, sound effects, or what is heard as naturalistic ambient sound fills the track. Directional microphones on booms are utilized to record sound on dramatic and comedy productions. Documentaries, interviews for news coverage, and talk shows may use small, lavaliere-type microphones worn on the clothing, although wireless microphones that are carried in a pocket or attached to a belt to permit greater movement have become more common. Compared to motion picture sound, television sound is far less sweetened, manipulated, and edited. Sound effects in television production are vastly fewer and always inferior in quality to those used in motion picture production for theatrical distribution. Another factor is that the systems in the typical television sets in the early 21st century still consist of smaller and vastly inferior speakers mounted within the television set itself. To compensate, home theater setups with stereo speakers amplify television sound.

What appears most definitive and distinctive of television style is a tendency toward accelerated pacing in nearly all genres. Quick cutting is a norm, although there are exceptions to this guideline. Multi-camera production in particular favors quicker cutting, with shot lengths typically three to five seconds in duration. Longer takes are less common in television. When long takes do occur, they frequently are instances of a camera moving, normally with a subject. The popular *ER*, for example, typically utilizes a Steadicam for about 70 percent of the shots on the show, especially for moving beside the paramedics rushing a gurney with a patient on it into the emergency room. This image is so typical of the program that it might be called a signature shot.

> The Steadicam is equipped with a special spring-loaded rigging that combines the freedom of a handheld camera with the stability of a dollied tracking shot. This creates the smooth, flowing appearing of the shot as the cameraman walks along. Although the weight is considerable at seventy pounds, it is reasonably distributed by way of a harness onto the hips of the cameraman. Instead of an eyepiece, the scene is viewed through a five-inch video monitor. (Pourroy, pp. 60–61)

During the 1950s and 1960s, television programming was decidedly slower-paced and more clearly based on principles of continuity than it is today. In the 1970s, cutting ratios quickened, so that shorter shots tended to be edited more quickly. As a general principle, the pace of editing has increased in all genres and types of television. However, as television programming has become as vast and as diverse as it did by the 1990s, generalizations about television style—and the prevailing aesthetic in the medium—must always be viewed cautiously. Made-for-television movies followed a slower pace of development and editing than dramatic and comedic television programming. Movies are longer, complete works. Most feature films that are shown on television are an hour and a half to two and a half hours in length. Music videos and commercials tend toward fast cutting, with pacing that often may be described as frenetic. As television producers in all genres manage and manipulate time—a phenomenon that descriptively is definitive of television—it is widely observed that generational tastes appear to dictate much about editing choices and pacing. Programming that is presumed to appeal to younger viewers, especially to teenage and young adult audiences, is more fast-paced than shows, programs, and types of television aimed at a middle-aged or older demographic.

Production Styles

Industry professionals often say that motion pictures are a director's and cinematographer's medium, while television is a producer's and writer's medium. This generalization points to a perception that defines the differences in production styles. Traditionally, feature films made for theatrical release explore a wider range of visual looks, camera setups and movements, and engage physical space in ways that are more ambitious aesthetically. Television production is far more cautious, economical, and standardized, being dependent upon turning out material on a regular basis in a uniform way. Drama and comedy produced for TV have been intended for episodic series, and that intention drives their style. News, information, and talk programming have to be regularized to repeat daily. Sports on television is an event, although the proliferation of sports channels in the late 1990s, the lengthy seasons of many professional sports—Major League Baseball (MLB) especially, but also the National Basketball Association (NBA), the National Football League (NFL), and the National Hockey League (NHL)—and the increased coverage of major college athletics have transformed the truism of "event" programming into the programming concept of covering a different event every three hours or so.

Art Direction

Production design, also known as art direction, plays an important role in television production. Studio production occurs in a defined space. Typical sets have three walls on a sound stage, usually decorated to look like familiar rooms in houses, hospitals, or offices. The fourth wall is left open for the camera equipment, lights, microphones, and a live audience if one is in the studio. Cameras are basically aimed in a forward direction like the eyes of the audience facing a stage, with side shots and close-ups as needed. The sets have open ceilings with rafters and lights. *ER* and *House* are exceptions to this norm with their four hard-walled, closed ceiling sets constructed to look like real hospitals. That is why viewers sometimes see the ceilings and overhead lights in the shots or follow the Steadicam, strapped to the camera operator's body, down the hallways.

Situation comedies have nearly always been taped in front of a live audience, even though the program that is shown is extensively edited after the actual taping, and normally does not air until several weeks later. The audience sits on raised bleachers on one side of the set, which normally consists of three stages built and dressed as the normal living, work, and leisure spaces of the characters. These are the places where the bulk of the show's action occurs, with another set built and added for specific scenes, in a bar or a restaurant, for example. These stages, all of which open to the camera personnel, are arranged in a line, like railroad cars, with the performance and its camera work most normally proceeding from left to right. Typically, these stages have scenery painted on backdrops to offer views out of windows from the set itself. For situation comedies, the décor and color combinations are brighter and lighter; for dramas, the look of the furnishings, the paint on the walls, and the costuming are more subdued. More reds and yellows are used in situation comedies; browns, grays, blues, and similar subdued colors are used for drama. Sets are detailed and dressed with props that look "natural" for the era and place, and for age and gender, as well as the economic or social status of the characters in a comedy or drama. Prop masters are in charge of selecting appropriate properties on the sets, and makeup artists and costume designers decorate the actors for their parts. *Sex and the City* was known for its designer clothing on the four principal actresses with the brand names of dresses, purses, and especially shoes written into the scripts.

The production designer or art director works hard at balancing any number of considerations. The driving aesthetic for such choices is naturalism, with a strong emphasis on creating spaces that the viewer will take as appropriate to, and believable for, the particular characters and episodes. Successful comedies and dramas run for years and then go into syndication, when they may be telecast daily. The distinct spaces where these dramas and comedies occur are very detailed parts of their overall aesthetic value.

Nonetheless, when thinking about the styles in television production, and, at some point commenting on a few of the differences between the production look of movies as compared to TV, a very basic and historic fact stands in the way of reaching any simple conclusion about television style. Because of their fundamental photographic nature, motion pictures and television aesthetically are considered to be strongly "naturalistic." From the inception of each of these media until the mid-1960s, however, production and presentation in them was in black and white. Little seems less natural than a visual world perceived and seen only in black and white, but many of the most highly regarded movies in motion picture history and all the classic television productions of the 1950s and early 1960s were in black and white. Moreover, reruns of *I Love Lucy* and *Gunsmoke,* for example, still entertain television audiences into the early 21st century. The telecasting of black-and-white classic feature films and significant historical documentaries on television has only grown with the proliferation of cable and satellite television and their many new channels.

The norms of spatial production design in drama and comedy produced for television tend to be stage-like, commonly with the action opened up toward the imaginary fourth wall of a set where the action occurs. The cast essentially plays to the cameras, much the way stage actors play to their audiences. Lighting for depth perspective and the use of filming techniques such as selective focus or deep focus have traditionally been minimized in production for television. Again, by the late 1990s and into the early years of the 21st century, HBO productions, notably series like *The Sopranos* and *Six Feet Under,* as well as special productions like HBO's *Angels In America,* directed by Mike Nichols, with Richard Edlund as its director of photography, pushed production for television toward motion picture artistry and its visual and performance aesthetic.

So much of what is on television is news, information, interview, and talk programming, and in these genres the stylistic conventions are standard. The set itself is generally functional, relatively unembellished, and the commentators, hosts, and guests are foregrounded. This means that their figures are prominently lit and that the backgrounds do not detract or draw attention away from their prominence in the frame. Such programming typically finds a satisfactory look and stays with it. There are differences, of course. The *Late Show with David Letterman* is produced in an older theater owned by CBS, and not coincidentally located on Broadway in New York City. *The Tonight Show* on NBC with Jay Leno is produced in a large studio in Burbank, California, and the production style is distinguished by beginning each show with shots revealing the entire studio, sometimes showing camera operations, and always zooming in to the host with a sweeping crane shot as he emerges on stage. More serious talk formats, such as *The Charlie Rose Show* on PBS or *Tavis Smiley* on the same network, utilize more minimal spatial and set design. Rose's interviews take place against a minimalist black background; Smiley uses two raisers in an unadorned space, which suggest a somewhat studied, but unnatural look for an interview. Serious interview shows and political and informational talk on television do not use an audience. Daytime talk shows and various similar genres, where talk is primarily with celebrities and entertainers, nearly always feature the audience in some way, typically taking the show's host into the audience at some point to interact with selected audience members in a great many of the shows.

The Split Screen

By the late 1990s, television news and informational programming on television in the United States discovered the split screen. Sometimes this is used purposefully, for example, to have a reporter at a location in one box discussing an event with the anchor in the studio, who is in the rest of the pictures. Other uses of the split screen appear more arbitrary or capricious. Splitting the screen is easy with the technology and frequently seems done for no other reason than that it can be done. A simple informational scroll of information in a line across the bottom of the screen—typically with stock prices, or the local weather—is a modest gesture that does not really split the screen.

Split screen use appears most effective on informational shows in which adversaries are discussing a public issue in debate style, and the screen is split between them for the conduct of what constitutes their debate. Perhaps even more so because they are separated physically and joined from different locations only as a visual convention on the TV screen, this visual format lends itself to the style of cross-talking and escalating exchanges that often seem to turn angry.

Any consideration of the style and aesthetics of television must keep in mind that the antecedents of television come as much, or more, from broadcast radio as they do from motion picture production. Sound is continuous in all types and genres of television. Silence is dead air, and even "natural" pauses in speech or response, whether in interviews, commentary, or delivering fictional lines are to be minimized. Part of the aesthetic of television is the constancy of sound, which in some instances, such as news coverage or reality shows like *Cops,* demands a prominent track of ambient location sound.

Directors

In motion picture production, successful directors gain recognition and fame. Their names appear prominently in the credits of a movie and on the marquees of the movie theaters. Such attention is not granted to television directors. If their productions are multi-camera, their work may be even more intense and demanding than directing for the single camera. Directors of sports television must be utterly engaged in what is going on in the game, quick-witted, and make instantaneous decisions. Their work is facilitated by the ensemble of veteran professionals around them. This is a slick business, whose positions are reserved for the best and the most reliable. Simultaneously, the director in live sports gives camera operators directions—"pan to the right," "get tight on the manager in the dugout," "hold a shot on the backfield," and so forth—while following the game and calling for the technical director, who works at a control board called a switcher, to take the correct shot and transmit it out to the audience. All this happens in a relative flash. The director also needs to be able to spot good reactions from fans in the stands, or at least amusing ones, for example someone who has fallen asleep in the late innings at a boring Major League Baseball game.

Studio multi-camera direction for talk shows or game shows is similar, but far less stressful. The action is predictable. Audience members at a show's taping most likely have been selected and seated by a production assistant well before the taping begins. Directing a newscast is even more predictable, unless breaking news interrupts the planned broadcast and the director must make an immediate decision about when to interrupt the newscast, how long to stay with the incident occurring in real time, and how to instruct the editor to use whatever camera coverage of it is available.

Multi-camera dramatic and comedy production for television requires the director to watch a large television screen with the pictures from each of the four cameras on that screen at once (called a quad-split), while simultaneously being engaged with what is going on with the characters. Directing is about camera setups, movements, and angles, but more deeply must be about what is going on with the characters and where each character's arc is in the story. Thus, directing most clearly for television drama and comedy comes down to being about capturing people and what is going on with them to fit the purposes and goals of the particular show. Television situation comedy directors must develop an uncanny feeling for a joke and also have a sensitive feel for catching a reaction shot from one of the other characters. For drama, something similar is the challenge, but the director watches for expressions of feeling and tension and is sure to cover those while also having made certain that appropriate reaction shots are covered for another character.

Actors

Television actors often have theater acting backgrounds, but acting for television is altogether different from acting in the theater. There are fewer rehearsals, with many last-minute changes and often little time to memorize lines. In the first few rehearsals before the camera crews arrive, actors may be relatively free to move about on the sound stage in accordance with where they feel they need to be. If the camera cannot make an adjustment, the actors change their movements to help out the camera operators. Often the floors of the sets are marked with quarter-inch paper tape that shows an actor where to stand and which way to angle his or her body, but the tape is removed before the cameras shoot. The directors block the actors to the furniture in situation comedies so that they do not look down when performing. Also, the blocking is for the director of photography so he or she lights where the actors will be. The actors (and the production staff and crew) for dramas put in extremely long hours, as many as 16 in one day, with many starts and stops while keeping consistency of character. They have to return to the set, bringing themselves back into character with the same voice, movement, and gestures.

Summary

The stylistic commonalities in television are many. The genres of production for television, however, are vastly diverse. Whatever is made for television and shown on television always is seen in a circumstance that varies greatly depending on the quality of the particular set on which the viewer is watching.

Will the horizontally expanded screen of HDTV and the brighter, more numerous pixels and more crisp resolution of the picture promised by digital television vastly change the viewing experience? At a simple, surface level, the answer is yes. But at a more complex depth of analysis, the question remains open. Television is about story and character. Any director of television understands that his or her job is less setting the cameras, framing the shots, and composing them than it is in understanding and conveying to viewers the sense of the story and what is going on with the characters in it. This is true for all television drama and comedy, but also for the news, informational reporting, celebrity coverage, talk shows, and whatever reality television may claim to be recording and portraying.

Exercises

1. Select examples from several types of programming—a situation comedy, a drama, a national or local news broadcast, a talk show, a game show, and/or a sports event—and turn off the picture and listen to a show for ten minutes. How much have you lost in your experience without the picture?

2. Record some situation comedies and dramas, then view them a couple of times to carefully determine and write down the use of close, medium, and long shots in the productions. What differences do you perceive between comedy and drama with regard to the use of close, medium, and long shots?

3. Analyze the same tapes that you used for exercise #2 and time the individual shots in the show. What do you perceive as the differences between comedy and drama in terms of the length of shots and the pacing with which the show is put together?

4. Again, using the same tapes of situation comedies and dramas, look carefully through them for the reaction shots. How frequently are reaction shots used? What patterns do you perceive in situation comedies and dramas? How are they different?

5. Watch a talk show to see how many reaction shots there are: of the host, of the guests, of the audience. Watch a public affairs show, on which guests or a panel representing different points of view are featured. See how many shots are reactions of someone when another person is talking. Watch a sports event throughout, such as a complete baseball or football game, and see how much coverage there is on players, coaches or managers, and fans in the stands.

6. Select an episode of a situation comedy with which you are familiar and watch it, concentrating on the number of reaction shots used on a character who is not talking. Do the same for an episodic drama.

7. What is the look of a particular show on television? Is the lighting bright or dark? Can you clearly see the characters at all times, or do the characters move into shadows where their features are obscured?

8. How would you describe the production design of any particular show on television? What do the sets, locations, or costumes suggest to you? What information is conveyed to you by the design elements? If it is a comedy or a drama, do the sets mesh with the mood or the theme of the program? If it is a nonfiction show, do the sets convey a sense of seriousness, authority, and/or objectivity?

9. When you are aware of a camera movement, either in toward a subject or out and away from it, or movement that follows a character from left to right or from right to left, can you explain what appears to be the motivation and intention of the camera being put into motion? Does this movement serve to reveal something in the scene to the viewer, or does the camera movement appear to be about mood and feeling?

10. Select a show with which you are familiar and have watched many times. Select one actor from the show and comment on the consistency of character (appearance, voice, movement, gestures, and attitude) over time.

Suggested Readings

Kingdon, Tom. (2004). *Total Directing: Integrating Camera and Performance in Film and Television*. Los Angeles: Silman-James Press.

Shelton, S. Martin. (2004). *Communicating Ideas with Film, Video, and Multimedia: A Practical Guide to Information Motion-Media*. Carbondale, IL: Southern Illinois Press.

Ward, Peter. (2003). *Picture Composition for Film and Television* (2nd ed.). Boston: Focal.

Zettl, Herbert. (2005). *Television Production Handbook* (9th ed.). Belmont, CA: Wadsworth.

4

Television, the Nation's Storyteller

Sing to me of the man, Muse, the man of twists and turns

driven time and again off course, once he had plundered

the hallowed heights of Troy . . .

Launch out on his story, Muse, daughter of Zeus

start from where you will—sing for our time too.

—Homer, *The Odyssey*

Introduction

As you have seen in previous chapters, television is a producer's medium, and most producers are the creators and writers of the stories that are told on television. Both fiction and nonfiction television tell stories, thus this chapter relates the important characteristic of television as a story-making medium. As a television critic, you will analyze the characteristics of narrative and the ways in which stories are crafted to fit the television medium. If you are a student of television production, this chapter will help you develop the stories you want to tell.

Structure and systematic organization are extremely important in television narrative. Because of frequent interruptions during the programs and week-long gaps between episodes, familiar structure enables viewers to stay with the stories. Time constraints for broadcast television require most stories to fit into 30- and 60-minute time slots, with the stories themselves taking up no more than 22 or 44 minutes, respectively. Half-hour shows are broken into two acts, while hour-long shows are broken into four acts. This allows for the commercial breaks and other interruptions. Programs on premium subscription television such as HBO are also broken into acts, although there is more flexibility because an episode is not interrupted by commercials. Formats are repeated week after week because television programming, for the most part, is episodic. Series and serial television have groups of recurring characters whose essential qualities and basic situations remain the same from episode to episode. In series television, novel events do occur, but the characters and their strategies and actions tend to remain similar. There is usually a resolution to a dilemma or problem in a single episode, but conflicts in interpersonal relationships may not get resolved. In serials, especially in soap operas, the situations continue from episode to episode. Each program in series and serials is composed of segments with a format holding the segments together, providing them with continuity and narrative progression. Like dramatic series, news programs are structured with breaking news stories early in the program followed by weather, sports, and human interest stories. News programs can be seen as a unified body exhibiting themes and patterns with heroes and villains. Narrative devices emphasizing community and rituals are used in news writing. News is put into frameworks that are easily understood and anticipated. Documentaries are structured as narratives, while sporting events are structured as rituals with stories about heroic players interspersed with the games.

Television's narratives and characters are familiar and reassuring to the audience. Paul Monaco explained, "Stories are best for television when they are highly accessible, easily understood, fall within a range of plausibility, and strike viewers as familiar enough to fit easily into patterns of repetition . . . They are best liked and most admired precisely in those instances in which a familiar formula is taken and modified slightly" (Monaco, 1998, p. 6).

Storytelling and the Human Condition

Storytelling is an ancient tradition. From the oral storytelling tradition of Homer to the stories told around the fireplace in the past to the electronic hearth of television today, people have enjoyed and participated in a narrative tradition. Narratives probably originated with human signifying practices, that is, the human ability to describe with language events and people in their absence. James Watson and Anne Hill (2003) define story as a social ritual that has the power to bring about a sense of shared experience and of social values. They quote Michel de Certeau's *The Practice of Everyday Life* (1984): "Narratives 'articulate our existences;' indeed, we as social, communal animals, are 'defined by stories' " (Watson & Hill, 2003, p. 187). Narratives take many forms, for they may be stories told orally or written or they may be visual stories told in stained glass windows, tapestries, or carved doors of churches and cathedrals. Many cultural and religious rituals are based on sacred narratives. For example, the story of American independence from Great Britain is celebrated on July 4; the Christian story of the birth of Jesus is marked each Christmas Day on December 25; the story of the rededication of the holy temple in Jerusalem after the Jews' victory over the Syrians in 165 BCE is celebrated during Hanukkah (or Chanukah) for eight days in November and December. Older stories are regenerated into newer versions. Shakespeare's *Romeo and Juliet* has provided the theme for many stories about star-crossed lovers; the legend of King Arthur and the Knights of the Round Table has been the basis for stories about chivalry, a quest, magic, and heroism; Homer's story of the Trojan Horse is a model for fooling an enemy. Themes from ancient stories, such as the prodigal son, the fall from innocence to experience, weaker persons defeating stronger forces, selling one's soul to the devil, succumbing to a temptress, and so on, proliferate in contemporary stories. As Roderick Hart pointed out in his discussion of narrative, "Sometimes these stories are complex, springing from deep cultural roots; often, stories told today are but updated versions of centuries old tales . . . they awaken within listeners dormant experiences and feelings" (Hart, 1989, p. 133).

Like most scholars, Walter Fisher, a rhetorician, made the assumption that humans are essentially storytellers and proposed in his book, *Human Communication as Narration,* that "all forms of human communication are most usefully interpreted and assessed from a narrative perspective" (Fisher, 1989, p. ix). He wrote:

> The world as we know it is a set of stories that must be chosen among in order for us to live life in a process of continual re-creation. [The] narrative paradigm sees people as storytellers, as authors and co-authors who creatively read and evaluate the texts of life and literature. A narrative perspective focuses on existing institutions as providing 'plots' that are always in the process of re-creation rather than existing as settled scripts. Viewing human communication narratively stresses that people are full participants in the making of messages, whether they are agents (authors) or audience members (co-authors). (Fisher, 1989, p. 18)

People tune in to television to be told stories, but they have a familiarity with the narrative forms in which the stories are told, thus they relate to these stories against a backdrop of the stories they know and become the coauthors, so to speak, in the story development. In order for a story to be successful, it has to engage the audience's own sense of narrative. This includes the ability to defer one's gratification, to supply connectives among the parts of the story, and to perceive events as significantly related to the point of a sequence or the entire story.

When my sons were young, I read bedtime stories to them every night. They enjoyed hearing the same stories over and over, often speaking the lines from the books before they could read them. Now my older son and daughter-in-law read to their daughter Elizabeth every night, often the same stories that I read to my sons. Elizabeth also loves the stories on television—*Clifford the Big Red Dog, Arthur (the Aardvark)*, and, when she was only three years old, she could expertly pronounce "aurora borealis" after seeing the Disney movie *Balto* (the story of a sled wolf-dog in Alaska). Like other children, she learned to produce and process stories at an early age. She enjoys repeated reading and viewing of stories and often tells me the stories that she has heard and watched. I am an avid reader of both fiction and nonfiction, yet I also regularly tune in to television stories on Tuesday, Thursday, and Sunday nights. My favorites are *Commander-in-Chief, CSI, Without a Trace, ER, The Sopranos, Mystery,* and *Masterpiece Theatre.*

The *Masterpiece Theatre* dramas, which are usually based on novels, and the made-for-television movies are self-contained and have closure, unless the movie is a pilot for a series. The difference between a self-contained novel or television movie that has closure at the end and a television series is that while a series episode may have closure of a given problem, there is seldom closure for the personal stories of the characters. As I watch series television over time, I learn about the characters, their relationships, and their ways of solving problems. They may solve a crime, figure out how the crime was committed, find a missing person, save someone's life or take it, marry, divorce, have babies, and so on, but the series continue each week with the same main characters and their ways of living and working together. Even when a series comes to an end, there is seldom closure. The exception was *M*A*S*H*, which in 1983 after 11 years on the air, had a 2½-hour finale celebrating the end of the Korean War with Hawkeye, BJ, Major Houlihan, Colonel Potter, and the rest of the 4077th Mobile Army Surgical Hospital returning home. (It was the highest-rated single program of all time with 106 million viewers.) *Friends* had somewhat of a closure when it ended in 2004 with Rachel getting back together with Ross and Monica and Chandler moving to the suburbs, but Joey's life was left unresolved because there was a spin-off, *Joey,* for the next season with Joey moving to Los Angeles. *Seinfeld* ended in 1998 with Jerry in jail for not helping a car hijacking victim and repeating some of the lines from the first show of the series. The last of the *Frasier* series in 2004 was a broad farce featuring Frasier's father Martin's wedding, an extravaganza planned by Frasier and his brother Niles with acrobats, a gospel choir, and a skywriter that was further complicated by Eddie the dog swallowing the wedding ring and Daphne, Niles's wife, delivering her baby in a veterinarian's office. Realizing that his family and friends had reached a turning point, Frasier accepted a new job in San Francisco as a TV advice host, but the last scene marked an ambiguous new beginning for Dr. Frasier Crane as he flies to Chicago, not San Francisco, and calls Charlotte, the woman with whom he has fallen in love, on his cell phone as the plane lands. This open-ended scene at the end of the last episode left viewers wondering if there would be a spin-off to *Frasier* sometime in the future. It is not unusual for viewers to anticipate a spin-off, for stories are narratives that are continually re-created into newer versions of themselves. Indeed, *Frasier* was a spin-off from *Cheers.*

The Nature of Narrative

Narrative recounts one or more events, thus a story is a series of events arranged in an order. Narrative can be about one event, as in "the hamster died" or "Marian left Simon." If an event is not recounted, then the expression of it is not a narrative. "Marian is the daughter of S. P. Haddock" is not a narrative because there are no events expressed in this sentence. It is assumed that a narrative will be expressed by someone to someone; a storyteller relates a story to an audience. Thus, a story can be viewed as being expressed in such a way that an audience can interpret its meaning. Whether the story is told as comedy or drama, news or sports, cooking instructions or infomercials, there has to be a pattern that viewers can anticipate. Narrative can be either fiction or nonfiction as long as events are ordered and recounted. A dramatic series on television is based on narrative, but the news, reality shows, and sporting events also have narrative structure. A narrative has two parts: (1) the structure that comprises the recounting of one or more events; and (2) the communicative act that involves the production and reception of the story.

A story almost always has temporal elements. Some of the events in the story may occur simultaneously; some may be successive; some may go back and forth in time. "Marian left Simon as he boarded an airplane to

New York" has a simultaneous temporal element. "After Simon left for the airport, Marian began to pack to leave him" is an example of successive events. "As Marian packed her suitcase to leave Simon, she reflected on the times in the past when they had been happy" is an example of going back and forth in time. In each case, the stories consist of at least one transformation from one state of affairs to another. Sometimes the events in a story may be linked by cause and effect. "Marian left Simon because he never helped with the dishes" is an example of causation.

The sequence of a narrative has to be structured in a systematic way in an order that makes sense to its audience. This allows the events, characters, and themes to develop and move forward in a coherent fashion. The television narrative should draw the viewers in, engage them, and keep them watching the program. Stories are structured so the scenes build on one another as the viewers gradually learn more about a character or the plot. Each stage of the narrative has a logical place and meaning in the sequence, and each stage influences the next one.

Narrative Theories

Aristotle's Narrative Theory

Narrative theory can be traced back to ancient Greece. Aristotle's *Poetics,* written in 330 BCE, is a treatise on the making of a dramatic work of art. Aristotle explained that drama is defined by its shape, composition, manner of construction, and purpose. While character, thought, dialogue, song, and spectacle were considered important, Aristotle said that plot is the most important part of the narrative. He said that plot is the unified arrangement of the incidents, which must have a beginning, middle, and end. Television programming appears to most strongly follow Aristotle's advice with tightly structured scripts that usually have to be 22 or 44 minutes long. Aristotle also said that unnecessary people and incidents should be omitted from a story's plot. Aristotle's guidelines are familiar to viewers of television in the 21st century. Television scripts must present the conflict in the first few minutes of the first act along with the hero, antagonist, and other essential characters who are related to the problem. The successive act(s) present complications and other incidents, and the final act presents a solution to the problem. We expect the familiar structure of the beginning, middle, and end; we expect unity of plot; we anticipate seeing only the essential characters with whom we are familiar; and we enjoy stories not only for the pleasure they give, but also for the order they offer.

Propp's Narrative Theory

Vladimir Propp, an early 20th-century theorist, influenced narrative theory with his 1928 book *Morphology of the Folktale*, although it was not translated into English until 1966. Morphology is the study of structure and forms which Propp developed into 31 functions of characters from the perspective of their fundamental meanings in a story. Propp argued that stories always contain the function of the *lack* and/or *villainy*. The story then proceeds to other functions, such as the hero and the villain joining in direct combat resulting in the defeat of the villain. When the hero's task is resolved, the lack is fulfilled, and Propp's last function has the hero marrying the princess and receiving an honor, such as ascending the throne. In other words, an initial equilibrium or harmonious state of a place or character is disrupted, most often by a lack of something or a villain. The narrative charts the course of the disequilibrium and ends with a resolution that restores equilibrium. A lack may be a missing person who is the subject of a search by FBI agents. If found, the missing person is restored to the family, and equilibrium is achieved. A lack may be overcome when police detectives find a criminal—the villain—and bring that person to justice. A person may lack love and a satisfactory relationship that can be achieved by meeting a desirable person. A teenager may lack the use of the family car until proven responsible enough to use it. Lack is also related to desire or wish fulfillment. If what is desired or wished for is not present, then there is a lack. Villainy does not have to be a person but could be an animal or an earthquake or some natural event that disturbs equilibrium. The movement to restore equilibrium drives the narrative forward, linking events together, providing insights and meaning, and fulfilling the desire to overcome the lack or the villain.

Barthes's Narrative Theory

The literary critic Roland Barthes (1974) described narrative as having a hermeneutic code. Hermeneutics is the science of interpretation. The stages of the hermeneutic code enable an audience to interpret and follow a story as follows:

First, there is an *enigma* that causes us to ask a question about the narrative's development: Who committed the crime? Who will win? How might a character react to a piece of news? How might a relationship develop? The enigma engages our interest and causes us to want to see how it is resolved. The enigma is like a riddle that teases us to guess the next piece of information to be revealed. Second, there is a delay that stalls or postpones the

solution to the enigma. The delay sequence may keep the enigma open causing us to dwell on it as suspense builds. Third, a resolution to the enigma is
found thus satisfying our curiosity and giving us pleasure.

Most narratives have an intricate series of enigmas, delays, and resolutions, with one resolution creating another enigma. For example, the criminal's identity is now known, but will he or she get caught? This drives the
narrative forward and sustains our interest. Not only do situation comedies
and dramas follow these patterns, but quiz shows, the news, and sporting
events are also structured in these ways. A quiz show has an enigma of who
will win the prize. A reality show engages us in an enigma, delay, and resolution as people, events, and actions cause the candidates for the prized position to be eliminated. For example, the enigma on *The Bachelor* is which
woman will he select? Will his parents like the woman he has brought to
meet them? (This presents another enigma.) They say that they like her
because she is an old-fashioned girl, but then he brings a second woman
home to meet them. This produces a delay and another enigma—will they
like her? They do not like the second woman that much, but he spends an
evening in the hot tub with her (delay), and picks her over the woman of his
parents' choice thus resolving the main enigma: Who will get selected to be
his bride? A sporting event has the "who will win?" enigma. When there is
more than one event leading to a bigger prize, the enigma builds suspense
over time. Smarty Jones, a remarkable but unlikely racehorse, won the
Kentucky Derby and the Preakness in 2004. The enigma was "Will Smarty
Jones win the Triple Crown?" The media provided many delays with stories
about previous winners and the horses and jockeys who would race in the
Belmont Stakes, the third race of the Triple Crown. Smarty Jones was compared to Seabiscuit, another unlikely winning racehorse, whose story had
been told in a recent best-selling book and a popular film. Suspense built up
until the day of the race, but Smarty Jones narrowly lost the race to a horse
named Birdstone, thus ending with a resolution.

Barthes also described an action code that makes complex ideas and feelings immediately recognizable to the audience while, at the same time, their
significance becomes apparent in the narrative. This requires the audience to
understand the action code within the context of the narrative, thus becoming the coauthor of the story. In other words, the audience senses what will
happen next. When Silvio in *The Sopranos* drives Adriana—who has been
an informant for the FBI—into the woods, the viewers sense that he is going
to kill her. How do they know this? She thought he was taking her to the
hospital to see her fiancé Christopher. Because he did not drive to the hospital, because the woods are isolated, and because she has been an informant, the viewer interprets the situation and recognizes, along with the

character Adriana, what the course of action will be. Of course, the viewer has learned, by watching the series, that the characters in *The Sopranos* execute their enemies as a way of obtaining revenge. Silvio is Tony Soprano's right-hand man and would logically be sent to do the dirty deed. The enigma of what will happen to Adriana now that she has told Christopher that she has been giving information to the FBI is delayed as she imagines that she is driving away with her suitcase in the car to enter a witness protection program. Carina Chocano, television critic for the *Los Angeles Times,* wrote: "The moment remains open to interpretation. But it at least hints at the idea that Adriana went to her death like a soldier" (Chocano, 2004, p. E25). When Silvio pulls into the woods, the viewer understands that she will be shot in an act of cold-blooded murder. Chocano wrote that Adriana "suffered like Antigone," thus comparing her story to the Sophocles play *Antigone,* written in 442 BCE. In the play, Antigone, the daughter of Oedipus, was executed (sealed alive in a tomb) by her uncle, the King of Thebes, because she buried her brother Polynices, who died fighting Creon's army. Creon considered him a traitor for whom state law forbade burial. It is a classic story of conflict of loyalty to family or the state.

Narrative Structure

Narratives rely on conflict and oppositions in their structures. Certainly the masculine/feminine opposition is used most frequently in both situation comedies and dramas. Other oppositions that are widely used are work/ home, legal/illegal, life/death, good/evil, healthy/sick, competent/incompetent, tolerance/intolerance, and so on. The oppositions that created conflicts on *Frasier* were youth/age and son/father as the two brothers, Frasier and Niles, had conflicts with their father. Sophistication/unrefined and high culture/low culture provided humor because both Frasier and Niles were pompous in their sophistication, whereas the father, Martin, was average and practical in his preferences.

Narrative structure provides a tendency for stories to fall into predictable patterns or formulas. Some formulas are unique to certain television genres and particular shows. The crime show will have a crime solved at the end; harmony will be restored in the family situation comedy; a life will be saved in the emergency room, and so on. Formulas that were successful in previous shows are repeated in new shows. Conventions are used that viewers recognize and come to expect. A convention is any kind of social or cultural practice used in a narrative that has a meaning that is shared by members of a culture. A musical signature at the start of a television program or a news reader looking directly into the camera are common conventions. As Watson and Hill (2003) point out, "Knowledge of conventions on the part of the audience and recognition when convention is flouted suggests an active union between encoder and decoder" (Watson & Hill, p. 188).

In order to keep an audience coming back each week to a series, multiple story lines, often without resolution, are developed and interwoven into the narrative structure of an episode. *Hill Street Blues,* on the air from 1981 to 1987, established this pattern with its ensemble cast, stories set within an institution (a police station), several intersecting story lines per episode, story arcs covering several episodes, and literate, witty writing (Stempel, 1996). *Hill Street Blues* had as many as seven story lines going on in one episode. When it did not get good ratings for its first season on the air, NBC renewed the show with the caveat that it had to complete at least one story line per show.

To aid viewer memory or to assist viewers who have missed an episode, script writers put in information that repeats previous episodes. Situation comedies recap the narrative situation after a commercial break to reorient viewers. The familiar "previously on . . ." is standard practice for the beginning of a drama series. As a series continues, some story lines are brought to closure, and new ones are introduced. Because writers have an entire season to tell a story, some story lines continue throughout the season.

Another form of structural repetition is the inclusion in the narrative of a number of redundant signs that reinforce a point, a character's personality, a theme, and suspense. These may be in the setting, costumes, details in the dialogue, and action. This kind of redundancy provides texture and tone for the audience and deepens the consistency and believability of the narrative. These are known as social codes and are discussed in more detail in Chapter 6, "Rhetoric and Culture," as cultural signs that are used conventionally for viewer recognition and meaning.

Narrative structure is also adapted to short sequences of action and rapid editing. This is done to try to prevent viewer zapping or channel-hopping. It is hoped that the viewer will not want to lose involvement in the ongoing narrative. Bignell analyzed the series *ER* with this in mind:

> The narrative of ER is patterned to include periodic bursts of rapid action interspersed with more leisurely character development, and the programme as a whole is segmented into a large number of relatively short scenes. The longer and slower scenes of character interaction draw on the conventions of soap opera, in which reaction by one character to events in the life of another is represented by frequent close-up, emotional cues provided by music and an emphasis on the viewer's memory of past events in the characters' lives to enrich what is happening in the narrative present. By contrast, the shorter

scenes of rapid activity, usually scenes in which the doctors respond to the arrival of a seriously injured person, use rapid hand-held camera shots, whip-pans and rapid editing. In these scenes the dialogue of characters overlaps, and the noises made by medical equipment accompanied by rapid percussion music add to the sense of urgency and confusion. (Bignell, 2004, p. 95)

It is impossible to separate art from the business of television. The objective of narrative is to attract viewers to the programs and hold them there during the show and keep them returning each week.

Intertextuality

Viewers are more likely to engage with a television program when they experience pleasure. One source of pleasure is recognition of references to other television programs or characters or events. Reference to or connection with other "texts" outside of the present one is known as intertextuality. If viewers recognize and understand an allusion, they can become party to it as an inside joke. For example, in an episode of NBC's *Law & Order* that aired on April 30, 2004, one of the leads, Detective Lennie Briscoe, is looking at a dead body in a park when a crime scene investigator suggests that the victim was hit on the head with a cane he has found. Briscoe says, "Leave the theorizing up to us." His attitude toward crime scene investigators is revealed later when the coroner finds a cell phone on the body during the autopsy and says the crime scene investigators missed it. Briscoe replies, "These crime scene guys are highly overrated," in a subtle reference to the CBS program *CSI*.

Intertextuality describes both the interpretive practice exercised by viewers and a strategy consciously used by television producers. Ott and Walter (2000) describe intertextuality as a stylistic device that writers and producers deliberately employ to invite a particular response. One reason for the popularity of the animated show *The Simpsons* is the parody created by many references to the media. *The Simpsons* deliberately invites viewers to tap into their knowledge of news stories, politics, current events, old movies, and other television programs, especially programs about families. In each half-hour episode, *The Simpsons* incorporates 15–20 allusions to outside events ranging from *The X-Files* to O. J. Simpson's chase in a white Bronco on the California freeway to the physicist Stephen Hawking talking about black holes. Intertextuality credits viewers with the experience necessary to make sense of these allusions, offering them the pleasure of recognition.

Collins attributes intertextuality as a hallmark of postmodern cultural production. He quotes Umberto Eco's description of the "already said"—that is, intertextuality—as the most distinguishing feature of postmodern communication. Revivalism in architecture, vintage clothing, antique furnishings, and so on are forms of recirculation and appropriation of older forms functioning in the present day. Collins writes, "There is no other medium in which the force of the 'already said' is quite so visible as in television, primarily because the already said is the 'still being said.'" (Collins, 1992, pp. 333–334)

Characters

Although Aristotle believed that plot was the most important part of a story, characters and their interrelationships dominate television stories. Characters, like the structure of the plots, however, also fall into formulaic types. Viewers recognize characters on television when they are acknowledged social types, defined by Reed, a sociologist, as "collections of real people who resemble one another in ways that could be quantified and measured if we wanted to do it" (Reed, 1986, p. 14). Characters may be popular ideal types and folk generalizations, representing the kinds of people one is likely to encounter superficially. Social types have certain noticeable behaviors and attributes that observers can easily identify and remember. Examples of well-known social types are rednecks, bullies, hillbillies, yuppies, hippies, Southern belles, groupies, snobs, gangsters, cowboys, bosses, maids, butlers, and so on. Because they are no more complicated than they have to be and have limited and predictable functions, they are likely to be minor characters on television. They are represented visually as well as through spoken accents, stock dialogue, and language.

Characters have to be introduced, their personalities defined, and their relationships to one another, to place, and to time have to be established. Characters are appealing because of their traits. The main characters have several traits, while minor characters may have only one or two traits. Character traits may be appearance, attitudes, skills, preferences, psychological drives, and any other specific quality created for a character. Chief Inspector Morse (his first name was never used)—played by the late John Thaw on PBS's *Mystery*—became a beloved character to television audiences. His character traits were that he was a cranky bachelor living in Oxford, England who loved classical music and opera, fast sports cars, and Scotch whiskey. He liked women very much but never had a sustained relationship. He was cynical and blunt, often insulting to his assistant Lewis, but always capable of admitting his own mistakes and ultimately solving the crime. No matter what plot was being acted out, Inspector Morse consistently had these traits. Consistency of character traits causes audiences to know the character and to look forward to seeing him or her each week. Viewers know that the main characters of a television show will be back again next week to experience similar conflicts and repeat similar acts. When a show goes off the air, viewers miss the characters because they have become part of their lives. They regard many television characters as their friends.

Steven Spielberg, who helped propel the project that became *ER* on NBC, said of the characters on *ER:*

> The secret to *ER* is that the characters are not overwritten. The audience has learned who the characters are the way people make friends with each other. A friendship evolves out of understanding who the other person is over a period of time, not overnight. So audiences who watch *ER* learn about the characters the way they would make a friend, slowly and with a great deal of respect and admiration. (Pourroy, 1995, p. 21)

As with long-term friendships in which friends reveal more of their personalities, television characters also become better known to us as the series progress.

Actors portraying television characters often become celebrities, and sometimes their fans confuse the actors with their characters. However, many actors deny being anything like the characters they portray. William Petersen who plays Gil Grissom, a scientist and a former forensic pathologist turned crime scene investigator, on *CSI* said, "Gil is the antithesis of me. I couldn't pass science in high school. Now I read science articles" (The William S. Paley Television Festival, 2001). *CSI*'s writers study science and employ consultants to give Petersen accurate scientific terminology.

Television scriptwriter Madeline DiMaggio also teaches scriptwriting. She advises creating back stories for characters, giving them a biography of significant events that happened in their lives before the television story unfolds. Although the back stories may not be part of the script, they are important in understanding the development of a character and may even help the writers determine locales and other characters. Many television program Web sites have back stories for the show's characters.

Because scripts for television programs are so tightly controlled, there is little time to show a character's personality except through action. Robert Hilliard explained, "Not only do the qualities of the characters determine the action, but the character is revealed through the action" (Hilliard, 1991, p. 75). The choices a character makes, especially at moments of crisis or conflict, bring out the qualities of the character. Character relationships, which are so important in television drama, reveal a character's personality and compelling characteristics. Also, because of the intimacy provided by television close-ups, the characters' inner feelings can be seen but not necessarily spoken about. We saw in Chapter 2 that this is known as a *subtext*. Marg Helgenberger who plays crime scene investigator Catherine Willows on *CSI* said, "It's a different style of acting because you look at the evidence without speaking and the audience knows what you are feeling" (The William S. Paley Television Festival, 2001).

Viewers know that the lead characters in a series will be back again the next week to experience similar conflicts and repeat similar acts. Most viewers tend to be more connected with the characters than with the plots, and they tune in week after week to see what adventures they will encounter and how they will resolve the enigmas that occur. By watching series and serials on a regular basis, viewers form a relationship with the characters and often identify with them. They see them go in and out of relationships, get married, have children, go to work, fight crime, settle disputes, enjoy leisure activities, and, of course, they see them encounter some form of disequilibrium and try to bring balance back into their lives. Each semester when I teach television criticism, I ask my students why they watch the shows they watch. Every semester different students offer the same answer as their predecessors: "Because the characters on television have such interesting lives, and we can vicariously live their lives." In other words, the television characters bring pleasure through identification and entertainment through vicarious experiences.

Characters in plays and made-for-television-movies that are not pilots must have their character traits established early in the script because there is not an entire season to develop them. Usually there is just one protagonist whose desire or lack catalyzes the story in these programs. Although there are delays in the narrative, there will be a resolution at the end of the program because there is no continuation unless it gets followed up later by a sequel. There may be more characters in a miniseries. For example, HBO's six-hour production of Tony Kushner's play *Angels in America* included many characters— invented ones such as rabbis, drag queens, housewives, nurses, doctors, and, of course, angels—as well as historical figures, such as Roy Cohn and Ethel Rosenberg. (Cohn and Rosenberg are strange bedfellows. Roy Cohn was a lawyer on Senator Joseph McCarthy's staff in pursuit of communists in the government. Ethel Rosenberg was executed for treason along with her husband Julius. They were accused of giving the secrets of the atomic bomb to the Soviet Union.) *Angels in America* starred important actors: Al Pacino as Cohn, a deep, complex, and surprisingly sympathetic character; Meryl Streep, who was outstanding in multiple roles as the ghost of Ethel Rosenberg, Hannah Pitt, and a male rabbi; and Emma Thompson as the angel, who crashed through the bedroom ceiling of an AIDS-stricken gay man and announced, "The messenger has arrived." The action ranged from the East Coast to Salt Lake City to Heaven itself and included encounters by and with gays, Jews, Mormons, African Americans, and WASPs. This outstanding production received 21 Emmy nominations in 2004, including best actress for Streep and Thompson and best actor for Pacino. The play's themes were about AIDS, relationships, pill addiction, loneliness, mental illness, homelessness, and sexual repression as well as the westward migration of Eastern European Jews to America and of Mormons to Utah, the Bayeux Tapestry, de Tocqueville's *Democracy in America,* the McCarthy hearings, and the decisions of President Reagan's judicial appointees. There were also archetypical and mythical themes such as initiation, flight, the journey, abandonment, separation, loss, forgiveness, and redemption.

Archetypes

Television characters are often modeled after classical archetypes such as heroes and villains, father and mother figures, leaders and sidekicks, wise elders and foolish youths, loyal friends and deceiving associates, and so on. Plots may be based on archetypal themes such as the ones in *Angels in America.* Images such as circles and bridges can be archetypal. Archetypes are recurrent patterns of actions, character types, or identifiable images whose expression is an unconscious product of the collective experience of the entire human species, an unconscious mental record of such experiences, the collective unconscious.

> The Swiss psychiatrist Carl G. Jung developed a theory of myth based upon his theory of the collective unconscious which he defined as, "a part of the psyche which can be negatively distinguished from a personal unconscious by the fact that it does not, like the latter, owe its existence to personal experience and consequently is not a personal acquisition . . . The contents [of the collective unconscious] have never been in consciousness, and therefore have never been individually acquired, but owe their existence to heredity . . . The content of the collective unconscious is made up essentially of archetypes." (Jung, 1971, pp. 59–60)

Through analysis of thousands of patients' dreams, Jung discovered a striking similarity among ancient myths, dreams, and symbols of widely separated civilizations and cultural groups. He found that the images and structures of the collective unconscious manifest themselves in regularly repeating forms that he named *archetypes.* He believed that these mythical images were present in all people, becoming activated in visual form in dreams and myths. He believed that they express desires, urges, and fears common to people of every age. People react to archetypes because they stimulate images that are already in their collective unconscious. Archetypes depict some eternal quality, some enduring feature of the human race. When people find them in a story, they experience immediate recognition.

Jung wrote that archetypes ". . . indicate the existence of definite forms in the psyche which seem to be present always and everywhere. Mythological research calls them 'motifs' . . . literally a pre-existent form" (Jung, 1971, p. 60). An archetype is a narrative pattern, a model, or a prototype reflecting cultural patterns that reveal and shape a person's psychic and social life. Some archetypes have human form, such as the hero, a monster, Earth mother, temptress, the innocent, unfaithful spouse, a magician, a martyr, or a warrior; some are experiences, such as a journey, a quest, a task, initiation, descent, ascent, the fall, or redemption; some are things, such as a bridge, fire, a door, or water; and some are metaphors, such as a mandala or magic-circle, light-and-darkness, or heaven-and-hell. There are too many archetypes to discuss fully here, but they can be found in the many writings of Jung and his followers. On television, heroes are obvious, as are villains, innocents, and temptresses. One archetype that deserves more consideration—because it appears so often on television programs—is the trickster, known for sly jokes, malicious pranks, preference for physical satisfaction above intellectual pursuits, the power to change shape, and sometimes a dual nature (half animal, half human). The trickster, although usually a negative type of hero, may transform what is meaningless into something meaningful (Samuels, Shorter, & Plaut, 1987). Jung identified the trickster in fairy tales such as *Tom Thumb* and *Stupid Hans,* but he also discussed the trickster in Native American mythology, often as a shaman or in the form of a coyote (Jung, 1969). The character Carla, the waitress on *Cheers,* was a comic trickster; whereas, in a drama, the trickster may be a clever criminal or a jealous rival.

Robert R. Smith found many archetypes in nonfiction television, such as tests of bravery in sporting events, wisdom in statements by government and world leaders, redemption in reports of medical breakthroughs and scientific advancement, Armageddon in news about floods, hurricanes, pollution, and starvation, paradise in holiday celebrations or vacation stories, and Dionysus (god of wine and revelry) in stories about rock concerts, parties, and other celebrations. Television is a natural medium for archetypes because of its visual appeal to a mass audience (Smith, 1976).

Rituals are also archetypal. Recreational, national, and celebratory events on television, such as the World Series, the Super Bowl, the Olympics, presidential inaugurations, state funerals, Macy's Thanksgiving Day parade, and tragic disasters, unify the audience as a collective body who observe and participate in these rituals from afar through a communal focus. These are narrative occasions as announcers and anchors tell the stories as the events unfold. Football players take on heroic dimensions in massive stadiums; inaugural rituals with visual and musical symbols of patriotism remind viewers of the stability and continuity of government and nation; state funerals, such as the 1963 funeral of President Kennedy, the 2004 funeral of President Reagan, and the 2007 funeral of President Ford; and televised accounts of tragedies such as the *Challenger* disaster, the Oklahoma City bombing, and especially the fall of the World Trade Center Twin Towers on September 11, 2001 enable the television audience not only to collectively mourn their loss but also to reinforce a strong sense of national unity. Meyrowitz (1985) explained that we respond to television images as if we were seeing them firsthand, thus physical presence is no longer required for the firsthand experience. Television is truly a "window on the world." The obsessively repeated images of tragedies on television burn them into our minds so that they seem to happen again and become part of our collective memories.

Myth

Myth and archetype tend to overlap, although myths are more closely related to individual cultures. Myths are important for television criticism because they have formed the foundation for narratives throughout the ages. Mythical themes occur and recur in narratives because they represent life experiences, beliefs, values, and behaviors that organize social interaction. Myths are generally known as fictitious tales, often with primitive or ancient origins, involving supernatural characters embodying timeless virtues and values. These virtues and values tend to be ideas to which people already subscribe. Myths offer examples of right and wrong, explain baffling or frightening phenomena, and provide models of good and evil. They are, according to R. Slotkin, "stories drawn from a society's history that have acquired through persistent usage the power of symbolizing that society's ideology and of dramatizing its moral consciousness—with all the complexities and contradictions that consciousness may contain" (Jasinski, 2001, p. 383). Rollo May explained that "a myth is a way of making sense in a senseless world. Myths are narrative patterns that give significance to our existence . . . Myths are like the beams in a house: not exposed to outside view, they are the structure which holds the house together so people can live in it" (May, 1991, p. 15). Myths are also based upon the norms of a culture and acceptable ways of resolving conflict. Rene Wellek and Austin Warren's definition of myth includes the notion of human origins and destinies: "Myth comes to mean any anonymously composed storytelling of origins and destinies: the explanations a society offers its young of why the world is and why we do as we do, its pedagogic images of the nature and destiny of man" (Jasinski, 2001, p. 383). Each society has its own myths that are related to its history, values, and beliefs. According to Roderick Hart, there are four characteristic types of myths based on their functions. *Cosmological* myths explain "why we are here, where we came from, what our ancestors were like" (Hart, 1990, p. 315). These myths come from family members, school books, church, films, and television. *Societal* myths "teach one the proper way to live" (Hart, 1990, p. 315). These may be stories of famous people, such as George Washington's refusal to lie and Abraham Lincoln's love of school and his long walks through the snow to get there. Although the facts of the myths may be erroneous, the "truth" of their messages is not. *Identity* myths preserve a culture's distinctiveness and provide a sense of collective identity. Stories of immigrants coming to America and succeeding in the fulfillment of their dreams and stories of the dedication of the United States to freedom and opportunity distinguish the nation from closed and authoritarian societies. *Eschatological* myths "tell people where they are going, what lies in store for them in the short run . . . and in the long run" (Hart, 1990, p. 318). These myths may promise success through hard work, discovery of a cure for disease, a heavenly reward, or an eternal punishment.

Bronislaw Malinowski, a cultural anthropologist, defined myth as "a body of narratives woven into a culture which dictates belief, defines ritual, and acts as a chart of the social orders" (Malinowski, 1961, p. 249). Joseph Campbell, the author of 13 books on myth, believed that there were two orders of myth: "the mythology that relates you to your nature and to the natural world of which you're a part. And there is the mythology that is strictly sociological, linking you to a particular society" (Campbell, 1988, p. 28). The former is a motivating power or a value system that is universal because it is of one's own body and of nature. The latter has to do with specific societies. In other words, a person is both a natural woman or man and a member of a particular group. Robert Scholes and Robert Kellogg (1966) in their book, *The Nature of Narrative,* use the terms "myth" and "traditional narrative" synonymously because this was the meaning of the Greek word "mythos." They further refined the definition of myth by elucidating three types: (1) the imaginative folktale designed to amuse an audience; (2) a legend, a quasi-historical tale of ordinary or fantastic events; and (3) the sacred myth, an expression of and justification for theology, manners, and morals (p. 217). The latter is the most tradition-bound of all forms of narrative in any culture and, as an embodiment of religious truth, is not to be tampered with or changed. Scholes and Kellogg pointed out that "traditional and rigidly preserved stories lend themselves to alteration or adaptation; they become rationalized and humanized or fancifully exaggerated . . . myth, in yielding up its special characteristics, dies only to be reborn. Because mythic narrative is the expression in story form of deepseated human concerns, fears, and aspirations, the plots of mythic tales are a storehouse of narrative correlatives—keys to the human psyche in story form—guaranteed to reach an audience and move them deeply" (Scholes & Kellogg, 1966, p. 220).

Earlier in this chapter, contemporary television narratives were described as forged from "older stories" and "themes from ancient stories." Today, myths can be found in our rituals, the visual arts, architecture, books, music, and on television programs. Television stories often have mythic themes already shared by large segments of the population. Television narratives often have characters, situations, and plots taken directly from known myths or mythic motifs. The enormously popular series *The X-Files* was analyzed by Leslie Jones as entirely mythical. Jones found that all the stories in the series were based on three myths in multiple versions and variants: "There's something in the woods," "There's something in the house," and "There's something in the government," depending upon the location of that week's story (Jones, 1996, p. 81). Jones described the equal weight given to each of the three categories in the episodes of *The X-Files* as "a kind of narrative osmosis, as characteristics of one category seep into another and all narrative traits become interchangeable. We find monsters of myth, space, and conspiracy equally out in the wilderness, at home in the sewers, and bagged, tagged, and filed for reference in the warehouses of the Pentagon" (Jones, 1996, p. 83).

Desperate Housewives has a weekly theme narrated by Mary Alice, a character who is dead. On December 4, 2005, the theme was "return of the prodigal son." At the conclusion of the episode, Mary Alice said in voiceover:

> The stories are as old as time itself. The prodigal son who returns home, the father who forgives him, the jealous wife who tricks the husband who trusts her, the desperate mother who risks everything for the child who needs her, and the faithless husband who hurts the wife who loves him so deeply. Why do we listen again and again? Because these are the stories of family, and once we look past the fighting, pain, and resentment, we occasionally like to remind ourselves that there is absolutely nothing more important.

Leading characters in television programs are often heroes with supernatural powers or superior abilities. Television series like *Xena: Warrior Princess*, *Buffy the Vampire Slayer*, *Ghost Whisperer*, and *Superman* featured characters who use their supernatural powers for the good of humankind. On the other hand, Karen Sisko, the lead character on the USA Network's television program that bore her name, is a small, delicate, and, of course, beautiful woman who can subdue a criminal much taller and heavier than she is. Sisko is supposed to be a U.S. Marshal, not a goddess or an Amazon, but she has superior abilities that enable her to hunt down criminals single-handedly and fearlessly. Athletes in sports may be seen to have superior abilities, consequently becoming heroes or fallen heroes. Barbaro is a racehorse who became a hero to thousands of admirers. Undefeated in previous races, he won the Kentucky Derby in 2006 by a thrilling 6½-length triumph. He was the favorite to win the Preakness Stakes on May 20, 2006 but suffered a life-threatening injury, shattering his right hind leg at the start of the race. Because of his heroic status, people sent cards, flowers, carrots, and apples to him following his surgery. The University of Pennsylvania School of Veterinary Medicine, the site of his surgery and convalescence, set up a Web site with reports of Barbaro's progress, photographs of him, and a link for people to send messages to the stricken horse, their fallen hero (www.vet .upenn.edu).

Campbell wrote that there are two kinds of deeds that mythical heroes perform: the physical deed, in which the hero performs a courageous act in a battle or saves a life, and the spiritual deed, in which the hero experiences the supernormal range of human spiritual life and returns with a message. He described the "usual hero adventure" as beginning with a lack—something has been taken from someone or something is lacking in normal circumstances. The hero takes off on a series of adventures beyond the ordinary to recover what has been lost or to find a remedy. It is a cycle of going and returning. The basic motif of the hero's journey is to leave one condition and discover that which will enable a movement to a richer or more mature condition (Campbell, 1988).

Television and myth are intimately related in many ways. Traditional tales of gods and heroes, folklore and fairy tales, and villains and supernatural forces are sources for television narrative. The patterns of characters in myth inform the destiny of the characters modeled on these myths. As you can see, there are many ways to analyze the mythical roots of characters in television stories. The following form of analysis combines myth and narrative structure.

Structural Analysis of Myth

The world of civil society has been made by human beings, and its principles are therefore to be found within the modifications of the human mind.

Humans create their own myths, most of which have their origins in actual experience of ancient peoples, representing their attempts to impose a satisfactory, graspable, humanizing shape on those experiences. The shape springs from the human mind itself, and it becomes the shape of the world that the mind perceives as natural or true. Myths involve the continual creation of recognizable and repeated forms that come from structuring. In other words, we look at our world in terms of relationships.

Structuralists can be found in many disciplines: Claude Lévi-Strauss in anthropology, Roman Jakobson in linguistics, Jean Piaget in psychology, and François Jacob in biology. All believe that there is in the human being an innate, genetically transmitted, and determined mechanism that acts as a structuring force. These structuralists believe that we have a universal capacity to formulate structure and to submit our own nature to the demands of structuring.

The human desire for structuring is manifest in the way a person spends time, manages money, or drives to school or work. Order tends to give people security, a plan, familiarity, balance, and development. Individual parts of the whole are not the same as when they were independent parts in a separate existence, but in combination they take on a special character. If separated, the parts help us to understand the whole. By examining the parts, certain meanings are engendered. By putting the parts together, certain rules of association are discovered. The end product is a reconstruction the reveals the rules of functioning.

As previously stated, what holds the elements of a television program together is its narrative and structure. Because the form is ordered in a certain way, the audience can engage with it. Narrative elements in television are also structural elements in society: themes of good and evil, heroes and villains, love and hate, gain and loss, life and death. All these are opposites or binary oppositions, according to Lévi-Strauss, because they stress their relationship to one another although they are opposite. An image of a person, for example, is structurally opposed to an image of a horse. They are opposite in that there are conceptual differences—like a person/not like a person. Another form of opposites is the mutually exclusive opposition, for example, married/not married. Some oppositions are simple and easily understood; others are remarkably deep and complex, for example, individualism versus community, freedom versus restriction, and tradition versus change.

A narrative is told in a sequence of events that form a story. Lévi-Strauss called this form syntagmatic because a syntagm is a chain, thus a chain of events unfolds across time in a story from the beginning to the end. This is the easily recognized structure of narrative in a television story. Deep structure, however, is known as paradigmatic because it reveals the latent meaning of a story. Patterns of opposition may be buried in the story, but they are what generate meaning. By analyzing binary oppositions, the relationships among the elements of the story, the patterns of the paradigmatic can be elicited. Specific oppositions are re-categorized under more general ones capable of being transformed. Transformation occurs through mediation or mediating terms that change the oppositions into resolutions of conflict and a plan for social action. This can reveal cultural laws and the moving force behind social systems. The end result is a myth.

Lévi-Strauss saw myth as a force generated to overcome contradictions, thus a myth can lead to the revelation of a society's model for resolving its conflicts. He defined myth as a model for social action and a story in which meaning is embodied in recurrent symbols and events. A myth is also an idea to which people already subscribe—a predisposition to act. It is an outer revelation of a person's inner experiences, feelings, and thoughts. Lévi-Strauss wrote, ". . . the purpose of myth is to provide a logical model capable of overcoming a contradiction" (Lévi-Strauss, 1963, p. 229). The structuralist method of myth analysis developed by Lévi-Strauss locates oppositions and binary differences and puts them in a chart in syntagmatic (chronological) and diachronic (vertical columns) sequences to show an amalgam of relationships in various layers that bring the meaning of the myth to the surface. Lévi-Strauss compared structural charts to musical scores. A musical score is laid out in chronology, but its structure is in its harmony, discord, and repetition of units. By naming the mythical units, which Lévi-Strauss called "mythemes," and arranging them in single columns, each exhibiting one common feature or function, while at the same time keeping the chronology of the myth in rows, the myth is organized according to its themes and motifs. In other words, to *tell* the myth, one would disregard the columns and read the rows from left to right, but to *understand* the myth, one reads the columns as units.

A chart can be constructed as follows. Watch a television program and note as many oppositions as possible in the order they are presented in the program. There can be oppositions in the story, characters, locations, ideas, values, sights, sounds, and dialogue. Use a few words for each opposition with a description from the narrative. For example, in *Frasier,* Frasier Crane drinks expensive wine, but his father, Martin, drinks beer. Frasier prefers opera, while Martin prefers football games. Use words like "wine/beer," "opera/football" to note the oppositions. After writing down all the oppositions, rework and reword the opposites into fewer columns of broader opposites, reducing the specific oppositions by clustering them under more general ones. For example, wine/beer and opera/football and other obvious oppositions could come under the single opposition of "high culture/low culture" or "snobbishness/ordinary." Put them into a chart like the one in Table 4.1.

Table 4.1   A Chart of Oppositions for a Structuralist Myth Analysis of *Frasier*

	Diachronic (vertical columns of binary oppositions)		
	Wine/beer	*Opera/football*	*Designer chair/ Barcalounger*
Syntagmatic (chronological events)	Martin offers a beer to Frasier, who declines and opens a bottle of fine wine.	Frasier brags about getting great seats to the opera; Martin watches football on television.	Frasier's chair is a designer chair by Eames; he is annoyed by Martin's chair, a Barcalounger recliner.

Second Level (reduction of oppositions to more general oppositions)

Snobbishness/ordinary	*High culture/low culture*
Wine/beer	Opera/football
Eames chair/Barcalounger	

Of course, there would be more opposites in the episode, but this example shows how to reorganize the story to emphasize the social oppositions while retaining the elements of the narrative. The chart has begun to reveal the themes and motifs of the myth. Going deeper into the themes, general oppositions can be determined, such as "frivolous/pragmatic" leading eventually to a mediated term that transforms the opposition. The mediator can be a term, a person, or an image. In *Frasier,* the mediator might be the housekeeper/therapist Daphne, who shows father and son how they can transform their differences into harmony that may lead to the myth of familial love being more important than social differences. On one episode of *Frasier,* Martin takes his sons Frasier and Niles (who is also a snob) to his favorite restaurant, the Timber Mill, where the server cuts off the ties of the nattily attired brothers and hangs them on the wall. Frasier and Niles are horrified, but Martin thinks it is hilarious. Niles and Frasier amuse themselves by making fun of the restaurant, the food, and the patrons, which annoys Martin. Once again, the snobbishness/ordinary and high culture/low culture binary oppositions become apparent. In this episode, the mediator who transforms the differences is the deceased mother of Niles and Frasier. Martin evokes the example of his wife, their mother, who was also cultured. He tells them that she was too classy to make anyone feel second-rate. Niles and Frasier tell their father that he is right and try to make amends—by eating all their chicken-fried steak.

What is interesting about a structuralist analysis is that you can go as far as your mind will take the analysis. Lévi-Strauss believed that "the human mind, regardless of the identity of those who happen to give it expression, should display an increasingly intelligible structure as a result of the doubly reflexive forward movement of the two thought processes acting one upon the other, either of which can in turn provide the spark or tinder whose conjunction will shed light on both" (Lévi-Strauss, 1969, p. 230). Several levels of abstraction may be discovered in a situation comedy giving it much more meaning than can be seen at a superficial level. By locating the myth, insight into society and its laws of social order can be determined. A police or detective story may reinforce society's violent solutions to social problems, while a family drama may celebrate compromise and sentiment. These are our myths, the stories our culture tells itself to purify and justify the values and beliefs that sustain it and provide it with an identity.

Close Analysis of Narrative Structure

Another way you can examine how a story is told is by examining a program scene by scene. Michael Porter defined a scene as a part in which all of the units are held together by continuity of time or place or parallel action in separate locations or a sequence of shots unified by a theme. He asked four questions of a scene in a television serial, either situation comedy or drama: (1) What does a scene tell about the story? (2) What does the scene tell us about the character? (3) What does the scene tell us about the setting? (4) What would happen if this scene was not here? Could I still understand the story? He examined scenes according to event, character, and details of the setting. These can be any kind of physical or mental action for events, any person or personalized entity for character, and any evocation of place for the third question. These are described in terms of functions with 15 functions for plot and 7 for character. Sometimes the setting may have a function as well. Porter also found that narrative analysis "focuses on how a culture presents the myths of a society to the members of that society" (Porter, 1998, p. 140).

Summary

The stories told on television challenge, tease, guide, and please the audience. There are stories that offer archetypal models, myths and folktales, morals and models for living. Roger Silverstone wrote, "Our stories are social texts:

drafts, sketches, fragments, frameworks; visible and audible evidence of our essentially reflexive culture, turning the events and ideas of both experience and imagination into daily tales . . . Narratives tell us how it is and it is how they tell us" (Silverstone, 1999, pp. 41 & 46). The television critic William Henry once wrote, "I run to television for solace. In times of personal turmoil it provides familiarity, emotional connections, and the promise of resolution" (Kubey and Csikszentmihalyi, 1990, p. 184). Television is the nation's storyteller. Understanding of narrative gives you, as a television critic, insight into how these stories are told and how they relate to social and cultural life.

Exercises

1. Describe the narrative according to its beginning, middle, and end on a news program.

2. Describe the "lack," according to Propp, in a situation comedy and tell how equilibrium is restored.

3. Watch a drama, a reality show, or a soap opera and identify the enigma, the delay, and the resolution.

4. Find an example of an action code (such as the one described in *The Sopranos* example) and describe how you sensed what was going to happen.

5. Read Bignell's description of the narrative structure of *ER*. Watch a different drama and describe its narrative structure.

6. Watch *The Simpsons* with a friend and list all the instances of intertextuality in one episode. See if you both find the same or different ones.

7. Look up *CSI* or *CSI: Miami*'s Web site and read the back stories of the characters.

8. Who is your favorite character on television? Explain why you like this character.

9. Give some examples of social types on situation comedies.

10. Discuss a particular character in a drama or situation comedy and describe how the character's relationship with another character or characters reveals his or her personality.

11. Cite an instance of an archetypal trickster in a situation comedy.

12. Describe archetypes in nonfiction television, such as sporting events and news.

13. Give an example of an archetypal ritual found on television.

14. Find a myth in a television drama and relate it to some deep-seated human condition.

15. Make a structuralist's chart of binary oppositions according to syntagmatic and diachronic columns, then reduce the oppositions to broader ones. Find the themes and motifs of the myth and what transforms the oppositions to the myth, a model of social action.

16. Try to analyze the structure of a 30-minute television program of your choice on a scene-by-scene basis, answering the four questions posed by Michael Porter.

Suggested Readings

Aristotle. (330/1995). *Poetics*. Cambridge, MA: Harvard University Press.

Barthes, Roland. (1974). *S/Z* (trans. Richard Miller.). New York: Hill and Wang.

Campbell, Joseph. (1988). *The Power of Myth*. New York: Anchor Books.

Jung, Carl G. (1969). *Four Archetypes: Mother/Rebirth/Spirit/Trickster*. Princeton: NJ. Princeton University Press.

Jung, Carl G. (1971). *The Portable Jung*. (trans. R. F. C. Hull.). New York: Viking Press.

Lévi-Strauss, Claude. (1963). *Structural Anthropology* (trans. Jacobson, Claire & Schoepf, Brooke G.). New York: Basic Books.

Propp, Vladimir. (1968). *Morphology of the Folktale* (2nd ed.). (trans. Laurence Scott.). Austin, TX: University of Texas Press.

5

Television Genres

"And the Emmy goes to Everybody Loves Raymond *for the Outstanding Comedy Series!"*

"The Emmy for Outstanding Lead Actress in a Drama Series goes to Patricia Arquette in Medium.*"*

"The Emmy for the Outstanding Game Show goes to Jeopardy!*"*

Introduction

The Emmy awards, perhaps the most important popular awards given to television programs, actors, writers, directors, and creators, are given in categories representing genres—comedy; drama; miniseries; reality/competition; made-for-TV movie; variety, music, or comedy; children's programs; animated programs; game shows; talk shows; commercials; and nonfiction programming. When a creator of a television program pitches a new show, it is identified as a situation comedy, a drama, a reality-adventure show, and so on. For television professionals, genre has been central to the organization and structure of the production industry. Although television shows are often blends of these categories, for example, the docudrama or the "dramedy," television programming continues to be based on the concept of genre. Television is known for its inventiveness in developing new genres, for example, the reality show. Another important aspect is the formulaic nature of television programming, which enables large numbers of people to recognize familiar types. Producers and viewers alike assume that genre categories exist and that they know what they are. The genres that prevail on television are those that yield a regular profit for their producers. As a television critic, you will recognize the genre, its conventions, and its departures from conventions when you conduct your analysis and evaluation.

Genre is a French word that translates into English as genus, family, or kind. It is a form of classification. In literature, the major genres are comedy, tragedy, novel, poetry, drama, prose, and nonfiction. In film, some major genres are romantic comedy, science fiction, horror, disaster, and film noir. In television, we recognize broad genres, such as situation comedy, drama, reality shows, talk shows, news programs, and commercials, as well as subgenres, such as daytime soap operas, detective or police shows, family melodramas, magazine-news shows, and docudramas, as kinds or types of programming. These tend to be tried and true formulae that have certain predictability and familiarity.

The opening sequence usually follows a familiar pattern. For example, in the police or detective drama, a crime takes place followed by detectives arriving on the scene and canvassing witnesses. A situation comedy usually opens in the same locale, for example, a family's kitchen or living room or an office or a coffee shop with a dilemma expressed by one or more of the characters. Because they are series, viewers recognize the locales as well as the personalities of the characters. Although each television program has its unique qualities, each one may be classified according to some genre or combination of genres.

The formula for a genre is based on certain familiar narrative conventions or common features that make it relatively easy for audiences to follow. Genre conventions prompt viewers to enjoy a program in a certain way. Conventions include program formats, subgenres, general characteristics, character types, and types of plots. The television audience not only recognizes conventions but also comes to expect them in particular genres. The audience also recognizes when conventions are flouted. This reveals the active union of viewers and television shows. As television programming continues to develop different approaches, traditional conventions are altered and blended with other genres to evolve into new genres and conventions. What is important is acceptance of certain basic assumptions and how much sense a new genre makes.

Television Genre, Production, and Scheduling

Genre is also used to organize the actual production process in the television industry. Comedies tend to be produced inside studios, with the final production presented in sequence before a live audience, followed by postproduction editing. Dramas tend to be produced more like films in that they are shot out of sequence, often filmed with a single camera, in studios and on locations, followed by postproduction editing. Comedies are produced to fill 30-minute segments, while dramas are usually in 60-minute time slots. Furthermore, genres are used to determine placement on television schedules. Soap operas and children's television are aired in the morning or early afternoon, while situation comedies are broadcast in early prime time for "family" viewing. Crime shows or adult dramas come later in the evening after the "family hour," presumably after the children are in bed. Morning news magazine programming takes place early in the morning before the workday begins, and local and world news programs come around 6:00 or 6:30 p.m. when the workday ends, and at 10:00 or 11:00 p.m. before bedtime or late-night talk shows.

The Rules for Classifying Genres

There are certain "rules" for classifying genres that relate to both cultural norms and production constraints. Such "rules" allow the mass audience to easily understand and follow familiar conventions. Viewers orient their reactions to what they see according to their expectations that have been generated by their knowledge of and experience with the genre. They expect to be amused by a situation comedy like *Two and a Half Men* or *Scrubs* but not necessarily by a detective show like *CSI*. They do not presume that a western such as *Deadwood* will have singing and dancing as they might in a musical. It is, however, difficult to isolate the characteristics that distinguish one genre from another because they change from season to season and from program to program.

Genres and their conventions change as cultural norms develop. Cultural themes reflect societal norms in a given time. Former situation comedies such as *I Love Lucy* or *The Dick Van Dyke Show* featured married couples who slept in twin beds. The men had careers and the women were homemakers who got themselves into funny predicaments. Today women on television have careers, may be single parents, and have sexual relations. Sometimes couples are gay as well as straight. Regardless of changing norms, a situation comedy has always been expected to be funny and often has laughter on the soundtrack. In the past, recorded laugh tracks were used, but today most laughter comes from a live audience in the studio watching the final performance. Indeed, the actors may even pause in their dialogue to allow for audience laughter. The audience is expected to laugh along with the studio audience, recognizing the humor in the dialogue or physical actions. Some situation comedies are not filmed in studios and may not have laugh tracks at all. Furthermore, what constitutes a comedy is not always clear, even to the professionals.

The popular *Desperate Housewives,* a show that is 60 minutes long, won the 2006 Golden Globe Award for Best Television Comedy although it is seldom funny, and it is not filmed before a live audience. Perhaps this is why the 2006 People's Choice Awards nominated it for Best Drama. Which genre is it? This show deals with divorce, death, murder, juggling career and parenting, and outrageous behaviors on the part of some of the characters in the manner of a television drama series, but it is also about friendship, love, domestic problems, comeuppance, and learning from situations in the manner of a situation comedy. The better classification would be "dramedy" because it fuses elements of both comedy and drama, therefore it is a hybrid genre. Marc Cherry, the creator of the show, calls it a "comedy-drama." Sometimes situations on *Desperate Housewives* provoke laughter, but more often we react to it with surprise and curiosity.

Joanne Ostrow, television critic for *The Denver Post,* wrote that hybrid shows were examples of "genre bending." She wrote, "Producers desperately seek ways to stand out in the increasingly competitive entertainment world, [and] the result is the number of hybrid experiments" (Ostrow, 2001, p. 1E). Ostrow also quoted Gail Berman, Fox Entertainment President, who said of Fox's mystery drama reality show, *Murder in a Small Town X,* which Fox produced, "It's not a hybrid for hybrid's sake; we want to constantly push the envelope creatively" (Ostrow, 2001, p. 1E). This brings home the point that the competitiveness for ratings is usually the driving force behind the push for novelty. Very often new television programs are blends of former successful shows and films. *Invasion,* a prime-time drama in 2005–2006 about a mysterious force that has taken over some of the residents following a hurricane in Florida, was also about divorced parents and the impact of divorce and new parental relationships on their children. It seems to be a merger of the film *Invasion of the Body Snatchers,* which was about aliens taking over the bodies and identities of the townspeople, and *Once and Again,* a popular television show in early 2000 that featured two divorced families and the impact of divorce and new parental relationships on their respective children.

Genre and Television Criticism

As television critic, you need to know about genres and conventions to be able to discuss subgenres, expected audience responses, and the conventions of formats, the characteristics of the subgenres, characters, and plots. You will ask how a genre helps us to understand how a story is told and how to identify and analyze the features of a program or a series. Knowledge of genres and conventions also explains an audience's ability to tune in to a new program midway through it and recognize the character types and progression of the plot. Genres, as discussed in *Key Concepts in Communication and Culture,*

> . . . limit the meaning-potential of a given text, and they limit the commercial risk of the producer corporations. But they are constantly transformed by the addition of new examples, so that in the end you have to conclude that there's no such thing as a "typical" Western, even though you can recognize one when you see it. (O'Sullivan et al., 1994, p. 128)

The characteristics of the subgenres especially tend to be reflective of cultural norms, concerns, and fears that change as times change. Topics such as sexual relationships, fertility, and homosexuality, which could never have been the subjects of situation comedies or daytime talk shows in the past, now are commonplace on television. Since the destruction of the Twin Towers of the World Trade Center in New York City by Al Qaeda operatives on September 11, 2001 and other terrorist acts around the world, the war on terror has been incorporated into many television dramas.

The history, features, and changes in genres are subjects worthy of an entire book, and there are several good ones (Creeber, 2001; Edgerton & Rose, 2005; Kaminsky, 1985; Mittel, 2004; Rose, 1985). There are also books devoted to single genres, especially comedy, drama, talk shows, children's programming, and reality shows. To present the aspects of genres in an efficient manner, the following table was developed to describe the genres, the subgenres, and common features or conventions in recognized genres. It is difficult to arrive at a finite list of all the genres and even more difficult to specify their individual characteristics. Yet, because television industry practice and viewer anticipation follow genre designations, it is important to include this information here. However, this table must include the disclaimer that these "rules" are frequently broken. The table is exten-sive but not all-inclusive because there are so many subgenres with differing characteristics. Some of the genres are self-evident and even have their own channels, for example, Food Network, Country Music Television, Cartoon Network, Home Shopping Network, and SOAPnet. The characteristics of each of the genres are discussed separately following Table 5.1.

Comedy

Situation Comedy

Situation comedies have been the staple of television programming for a long time. In the 2004–2005 season, their numbers significantly declined. Many pilots were made, but few made it onto the air. Plenty of people in the television industry were disappointed. Producers tend to prefer the econom-ics of situation comedies because they are often less expensive to make than other types of programs. A situation comedy is usually located in a domestic or workplace setting. Therefore, the same set can be used over and over, and a limited number of actors are employed, although the casts of very success-ful shows such as *Friends* demand and receive extremely high salaries. The family and workplace settings are convenient places to bring people together. In the workplace, people have a common goal to get a job done, thus they have to interact with one another. The workplace provides an opportunity to develop characters of different backgrounds, ethnicity, gender, and race.

Situation comedies are generally known as escapist fare and provoke laughter through jokes, humorous dialogue and situations, and slapstick. As series, they are broadcast at the same time each week for 30 minutes during the television season and tend to be complete in each episode. The characters are the same each week, although there may be a guest actor playing the role of an outsider who sets the plot in motion. There may be a lead actor, such as Kelsey Grammer was in *Frasier*, although usually there is an ensemble of actors playing the family or the staff in the workplace. The plot customarily involves some minor dilemma or a test, known as "the problem of the week," for example, getting a date, having a disastrous date, avoiding a visit by an in-law, losing something valuable, forgetting an anniversary, wrecking the family car, buttering up the boss, coping with jealous coworkers, or convinc-ing a coworker to go out on a date. The dilemma or disruption gets resolved by the end of the episode, and usually there is some sentimental reconcilia-tion, a lesson learned, or moral growth. Equilibrium is achieved in 30 min-utes, so there is a happy ending that the audience has come to expect. The basic nature of the characters and their situation is reaffirmed.

(Text continues on page 110)

Table 5.1 Genres, Subgenres, and Their Conventions

Genre	Subgenre	Conventions					Examples
		Format	Characteristics	Characters	Plot		
Comedy	Situation comedy	30 minutes, usually filmed before a live audience and edited later	Provokes laughter through jokes, humor in dialogue, or slapstick. Domestic or workplace setting.	Ensemble actors, one or more leads, often stereotypical, guest stars.	A dilemma or test is solved by the end of show. Learning or moral growth.		*Joey* *My Name is Earl* *Will & Grace* *Scrubs*
	Animated comedy	30 minutes, animation with voices, often celebrity voices	Provokes laughter through parody, sight gags. Multiple story lines, intertextual references.	Cartoon characters, regulars and guests.	Domestic dilemma, event, or parody of real life.		*The Simpsons* *King of the Hill*
	Variety comedy	60 minutes, live before an audience	Provokes laughter, enjoyment. Comic skits, musical numbers.	Ensemble cast, guest host	Satire and parody		*Saturday Night Live*
Talk Show	Nighttime talk shows	60 minutes, recorded before a live audience Broadcast late at night five nights/week	Provokes laughter, entertainment. Opening monologue, improvisational and scripted dialogue, skits, music. Desk for host, sofa for guests,	Single host, band leader, and sometimes a sidekick. Celebrity guests, exotic animals.	Topical humor and variety		*The Tonight Show* *Late Show With David Letterman* *The Late, Late Show*

(Continued)

Table 5.1 (Continued)

		Conventions				Examples
Genre	Subgenre	Format	Characteristics	Characters	Plot	
			performance space in studio.			
	Daytime talk shows	60 minutes, recorded before a live audience 5 days/week	Informative, sometimes shocking, guests reveal sensitive and personal experiences. Host and guests sit on chairs on the stage. Studio audience reacts boisterously.	Host and guests who are often ordinary people, sometimes high-profile celebrities	Explores cultural oddities, usually domestic	Oprah Dr. Phil Jerry Springer
	Informational talk shows	Usually 60 minutes	Informative discussion of current topics, conversational, face-to-face, and remote interviews	Single host with experts, sometimes celebrities	Topics: current issues, books, films	Larry King Live Charlie Rose
News	National and world news	Usually 30 minutes, live with recorded segments	Informational, anchor announces news with pre-recorded reports, brief news clips.	Anchor sits behind desk, network field correspondents report live or recorded	Global, national current events, business, human interest, health advances	ABC News CBS News NBC News Fox News

Conventions

Genre	Subgenre	Format	Characteristics	Characters	Plot	Examples
	Local news	Usually 30 minutes, 60 minutes in some large markets	Similar pattern regardless of place of origin, brief recorded clips and field reports	Two or 3 anchors and sportscaster, mixed gender and race, they also chat "happy talk."	Local news, "breaking news," about crime, accidents, disasters, lifestyle, sports, weather. Larger markets may include some global news.	Local television stations
	News-talk	Usually 60 minutes	Informational, 3-4 in-depth stories, news staff stays with story and asks questions	Host with other staff reporters	Global, national current events, business, and health news	News Hour with Jim Lehrer
	24-hour news	24 hours of news, both live and pre-recorded	Informational news repeated throughout the day, other news on captions, special reports	Several different anchors in shifts, correspondents are prominent	Global, national current events, business, health, and human interest news	CNN Headline News Fox News
Magazine Show	News-talk-entertainment	1–3 hours with pre-recorded segments	Informational and entertaining news, interviews with authors, celebrities,	Two anchors, one male, one female who interview guests plus other	Multiple segments similar in layout to a print magazine	Today Good Morning America The Early Show

(Continued)

Table 5.1 (Continued)

Genre	Subgenre	Conventions				
		Format	Characteristics	Characters	Plot	Examples
			politicians, health professionals. Segments about food, music, fashion, new products.	talent reading news, weather, human interest stories. Anchors chat, tell personal stories.		
	Investigative or public affairs	60 minutes, pre-recorded	Informational, entertaining, shocking stories with reenactments and interviews	Anchor with field correspondents	Usually one primary story about an event, scandal, illegal or immoral acts.	*60 Minutes* *48 Hours* *Nightline*
	Celebrity news	Information about film and TV stars' private and professional lives, 30–60 minutes	Male and female hosts announce stories with pre-recorded, edited segments.	Hosts are youthful and attractive.	Stories about the stars to reveal them as people who date, marry, divorce, have children.	*E! News* *Entertainment Tonight* *Insider*
Drama	Crime stories, detective/ police/FBI, forensic science	60 minutes recorded outside and on indoor sets, episodic	Audience follows case step by step, anticipates the outcome. Case is solved within the hour, interpersonal conflicts may carry	Ensemble cast with character development over time. Major and minor characters, mixed gender and race.	Crime is committed or person goes missing; law enforcers arrive at scene, interrogate	*NYPD Blue* *The Shield* *Cold Case* *NCIS* *Criminal Minds* *Without a Trace*

Conventions

Genre	Subgenre	Format	Characteristics	Characters	Plot	Examples
			over to subsequent shows. Character and dialogue are central to show. Usually set in urban area. May use flashbacks. Emphasis on law, order, and justice.		witnesses, examine evidence at crime scene or in laboratory, make arrest, solve crime, find missing person.	
	Workplace drama	60 minutes recorded outside and on indoor sets, episodic	Audience follows several events, anticipates the outcome. Workplace crisis or conflict is usually settled within the hour. Set in hospital, law office, courtroom, government facility, prison. Interpersonal attraction between and among people at workplace. May have flashbacks.	Ensemble cast, young attractive women and men with few older adults, mixed racially. Interpersonal relationships develop over time.	Crisis or conflict, teamwork to arrive at a solution within the hour, interpersonal affairs carry over.	*ER* *House* *Grey's Anatomy* *Law & Order* *Boston Legal* *The West Wing* *The Nine* *Lost* *24* *E-Ring* *Prison Break*

(Continued)

Table 5.1 (Continued)

		Conventions			
Genre	Subgenre	Format	Characteristics	Characters	Plot	Examples
	Family drama	60 minutes recorded outside and on indoor sets, episodic	Audience identification with characters, familiar conflicts, set inside home and surroundings in the present time.	Ensemble cast with young adults, children, some senior citizens.	Multiple interpersonal conflicts carry over from week to week.	*The O.C.* *Wildfire* *The Sopranos* *Smallville* *Brothers and Sisters*
	Hybrid dramas	60 minutes recorded outside and on indoor sets, episodic	Family drama fused with mystery or science fiction. Audience anticipates outcome, may identify with characters.	Lead actor(s) with ensemble cast.	Dilemma may or may not be solved within the hour, may be crime, espionage, or interpersonal conflict.	*Invasion* *Medium* *Ghost Whisperer* *Jericho*
	Telefilms	Audience may have familiarity with story Miniseries over 3 or 4 nights or 90- to 120- minute movie, possible pilot for a proposed series	Audience identification with characters. Adapted from a well-known book or original screenplay. Full-length drama, may be romantic, adventure, or melodrama.	Actors may or may not be famous. Heroes and villains.	Characters established and followed through story to the end.	*The Five People You Meet in Heaven* *Tuesdays with Morrie* *Empire Falls* *Lackawanna Blues*

Genre	Subgenre	Conventions				
		Format	Characteristics	Characters	Plot	Examples
	Docudramas	Audience may know something about the biographical person but expects to learn more. Audience is expected to know it is watching impersonations, not file footage. Blend of fact and fiction. Miniseries over 3 or 4 nights or 90- to 120-minute movie.	Based on a true story, biography or crime in dramatic form, includes imaginary dialogue. Often melodramatic.	Some resemblance to actual people, actors may not be well known.	Tends to rely on family melodrama, a specific time in the life of a famous person, often features mature and personal topics such as spouse abuse or eating disorders.	*The Elizabeth Smart Story* *For the Love of a Child* *The Burning Bed* *The Karen Carpenter Story* *Elvis*
Soap opera	Daytime drama, some nighttime drama	30–60 minutes, daily, continuous serials. May run for years. Audience has to stay tuned to follow narrative.	Interpersonal relationships, domestic crises, overlapping storylines, cliffhangers.	Regular cast of familiar characters, attractive young adults, a few older adults. Familiar setting in homes or work places.	State of equilibrium is disturbed, rarely a solution or a climax that ties loose ends. Resolution is endlessly deferred.	*The Young and the Restless* *As the World Turns* *General Hospital* *All My Children*

(Continued)

Table 5.1 (Continued)

Genre	Subgenre		Format	Characteristics	Characters	Plot	Examples
		Conventions					
Science fiction			Feeds audience imagination 30–60 minutes, episodic On Sci Fi channel	Usually takes place in the future and in space, features fantastic technology. Stories reflect contemporary problems of the present such as nuclear threat, racism, multiculturalism, ecology.	Ensemble space ship crew, aliens	Heroes save humanity from aliens and Armageddon.	*Star Trek* *Battlestar Galactica*
Reality shows			Encourage audience voyeurism Usually 60 minutes, usually episodic, almost never appear as reruns	Ordinary people compete for expensive prizes. Competitive, winners chosen by group vote or judges. Real-life police responses to crime, sting operations.	Non-actors audition for places and opportunity to compete.	Contestants are given tasks to complete in blocks of time; contestants are eliminated by group members, judges, or authority. One team or one winner emerges. Police arrest offenders.	*The Biggest Loser* *The Apprentice* *Survivor* *Fear Factor* *American Idol* *Cops* *The Bachelor*

			Conventions			
Genre	Subgenre	Format	Characteristics	Characters	Plot	Examples
Sports	Football, basketball, baseball, hockey, tennis, golf, soccer, water sports, volleyball, Olympics	Audience sees live broadcast of full-length games	Sports announcers describe and comment on the game.	Live competition	Stays on the air until a winner emerges.	Network and sports channels coverage of various sports such as Super Bowl and college bowl games, NBA, World Series
Children's television	Live and animated programming.	30 minutes, 5 days/week, daytime Appeals to children of various ages	Ranges from educational entertainment to cartoon violence.	Often has familiar characters such as Big Bird.	Educational programs have combination ensembles of puppets and live actors. Cartoons have heroes and villains.	*Sesame Street* *Mister Rogers' Neighborhood* *Scooby Doo* *Sponge Bob*
Game shows		Television audience can match answers or guesses with contestants, 30–60 minutes. Recorded in front of live audience, weekly or daily.	Contestants compete for prizes within the program or over several weeks.	Host and attractive woman to work the game board. Contestants.	Categories of quiz questions. Correct answers increase value of prizes, suspense is built as contestants struggle to give correct answers.	*Jeopardy!* *Who Wants to Be a Millionaire* *The Price is Right* *Wheel of Fortune*

(Other genres are mostly self-evident: religious broadcasting, shopping networks, food networks, award shows, music performances, movie channels, History Channel, Discovery Channel, *Nova, Nature,* Animal Planet.)

(Text continued from page 100)

The main characters are likeable, and audiences identify with them because the foibles of the characters are recognized as similar to their own shortcomings. Carl Reiner, who wrote, directed, and produced many outstanding situation comedies, such as *The Dick Van Dyke Show,* said it was important for the characters to have "warmth." "You laugh easier when funny things are happening to nice people" (Rose, 1985, p. 117). James Burrows, director of *Cheers, Will & Grace,* and many other situation comedies, echoed Reiner when he said, "The successful key to a situation comedy is to create warmth which transfers to the audience. Good shows are stories told from the heart" (O'Donnell, 1996). In his book *Comic Visions,* David Marc wrote, ". . . sitcoms depend on familiarity, identification, and redemption of popular beliefs" (Marc, 1989, p. 24). While the situation comedy endorses cultural norms, it may also advance certain new ideas.

The late Sheldon Leonard, producer of many successful situation comedies, such as *The Andy Griffith Show,* said, "We can, within a framework of good showmanship, advance valid social comments, valid ethical concepts, valid generalizations about the human condition which have meaning for the audience" (Rose, 1985, p. 119). In the situation comedy about a television news staff, *Murphy Brown,* not only did the lead character (played by Candice Bergen) have a child out of wedlock, but in a later episode, Murphy had breast cancer and subsequent surgery for which she chose a lumpectomy rather than a mastectomy. Breast cancer was also a theme in some of the last episodes of *Sex in the City* as Samantha (Kim Cattrall) lost her hair due to chemotherapy. These problems were not treated as comedy but rather as real-life situations. Thus, the situation comedy, though generally funny, also enables the audience to identify with real-life situations and embrace the characters as more human.

Animated Situation Comedy

Animated situation comedy has once again become popular on prime-time television, especially since *The Simpsons* became a regular series in 1990. Animated situation comedy tends to have everything a human comedy has—a family, an ensemble of regular characters who do things to provoke laughter, multiple story lines, a "problem of the week," and restoration of equilibrium at the end of 30 minutes. Spin-offs of *The Simpsons* include *King of the Hill, South Park, Family Guy,* and *American Dad. The Simpsons,* which began as 30-second inserts in *The Tracey Ullman Show* in 1987, has been running as a regular 30-minute series since 1990, holding the record for the longest-running situation comedy, and has surpassed the longest running prime-time animation series, *The Flintstones.*

Photo 5.1   Bart and Lisa Simpson.

Animated situation comedy is characterized by parody and satire. The brochure for the Museum of Television and Radio's seminar on *The Simpsons* describes it as "a gonzo attack on mainstream television, melding sharp, clever writing with animation to reinvigorate the conventional sitcom format as a cartoon satire on contemporary America" (Creating Prime-time Comedy, 2003, p. 9). The references to television, film, organized religion, political figures, and advertising give the show its special edge. To appreciate this aspect of *The Simpsons,* a viewer has to be familiar with classic films like *Citizen Kane* as well as television's *The X-Files.* The Simpson family watches a lot of television, thus there are many references to actual series. On one episode, the little sister Lisa is trying to make new friends while on vacation at the seashore by telling them about hermit crabs. One child asks Lisa, "Did you learn that from a teacher?" "No," said Lisa, "I learned it on *Baywatch.*" These intertextual references are enhanced by the audience's knowing complicity and recognition of famous guest voices such as Meryl Streep and Patrick Stewart. To understand the intertextual humor, the audience has to be familiar with the events, names, voices, films, and television programs that the show parodies. In one episode, Lisa gets in trouble because a career test indicates that her future work should be that of a homemaker. The school principal asks her, "What are you rebelling against?" Her response refers to Marlon Brando in *The Wild One* when she says, "Whattaya got?" It is possible to enjoy *The Simpsons* without intertextual recognition, but when the allusions are caught, the enjoyment is enhanced. Thus, children and adults alike enjoy the show. Because it is an animated cartoon, it gets away with antics that might not be acceptable in human situation comedy.

Variety Comedy

The variety comedy shows of the past, such as *Your Show of Shows* with Sid Caesar and Imogene Coca or *The Carol Burnett Show,* had a regular host, an ensemble cast, music, and humorous skits. While many variety comedy shows have come and gone, *Saturday Night Live* has been on NBC since 1975 with weekly guest hosts, including Sting, Queen Latifa, and Cameron Diaz, an ensemble cast of improvisational comics who do impersonations and put on funny and satirical skits, and breakout musical acts. This show has launched the film and television careers of comic performers like Steve Martin, Eddie Murphy, Dan Aykroyd, Bill Murray, Adam Sandler, Julia Louis-Dreyfus, and Jane Curtin. It is telecast live before an audience in New York City at 11:30 p.m. and has followed the same formula since its inception. The skits, performed by the ensemble cast as well as the guest host, satirize current events, politicians, newscasters, or relationships. *MadTV* on Fox follows a similar formula although its cast is not as well known.

Talk Shows

Nighttime Talk Shows

Steve Allen launched the nighttime talk show genre in 1954 with comedy, music, and guests on *The Tonight Show.* When Johnny Carson became the show's star in 1962 and remained there for 30 years, it became a late-night institution. The format Carson used has hardly changed. There is a single host sitting behind a desk who talks to guests who are sitting on a sofa. The host has a sidekick or a band leader with whom to banter, and there is a performance space for musical numbers. The guests may be celebrities, politicians, or zoo keepers who introduce exotic animals to the host.

Writers meet with the host to develop a "script" that is placed on the host's desk, but much of the dialogue is improvisational. As Rob Burnett, head writer on the *Late Show with David Letterman,* said, "Everything is planned and nothing is planned" (Writers Guild of the East, n.d.). The late-night talk shows are taped before a live audience earlier in the evening and broadcast late at night, after the news, five nights a week. Each show opens with a monologue, usually a parody of that day's newspaper headlines, followed by talks with guests who may be promoting films or books or themselves (Arnold Schwarzenegger announced his candidacy for governor of California on *The Tonight Show* with Jay Leno), musical events, and comic skits. Letterman does remote acts outside the studio, but they are filmed and edited in advance. These late-night talk shows are 60 minutes long. *The Daily Show With Jon Stewart* is 30 minutes long and runs four nights a week. Stewart satirizes the news and current events, but he also has comic skits and guests who visit in the talk show format.

Bernard Timberg called this "television talk" rather than "television talk shows" because it is a special kind of talk. "It is often directed to an individual in the studio (guest or sidekick) but also, simultaneously, to a national television viewing audience of millions" (Timberg, 2000, p. 359). He also indicated that television talk "begins and ends with the host. Talk shows are, to use the words of one producer, 'he' or 'she' shows. The producers and talent coordinators line up guests and topics for 'him' or 'her'; the writers write lines that will work for 'him' or 'her,' to be spoken as he or she would speak them. The tone and pacing of everything that happens with the show is set by the host" (Timberg, 2000, p. 361).

Daytime Talk Shows

Daytime talk shows are taped before a live audience for 60-minute time slots, five days a week. The host and guests tend to explore cultural oddities. The guests are seldom famous—rather they are people who reveal sensitive problems, usually domestic or criminal, and disclose their most private experiences to the host or hostess. Often these people are from marginalized or stigmatized groups. They may be incest or rape victims, unwed mothers, transsexuals, prostitutes, or people with incurable diseases. In some cases, the guests and the studio audience have been rehearsed. Oprah Winfrey will not pander to anything vile or mean-spirited on *Oprah,* which is regarded as a "talk service" show. However, Jerry Springer and Maury Povich, whose talk shows bear their names, emphasize the vulgar and crude, often with fistfights between guests, nasty repartee, and outbursts from the audience. Media psychologist Dr. Phil, on the show of the same name, teaches through interpersonal discussion and psychological analysis of his guests. The audience can observe how others with problems and personal conflicts in relationships work through them. Daytime talk shows highlight moral conflict and confrontation between and among the guests and sometimes the audience members. The approach is to "tell all" no matter how distressing.

Photo 5.2   Oprah shows compassion for her subject.

Information Talk Shows

Information-oriented talk shows include discussion of current issues, books, films, and other serious topics. They are conversational and guest-oriented. Larry King, on *Larry King Live,* conducts both face-to-face and remote interviews and takes telephone calls from the viewing audience. Since Ross Perot announced his presidential candidacy on King's show, appearances on the show have been a must for politicians. Charlie Rose, on *The Charlie Rose Show,* leads serious discussions with one or more guests who sit at a table with him. The viewing audience gains information from experts.

News

News includes the elements of "timeliness, consequence, prominence, rarity, proximity, conflict, change, action, concreteness, and personality" (Metzler, 1979, pp. 23–24). News reporting is interpretative and creative, therefore it is a symbolic strategy that contains an attitude toward the events that are recounted (Wilkins & Patterson, 1987). Communication satellites, radio relay stations in space, carry press agency news feeds and global television bringing news from remote regions around the world and up-to-the-minute reporting from conflict zones. Interviews, correspondent reports, and actual footage are structured to fit the news format and time.

National and World News

The national half-hour news report at the end of the workday follows a standard format of news stories sprinkled with advertisements for remedies for indigestion and headaches. An anchor sitting at a desk reads the news reports with taped or live visual images to convey the stories. Satellite transmission of images allows the viewers to feel a sense of immediacy and involvement. The nightly telecast of the war in Iraq "exerts a powerful effect on the audience. Suddenly everyone watching television is dragged into war. When there is a sandstorm, the audience can't see any better than the troops . . . the viewer feels a part of the invading army" (Boxer, 2003, p. 2). Network correspondents report from Washington, DC, the White House, Capitol Hill, the Pentagon, and from around the globe. Cuts in budgets have reduced the number of correspondents in the field, resulting in "parachute journalism." Correspondents based in a foreign city have to fly at a moment's notice to a location where the news is breaking (Foote, 1998). National news anchors have become stars. Former anchors from the three networks—ABC, CBS, and NBC—Peter Jennings, Dan Rather, and Tom Brokaw became institutions in our living rooms. Katie Couric, already a star from NBC's *Today,* is now the anchor on *CBS Evening News.*

When CNN, the 24-hour news channel, appeared in 1980, the three networks redefined their approach to news to compete. "Assuming that viewers watched the big stories before the evening news was broadcast, networks opted for more reflection, stylized reporting, longer trend stories, and a hint of 'infotainment.' What they lacked in immediacy and news-gathering ability around the world, they tried to make up for with a well-regarded anchor name and segments" (Foote, 1998, p. 12). In addition to national and international current events, the nightly news also includes segments of business news, advances in medicine, and human interest stories, all of which are very brief.

Local News

The local news is usually on for 30 minutes before network national and international news and late at night before the nighttime talk shows. Local news broadcasts tend to have a similar format regardless of their origins, thus the local news in New York City resembles the local news in Los Angeles. Typically, there are two or three anchors behind a desk, a man and a woman plus a sportscaster, usually male. Often one or more of the anchors is African American, Hispanic American, or Asian American. In addition to reporting the news, the anchors chat with one another. The weather person is not behind the desk, but rather he or she appears to be standing in front of a map for the weather spot on the program. Promotions and lead-ins are used to grab viewer attention. ("Arson suspected in home fire. News at 6:00.") Local news often emphasizes "breaking news" with live images of car chases, people being carried by stretcher to a waiting ambulance, burning buildings, and so on. In addition to crime and disaster news, local stations usually have some soft news. ("Fireman rescues kitten from sewer pipe.") In addition, there is health news, local and national sports, and celebrity items. Local news from large urban areas has some national and international reporting. For example, the ABC local affiliate in Los Angeles had its own correspondents in Israel reporting on Prime Minister Ariel Sharon's stroke in 2006.

News-Talk

PBS's *The NewsHour with Jim Lehrer* is on five nights a week for 60 minutes. It has in-depth news stories, usually only three, with reporters staying on the story for greater understanding. Lehrer stops and asks questions during each report. The stories are about national and international news, business news, and education, and there are interviews with heads of state, writers, and politicians. When the stock market report comes up, the reporter tells the audience what it means. A seminar at the Museum of Television and Radio in 1989 included Lehrer and his former coanchor Robert MacNeil, who said, "We intended our show to be different . . . to expand time devoted to a story to fit its importance. [You] stay with the topic or interview until you find its importance." They do not consider their audience elite, but very broad in scope. Lehrer said, "We do not assume a certain body of knowledge in the audience. We are very basic, we use maps and other information helpful to understanding the issue. We ask, 'would so-and-so understand this and would he care?" (*MacNeil/Lehrer NewsHour*, 1989).

Other news talk shows are more specific in their focus. For example, *Meet the Press* reviews weekly news events on Sunday mornings. Network and cable channels feature shows with pundits, self-appointed experts who express their own opinions and argue with one another about issues of the day.

24-Hour News

The Cable News Network (CNN) began to broadcast news 24 hours a day, seven days a week in 1980. Although it had anchors, emphasis was placed on the news, not on personalities, and the correspondents' reports were given importance. News bureaus were set up across the United States and around the world. In 1982, Ted Turner initiated a second CNN service, *Headline News* with updated newscasts every half hour. When President Ronald Reagan met Mikhail S. Gorbachev at the summit that would signal the end of the Cold War, CNN had 17 correspondents onsite. By 1989, CNN was available in 65 countries. In 1991, CNN was the only television network operating live from Operation Desert Storm in Iraq and Kuwait.

Other 24-hour news channels emerged—MSNBC and Fox News—to challenge CNN. Stuart H. Loory, who was Washington managing editor and vice president of CNN for 18 years, believes that there are four reasons why CNN has fallen behind Fox News in the ratings: (1) CNN "abandoned its founding concept [by promoting] anchors and correspondents instead of allowing their work to speak for itself"; (2) "CNN has abandoned the emphasis on hard news coverage—the pursuit of stories by its reporters—for discussion of the stories by experts, analysts, and consultants"; (3) "CNN too often abandons the general news of the day to dwell on one story only"; (4) "CNN puts too much emphasis on video often forgoing a story because it cannot be illustrated well enough" (Loory, 2005, pp. 342–343). What made CNN so successful in the past seems to have been exchanged for attempts at higher ratings. On the other hand, the CNN Web site, celebrating its 25th anniversary, had an essay by Christiane Amanpour, who wrote: "CNN still is one of the most recognized brand names in the world. Its chunky bright red logo is the eternal symbol of excellence, credibility, truth and trust. We plan to keep it that way for the next 25 years!" (Lule, 2006, p. 339)

Magazine Shows

News-Talk-Entertainment

News-talk-entertainment shows are generally on in the early morning. To attract the working audience, 22 minutes of commercial-free hard news is reported at 7:00 a.m. The next hour, from 7:30 to 8:30 a.m., has hard and soft features aimed at a female audience, and the final half hour is aimed at senior citizens, with health-oriented pieces. The content includes interviews with celebrities, authors, politicians, and doctors. Consumer advice, health news, cooking tips, film reviews, and fashion are presented by the anchor-hosts and guests. Much of the fare is light-hearted, and the anchor-hosts, usually one woman and one man, chat with one another. More serious news is handled by a regular news reader, and another regular on the show talks about weather. These multiple segments are similar to a print magazine, for they are short, informative, and basically entertaining. *Today* has been on NBC since 1952. Meredith Vieira, Matt Lauer, Al Roker, and Ann Curry are the stars who go outside to chat with the crowd that gathers as early as 5:00 a.m. in Rockefeller Center. In the summer, they have live music on Fridays. *Good Morning America* hosts are Diane Sawyer, Robin Roberts, Chris Cuomo, and Sam Champion. Their show is similar to *Today,* although the crowd outside waves behind a glass window. The CBS *Early Show* also follows a similar pattern with hosts Julie Chen, Harry Smith, and Hannah Storm. Needless to say, these news-talk-entertainment shows are very competitive. Although Fox News on cable has a similar show, *Fox and Friends,* it began a new, one-hour morning show in January 2007. Fox's new show has no hard news, however, just entertainment and lifestyle segments.

Investigative or Public Affairs

Investigative or public affairs television shows were developed "to offer an alternative to the television presentation of news" (Stark, 1997, p. 188). Each of these shows has one or more anchors and investigative field reporters. They may focus on single or multiple stories of a scandalous or disturbing nature, such as kidnapping, organized crime, unsafe food in restaurants, scams, and frauds, although sometimes they do positive profiles on people who have done good deeds, recovered from adversity, or are effective leaders. They may use taped footage, but some are inclined to use reenactments with actors. *60 Minutes* has been on the air since 1968, and reporters such as Mike Wallace, Morley Safer, and Andy Rooney have been with the show for many years. The late Ed Bradley was a very popular reporter on the show. Diane Sawyer joined the show as its first woman in 1984. When she left in 1989, Lesley Stahl replaced her. When host Harry Reasoner introduced the first broadcast of *60 Minutes,* he said, "It's kind of a magazine for television, which means it has the flexibility and diversity of a magazine adapted to broadcast journalism" (Stark, 1997, p. 189). The first show had a story mix of political campaigns, conflicts between police and citizens, an animated film, and a humorous essay. In later years, *60 Minutes* altered its focus with fewer lighter features and more investigative pieces. In keeping with popular tastes, it also featured profiles of film stars and athletes. Steven Stark wrote, "*60 Minutes* changed the face of programming and journalism . . . [it] made journalists into national icons" (Stark, 1997, p. 189). *60 Minutes* spawned a trend in news magazine shows. *48 Hours* covers one story with multiple angles, whereas *Dateline* is known for its surprise visits and hidden cameras. *20/20* features sensational stories, often using reenactments.

Celebrity News

The 21st century has seen an increased obsession with the lives of celebrities, and many television shows concentrate solely on the private and personal lives of film and television stars. *Entertainment Tonight* or *ET* began in 1981 with Mary Hart and John Tesh in an upbeat, gossipy, and glitzy show about the stars, award shows, new films and television shows, and musicians. Soon other shows followed—*Insider, Hollywood, True Hollywood Story,* and an entire cable channel, E! Entertainment Television, devoted to entertainment news. Described as "hysterical cheer" and "tabloid TV," the fast-paced style of celebrity news shows with attractive and young female and male hosts revealing the intimate details of the lives of the stars has influenced the style of local news programs and reality shows.

Drama

Drama on television may be serial, a miniseries, or a single play that may last for one hour or several hours spread over a fixed number of nights or weeks. Drama is the most varied, complex, expensive, and popular television genre. Series drama tends to be formulaic, whereas miniseries and single plays are formatted to fit the allotted time in the schedule. Series consist of 22–26 episodes per season and are broadcast weekly. Because a single episode of a drama series costs $2 million or more to produce, the plots tend to be self-contained with a resolution at the end of the hour. This is convenient and cost-effective for reruns because viewers do not have to know what happened in the previous episode. Not all series are self-contained, however, for unresolved issues keep the viewers tuning in to find out what happens next.

Most dramatic series have ensemble casts of actors who play the same roles from week to week. Audiences prefer familiar characters and story lines. In a study conducted by the Corporation for Public Broadcasting to find out why American audiences were not watching imported British dramas more frequently, participants in focus groups said that because they did not know the characters, it required too much effort to watch a new program with so many new actors. Their preferences were for familiar characters, sets, and story lines (Kubey, 2004). Familiarity with the characters and narrative structure also enables the audience to pick up a story line when the holiday seasons interrupt series for several weeks.

Crime Shows (Detective, Police, FBI, and Forensic Science)

The crime series are 60 minutes long, starting at point A with a dilemma (a murder, a missing person, a theft, a rape, a kidnapping, or an arson in an urban or suburban area) that is resolved (by detectives, the police, FBI agents, or forensic scientists) at the end of the hour at point B. Although they are part of a series, individual episodes can stand alone because of the resolution at the end of each show. Since September 11, 2001, terrorism has become a common theme on crime shows, especially those that feature the FBI.

Crime shows have ensemble casts playing crime fighters who have weapons and know how to use them. These characters also have interpersonal relations with one another. While a crime gets solved, the suspense and conflict in these relationships are not necessarily resolved at the end of an episode, carrying over to the next week. The casts are usually mixed in gender, race, and age, with characters who develop some depth over time. However, these shows are not so much about crimes but rather about those who try to solve them, thus they depend upon characters and their dialogue. Although each individual crime series has its own uniqueness, they tend to follow a similar structure: (1) a crime is committed; (2) the detectives-police-FBI-crime scene experts arrive at the scene to view the body or fire or other criminal act; (3) they interrogate witnesses and family members and follow the leads; (4) they search for and ultimately detain or arrest the suspects; (5) they solve the crime.

Sometimes there will be internal conflict when the police or detectives disagree or go beyond the boundaries of their duty. The Internal Affairs Bureau (IAB) officials, although on the side of the law, are often depicted as villains who get in the way of the detectives who are trying to solve a crime. *NYPD Blue* and *The Shield* are about crime in New York City and Los Angeles, respectively, with very well-drawn characters, especially Dennis Franz's character, Andy Sipowitz, a recovering alcoholic with bigotry issues, and *The Shield*'s Michael Chiklis, who plays Vic Mackey, good cop and bad cop rolled into one. Over the years, their characters have developed through both their work and personal lives. *Cold Case*, set in Philadelphia, is about investigating unsolved murders from the past, while *Close to Home* is about crimes committed in suburban neighborhoods. Both of these series feature female leads, Jennifer Finnigan as Annabeth Chase on *Close to Home* and Kathryn Morris as Lilly Rush on *Cold Case*.

The crime scene investigator characters of *CSI*, *CSI: Miami*, and *CSI: New York* collect evidence that they examine in the laboratory and almost always examine bloody, bruised, and mutilated corpses with medical examiners explaining the cause of death. A trademark of these shows is expensive equipment donated by publicity-seeking manufacturers (a $50,000 forensic microscope and a $500,000 ballistic identifier on *CSI*) and special visual effects known as "snap-zoom" that snap into a body or zoom into a piece of evidence (Stein, 2003, p. 72; Gliatto, 2002, pp. 113–115). The viewer looks at the evidence along with the characters in the show. Correct scientific vocabulary, often in Latin, is used for realism.

Without a Trace features FBI agents searching for missing persons. This show uses flashbacks as acquaintances of the missing person remember details with ghostly images as the agents re-create their movements. Hank Steinberg, the show's creator, said, "The essential distinction between our show and every other cop show on television is the possibility that the missing is still alive" (Hinson, 2003, p. 10AR). Most of the time, the FBI team manages to locate the person who has gone missing, but not every person is found alive. Each of the agents has a personal story too, which affects how he or she acts in the investigations. *Criminal Minds* features FBI profilers who track criminals to try to prevent them from attacking again. *Numb3rs* has an FBI agent who recruits his brother, a mathematical genius, to help solve tough cases. A variation on the FBI is the Naval Criminal Investigative Service featured in *NCIS*. This series chronicles the operations of an elite team of special agents whose mission is to investigate any crime that has a shred of evidence connected to Navy and Marine Corps personnel.

The long-running *Law & Order* series effectively combine the police and lawyer subgenres. Not only is each crime solved by the end of the episode, but the court case that brings the criminal to justice is also completed. The characters on *Law & Order* are strictly revealed as professional with very little reference to their personal lives.

Essentially, crime series emphasize law, order, and justice as well as the determination and ability of law enforcement officials. It is not unusual, however, for some of the law enforcers to break rules or to work against their associates. In fact, this is a common theme in *The Shield*, which has the tag line, "The road to justice is twisted."

Workplace Drama

Workplace dramas are about groups of professional people in a hospital, law firm, government office, casino, the military, or a prison. An ensemble cast of young and attractive men and women with a few older adults is likely to be racially mixed. The characters they play undergo personal growth over time in both their work and their personal relationships. The settings provide the work-related action as well as the characters' personal affairs. In most workplace dramas, several events occur simultaneously, with work-related crises or conflicts usually settled within a 60-minute episode, while the personal affairs continue over several episodes.

The hospital has been a popular setting for television workplace dramas with various illnesses, accidents, last-minute surgical saves, compassionate doctors, and a multitude of patients who provide opportunities for guest actors. *ER* has been on television since 1994, but the cast of characters has changed over the years with younger actors added as the older ones leave the show. Alex Kingston, who played the surgeon Dr. Corday on *ER,* left the show at the end of the 2004 season. In an interview with the British publication, *Radio Times,* Kingston, who was 41 at the time, said "her contract wasn't renewed because the program was increasingly focused on young characters 'and apparently I, according to the producers and the writers, am part of the old fogeys who are no longer interesting.' Producer John Wells, in a statement, said the Corday storyline had run its course" (Kingston ends *ER* shift, 2004, p. D1). Much more a personal drama than a medical drama, *Grey's Anatomy* follows a group of young, attractive doctors through their first-year surgical residency at a Seattle hospital and the older doctors who guide and harass them. *House* has a lead actor, Hugh Laurie, who plays Dr. Gregory House, a brilliant diagnostician with a dysfunctional personality, who delivers surly, acerbic lines with a wry sense of humor. He supervises a group of young doctors and argues with the hospital administrator about a single case on each episode.

Fictional presidents of the United States, both female and male, and their staffs coping with national and international crises have been featured on the political workplace dramas *Commander-in-Chief* and *West Wing.* Although each program has a lead actor (Geena Davis and Martin Sheen, respectively) playing a principled president, the other characters are played by strong ensemble casts. National and international crises usually get solved (unrealistically) within the hour, although occasionally the crisis lasts for two episodes. Audiences may enjoy an imaginary glimpse into the activities in the White House, and, because the president's family has domestic quandaries similar to those of ordinary families, audience identification is likely to occur. When the ratings declined, *West Wing* was cancelled in 2006 after seven award-winning seasons. Kevin Reilly, NBC entertainment president, said, "There's a point when you look at the ratings and say, it feels like it's time" In addition to critical acclaim, *West Wing* had "the most upscale audience on television, an important drawing point for advertisers" (Bauder, 2006, p. 1).

Other workplace dramas take place in a casino (*Las Vegas),* in the Pentagon (*E-Ring),* in the CIA (*24*), and even in prison (*Prison Break*). With the exception of *24*, which positions each episode into one of 24 hours—requiring weekly viewer commitment—each of these programs solves a crisis within the hour. *24* and *E-Ring* have narratives about fighting terrorism; *Prison Break* has a story about a man getting imprisoned to help his brother escape.

Family Drama

Family dramas are melodramas, for they depict ordinary suffering as special and meaningful (Deming, 1990). Personal life as revealed through close relationships is at the core of melodramatic narrative that also is replete with extraordinary conflicts and catastrophes (Ang, 1990). Family dramas have their own network, ABC Family, where viewers can watch youth-oriented series such as *Wildfire* and *Smallville*. *The OC* on Fox features an affluent California family in soap opera fashion with parents and teens who get involved in various interpersonal conflicts and crises outside the home.

The Sopranos is a family drama, but instead of going to the office, Tony Soprano, a besieged, Prozac-popping boss of a group of unsavory gangsters, conducts business in the back room of a strip club. His extended family consists of uncles and cousins as well as the "family," in the sense of organized crime. The show's creator David Chase said, "It has to do with the limitations of family and friendship in a materialist world" (Meyers, 2004, p. 18). The family dynamics range from Tony's conflicts with his wife, son, and daughter over domestic issues to fights with his sister to vicious and illegal activities with his brothers in crime. Tony's therapy sessions and his dreams allow the viewer to see his internal fears and suffering. Because *The Sopranos* is an HBO production, its format is 54–58 minutes of drama without commercial interruption, and it is replayed three times each week. An entire year of repeats ran in 2005 while the producers took a year off to prepare the new episodes to begin in March 2006. Without censorship, HBO allows nudity in the Bada Bing! strip joint, very strong language, and gruesome killings. TV critic Robert Bianco wrote, "It should be noted that this 'family' drama is hardly family entertainment. *The Sopranos* is sexually explicit, incredibly profane, and shockingly violent . . . You're not meant to empathize [with Tony Soprano]; you're meant to recoil" (Bianco, 2004, p. E2).

Hybrid Drama

Hybrid dramas on contemporary television are police or family dramas blended with elements of science fiction or the supernatural. *Medium* is a self-contained, hour-long drama that is part family drama and part police show and features a mother of three young daughters who is married to an understanding and helpful husband. She works for the district attorney because her dreams reveal the identities of killers, and she has visions of their crimes when she confronts suspects and crime scenes. *Invasion* was a continuous story about a divorced couple, each of whom has remarried, who struggle to get along for the sake of their children in the midst of a mysterious extraterrestrial invasion wherein citizens of a South Florida community are taken over by aliens that appear as lights in the water. *Ghost Whisperer* features a beautiful newlywed woman who speaks to confused dead people before they "cross to the other side." Each episode has a resolution at the end when the dead person resolves the conflict with his or her family member and goes "into the light." Producers of shows with a supernatural twist apparently believe that the American public is concerned with death and interested in the supernatural.

Jericho is a hybrid drama about what happens when a nuclear mushroom cloud suddenly appears on the horizon, hurtling the people of a small Kansas town into chaos. They do not know if they are the only Americans left alive because all communication and power are shut down. This show is a reflection of our fear of terrorism, but ultimately, it is about nation rebuilding as the citizens of Jericho pull together to cope with a tragic situation. The characters' actions are heroic as they discover their inner strength.

Teleplays and Telefilms

Teleplays or films cover a wide variety of stories, for they may be based on well-known books, historical characters or events, or original adventure, romantic, or melodramatic scripts. They may be in the format of miniseries spread over three or four nights, or a 90- to 120-minute movie that could also be a pilot for a proposed series.

Imported teleplays from England are shown weekly on *Masterpiece Theatre* and *Mystery!* on PBS. There is no *Masterpiece Theatre* or *Mystery!* on British television; rather the shows that appear on PBS are dramas from England's BBC, Channel 4, and other television stations. *Masterpiece Theatre*, on the air since 1971, has dramatizations of classic literature, history, and contemporary stories, such as *David Copperfield, Great Expectations, The Lost Prince, Henry the Eighth,* and *House of Cards.* Hosted by the venerable Alistair Cooke for 20 years, who was succeeded by Russell Baker, these programs often stretch over two to eight weeks and feature well-known British actors such as Derek Jacobi and Miranda Richardson. *Mystery!* is a weekly program on PBS that features short series such as *Prime Suspect, Foyle's War, Inspector Linley, Miss Marple,* and *Brother Cadfael* that run from two to six weeks. *Mystery!* also features famous actors such as Helen Mirren and the late Alan Bates. Both programs come from PBS affiliate WGBH in Boston, which originally promised to present a fair number of American works or productions, but rarely did so. A producer said, "It's cheaper to import productions which the BBC or other British companies have already done" (Stark, 1997, p. 174).

Hallmark Hall of Fame has high-quality dramatic productions on network television with reruns on the Hallmark Channel. HBO has adaptations of books that run for two or more weeks, such as *The Five People You Meet in Heaven, Tuesdays with Morrie,* and *Empire Falls,* as well as original dramas such as *Lackawanna Blues,* based on the true story of Ruben Santiago, Jr. and his relationship with Rachel Crosby, set in 1950s and 1960s Lackawanna, New York, and *Warm Springs,* a story about Franklin D. Roosevelt's early battle with polio. *Angels in America,* an award-winning Broadway play, was adapted for HBO by playwright Tony Kushner and directed by Mike Nichols. It cost $60 million for a six-hour production with stars including Meryl Streep, Emma Thompson, and Al Pacino.

Docudrama

Once a staple of network broadcasting, the made-for-television movie is now more likely to be a docudrama on a cable channel about a biographical person or event. These films are based on a true story, biography, or crime such as *The Elizabeth Smart Story,* about the abduction of a young Utah girl; *Elvis,* about the early career of Elvis Presley; *For the Love of a Child,* a true-life drama about the two women who founded Childhelp USA and rescued more than five million children. Viewers are expected to know they are watching impersonations, not file footage, and that these films are a blend of fact and fiction. They tend to rely on family melodrama and mature topics such as spouse abuse (*Burning Bed*); eating disorders (*The Karen Carpenter Story*); and other private topics and personal stories.

Soap Opera

The soap opera could be considered a subgenre of the drama, but it has become so prevalent and popular that it is considered a genre unto itself. As a genre, soap operas are best known for daytime dramas such as *All My Children*; however, nighttime serials such as *The O.C.* have soap opera qualities. Daytime soap operas are daily, 30- to 60-minute, continuous serials without end, running year-round for many years. Because they are performed daily, the actors have little rehearsal time. They are performed in broadcasting studios, taped, edited, and aired two weeks later. The settings are urban or suburban, but nearly all the action takes place indoors. Open narratives with unresolved stories keep the viewers coming back. Agnes Nixon, creator of *All My Children,* said her philosophy for viewers was "Make them laugh, make them cry, make them wait" (Stark, 1997, p. 204). Many fans record the soaps when they cannot watch them at scheduled times, but they also have access to the Disney Channel reruns of ABC-owned soaps and, since 2000, the SOAPnet channel repeats those in syndication.

> "Soap operas," Robert C. Allen explains, "implicitly assume they will never end, and they very seldom produce narrative closure within a given episode. Every plot line continues across a number of episodes . . . Soap operas disperse their narrative energy among a constantly changing set of interrelated plots, which may merge, overlap, diverge, fragment, close off, and open up again over a viewing period of several years. Individual episodes advance the plot incrementally, but no one watches a soap opera with the expectation that one day all of the conflicts and narrative entanglements will be resolved so that the entire population of the soap opera universe can fade into happily-ever-after oblivion." (Allen, 1992, pp. 107–108)

Soap opera casts are very large and may include as many as 40 regular cast members who have an array of melodramatic problems. The young adults have ideal bodies and faces and wear the latest fashions. Steven Stark summarized some conventions of the soaps:

> Women who want to get pregnant never can, but those who don't want to usually end up with a child, even after a presumedly safe one-night dalliance. Amnesia is almost as frequent as the common cold. No one accused of murder is ever the guilty party. The parents of characters often are not the "real" parents . . . People get killed in accidents, only to have long-lost twins somehow mysteriously show up months later, when an actor or actress playing the character returns to the soap from another engagement . . . Characters seldom talk on the telephone, preferring instead to drop in on people, even if they have to drive a long distance. (Stark, 1997, pp. 205–205)

The soaps are known for taking on major social and personal issues, for example, mental illness, spouse abuse, interracial romance, date rape, homosexuality, and infertility. In an attempt to attract younger viewers, according to Seiter and Wilson, soap opera narratives also have supernatural story lines such as demonic possession and witches and angels wreaking havoc on towns-people (Seiter & Wilson, 2005). Soap operas are popular among high school and college students as well as older adults How popular they are was made clear when I supervised a graduate project on soap operas and asked under-graduate students in my large film and television class to be subjects in three categories: nonwatchers, moderate watchers, and heavy watchers. In a class of 100, only one student was a nonwatcher of soap operas.

Science Fiction

Science fiction as a genre is easily recognizable because the action usually takes place in the future and often in space, although this is not always the case. When science fiction is set in the future, the societies tend to be utopian, that is, progressive and positive, or dystopian, that is, apocalyptic and pessimistic. Plots tend to be about saving humanity from aliens, although sometimes the aliens are peaceful. Both aliens and humans utilize fantastic technology. The best-known science fiction television program was *Star Trek,* in which an ensemble of mixed ethnic and racial characters explored outer space but also dealt with contemporary problems of the present day, for example, racism, nuclear warfare, overpopulation, multiculturalism, and ecology. *Star Trek* spawned four prime-time series. Conventions of the science fiction genre are often mixed with other genres, such as comedy in *Third Rock from the Sun* and crime in *The X-Files.*

Reality Shows

The proliferation of reality shows in recent years may cause people to think that they are a new phenomenon; however, the reality show can be traced back to 1973. (A case could be made for *Candid Camera,* which began in 1948, as the first television reality show. The show's surprise contrivances were set up without the contestants' knowledge until the end when they were told, "Smile, you're on *Candid Camera.*") The first modern reality show was the PBS series, *An American Family,* a documentation of the daily life of the Loud family that included the parents' divorce and the son's coming out as a gay man. Seven months of filming resulted in 12 weekly one-hour install-ments. *An American Family,* however, did not immediately bring about other reality shows. *Cops,* a half hour of edited footage taken by camera and sound professionals who ride along in a squad car as the police answer calls, began in 1989 and is still running on Saturday nights on Fox with reruns on Court TV and Fox's Reality channel. Each week the veteran reality show gives its audience "a dose of unscripted chaos" from various cities and towns around the nation with "cops breaking up domestic squabbles, cops hassling drunks, cops busting down doors, cops bagging bad guys" (Farhi, 1998, p. 21). Nothing is rehearsed, for the people in the police squad car do not know where they are going until they get the call from police headquarters. *Cops,* like many reality shows that followed it, is cheap to produce because there are no actors or sets.

The new trend in hour-long reality shows began in 2000 with *Survivor,* a blend of soap opera elements, quiz show, and adventure program, which spawned many imitators such as *Fear Factor. Survivor* has a very large production crew—more than 20 camera people and 13 editors. Three hundred hours may be taped to be edited for a single 42-minute episode (Simon, 2005). Romance and rejection are featured on *The Bachelor* and *The Bachelorette* while the world of business is the theme of *The Apprentice.* Makeovers are popular themes in *The Biggest Loser* (obese people try to lose weight); *Extreme Makeover* (contestants undergo plastic surgery); and *Extreme Makeover: Home Edition* (homes are refurbished). The top-rated *American Idol* has inspired many copycat shows that stress talent competition and harsh comments from the judges. There may be as many as 50 reality shows running on various channels on television. In most cases, the production process manipulates and contrives the action on these shows, and they are partly scripted for the non-actors who compete with one another for expensive prizes. Contestants on some shows vote to eliminate fellow players, and they can be quite cruel to one another. Reality shows encourage audience voyeurism as viewers watch people undergoing difficult tasks, competing with one another, and being humiliated, rejected, or victorious. Audiences like to watch reality shows because, as Ron Simon explained, they refer "back to the commonplace world we experience and live in every day and especially how real people interact in undirected situations" (Simon, 2005, p. 180). Viewers also are likely to feel superior to the contestants and judge them as uncouth and disgusting. The popularity of reality shows may reflect the urge for a sense of contact with what is real rather than what is fiction.

Sports

Television is a very popular medium for watching sports. One can watch practically any sport on one of the cable sports channels or subscribe to specialized events such as baseball games and boxing matches. Networks preempt regular programs to broadcast basketball tournaments, college and professional football, horse racing, and specialized sports like the Olympics. While one game is being broadcast, regional "splits" show another game that is being played simultaneously, or inserts keep viewers informed of the progress of other games. Viewers can watch live games, interrupted by commercials, through to the finish while listening to sportscasters describe the plays and comment on the players. Television has changed sports because instant replays cause time-outs. In professional baseball, pitchers' mounds were lowered in 1969 to make it harder for pitchers to strike out batters, thus making the sport more visually appealing (Bellamy & Walker, 1996). Sportscasters such as Bob Costas and Billy Packer have become celebrities who bring life to the games.

Children's Television

Children's television is the only genre to use age as its defining characteristic. It may be aimed at toddlers, young children, preteens, or teenagers. It incorporates other genres—comedy, drama, game shows, talk shows, cartoons, and news. PBS's *Teletubbies* is for very young children, while *Sesame Street* with its well-known characters like Big Bird, Kermit, and other Muppets (meant to be the emotional voices of children) is for preschool and kindergarten children. PBS has a large variety of daily animated programs, for example, *Arthur* and *Clifford the Big Red Dog* with stories about sharing, acceptance of others, and friendship. The Disney and Nickelodeon channels are aimed at younger children, while MTV and the Cartoon Network attract teens. Norma Pecora pointed out that commercial stations have catered to 6- to 11-year-olds because they could pressure their parents to buy things, whereas preschoolers had no consumer value. With the introduction of cable channels, teens became more important to the market, thus teen dramas such as *Felicity, Dawson's Creek,* and *Buffy, the Vampire Slayer* provided outlets for stories about identity, sexuality, and relationships (Pecora, 2005). The January 24, 2006 merger of WB and UPN into a new channel, CW, was done to attract young viewers and advertisers.

The Children's Television Act of 1990 requires all television broadcast stations to program for the educational and entertainment needs of the young audience. The Three-Hour Rule was added in 1995, requiring broadcasters to program an average of three hours of age-specific educational programming each week (Pecora, 2005).

Game Shows

Game shows either ask competing contestants questions or get them to do something to win very large amounts of money (*Who Wants to Be a*

Millionaire, Jeopardy!) or prizes such as cars, furniture, and vacations. They feature a host, usually male, an attractive woman assistant, and preselected contestants on a studio stage filled with a spectacle of flashing lights, bright colors, and carnival-like sound effects. These shows are taped live in front of an audience and are on the air daily or weekly. Some of the game shows have been on the air for many years—*Jeopardy!* since 1964 and *The Price is Right* since 1973. Prior to 1967, all game shows were on prime time, but they were moved to daytime and prime-time access, the alleyway to prime time at 7:30 p.m. The viewing audience can match wits with the contestants with its own answers. The answers must be given within seconds, so there is no time for reflection. Competition, winning, and materialism are the values featured in these shows. Like so many other genres, game shows have their own network, GSN, The Game Show Network.

Other Genres

There are many other genres, but their characteristics are self-evident, for they focus on a single theme: movie channels, History Channel, Discovery, Animal Planet, award shows for film and television, religious broadcasting, shopping networks, food networks, country music, and so on. The Weather

Photo 5.3   *Jeopardy!* host Alex Trebek gives a question to the contestants.

Channel drew record numbers of viewers in 2005 as devastating hurricanes hit the southern part of the United States. There is a cafeteria of genres on today's television, something for everyone, that supports the importance of television in our lives.

As a television critic, you will examine the characteristics of the genres in light of society and culture. The television medium stresses immediacy, thus context and culture are extremely important. Jason Mittell pointed out, "Genres operate in an ongoing historical process of category formation—genres are constantly in flux, and thus their analysis must by historically situated" (Mittell, 2004, p. xiv). Mittell emphasized that genres do not come from the television texts but rather from the television industry, its audience, and historical context. He asks us to look at a genre's operative coherence. "Does a given category circulate within the cultural spheres of audiences, press accounts, and industrial discourses? Is there a general consensus over what the category refers to in a given moment? Do so-called 'subgenres' play a useful and widespread role in classifying, interpreting or evaluating programs?" (Mittell, 2004, p. 11). Mittell suggests that we examine circulating generic practices and the ways they are culturally operative. In other words, what do they mean to a specific audience and why do people enjoy and regularly watch genres? How do they derive pleasure from genres? Horace Newcomb, in a similar approach, asks, "What is the relation of television's stories and storytelling strategies to American society and culture?" (Newcomb, 2005, p. 25). This question, according to Newcomb, together with asking "How does television tell its stories?" is central to the study of television. He supports the idea of examining industrial practices and ideological formation contained within genres. Social issues are treated in genres, but you, as a television critic, need to be aware of how the same social issue is shaped differently in different genres.

Summary

Genre is an acknowledged form of television industry categorization that is recognized by viewers who develop certain expectations about what they watch and enjoy. Successful genres on television are those that bring in profits for their producers. Genres and subgenres, of which there are many, have formulaic conventions that render them identifiable. As society changes, so do the genres and their conventions. Television blends and bends genres, but the viewing audience continues to recognize the various characteristics within them. The television industry organizes production of shows according to genre and schedules them accordingly. Knowledge of genres enables a television critic to understand how a television story is told, organized, and resolved. Such knowledge also enhances the television critic's awareness of the relationship of television storytelling to society and culture.

Exercises

1. What are the conventions of genre? Select a favorite television show, identify its genre, and describe the conventions.

2. How are genres used in the television scheduling process?

3. Select any genre and list your expectations of it before you watch it.

4. Why is it important for the television critic to know about genre?

5. Why is a situation comedy generally cheaper to make than some other types of programs?

6. What are the genre characteristics of plot in a situation comedy?

7. Why do intertextual references on *The Simpsons* enhance viewer enjoyment?

8. Why are talk shows called "he" or "she" shows?

9. Watch the national and international evening news to see how much of it is news and how much is infotainment. List the news stories and list the infotainment stories. Now watch PBS's *The NewsHour with Jim Lehrer* for one of the stories you watched on the national and international news. Compare and contrast the coverage.

10. Select a crime series (police, detective, forensic science, FBI) and record your thinking as you watch it. Do you participate in examining the evidence and selecting a suspect? What led you to your selection? Did you pick the same one that the characters on the show did?

11. Select a workplace drama (hospital, law firm, the White House). Describe how the story is more about character and dialogue than workplace.

12. What is a hybrid drama? Give example and identify the genres in it.

13. Watch a daytime soap opera and count the number of characters and plot lines in a single episode.

14. Select a reality show. What elements of the commonplace world do you observe? How does it reflect our cultural norms? Why do you think it is popular with viewers?

15. Watch a sporting event on television with and without a sportscaster's comments. Describe the differences in your experience of watching the game.

16. Select a children's television program and estimate the age of the children at whom it is aimed.

17. Select a science fiction show and describe its characteristics. Does the story take place in the future? In space? Is it utopian or apocalyptic?

18. Watch a game show and try to give answers to the questions. How do you compare with the contestants? Why do you think the contestants know so much about what seems to be trivial information?

Suggested Readings

Creeber, Glen (Ed.). (2001). *The Television Genre Book*. Berkeley, CA: University of California Press.

Edgerton, Gary R. & Rose, Brian G. (2005). *Thinking Outside the Box: A Contemporary Genre Reader*. Lexington, KY: University Press of Kentucky.

Kaminsky, Stuart M. (1985). *American Television Genres*. Chicago: Nelson-Hall.

Mittell, Jason. (2004). *Genre and Television: From Cop Shows to Cartoons in American Culture*. New York: Routledge.

Rose, Brian G. (Ed.). (1985). *TV Genres: A Handbook and Reference Guide*. Westport, CT: Greenwood Press.

PART III

Theoretical Approaches to Television Criticism

6

Rhetoric and Culture

We make our meaning together with a text, we wrestle with what we see and talk back to it, and we become more fully ourselves in the process.

—Edward Hirsch (1999, p. 260)

Introduction

Rhetorical criticism and cultural criticism are different intellectual practices with very different pasts. Rhetoric had its beginnings in classical Greece 2,500 years ago, whereas cultural studies had its current roots in Great Britain in the 1970s. Rhetoric locates and analyzes what are the available means of persuasion and information and how they work; cultural analysis examines the strands of meanings that can be made from discourse and how they relate to social practices. Rhetoric examines the intention of symbolization; cultural criticism examines the struggle and conflict over meaning. Neither rhetoric nor cultural studies is monolithic, however. Both practices have a repertoire of methodologies, some more explicit than others. Each practice can be useful to you as a television critic, or combinations of the methodologies may yield answers to questions one asks about television.

There are areas of overlap, as exemplified in Thomas Rosteck's book *At the Intersection: Cultural Studies and Rhetorical Studies*. Both rhetoric and cultural studies "address specific and parallel questions about culture, critical practice, and interpretation" (Rosteck, 1999, p. viii). Rosteck cited Cary Nelson and Dilip Gaonkar, whose review of some early cultural studies concluded that "cultural studies has been deeply, if broadly, textual and rhetorical in its methodology" (Rosteck, 1999, p. 9). Both perspectives recognize that meanings are related to particular contexts. Rosteck wrote:

> Rhetorical studies offers a mode of analysis for thinking about how texts are produced (intent), what they are (textuality), and what they do (consumption/ effects.) A more properly "rhetorical cultural studies" recognizes that the perspectives of rhetoric define an approach that holds in suspension text and producer, text and reader, text and society . . . Cultural studies . . . delivers to rhetorical studies a richer and more fully realized model of how discourse is always a product of wider social formations and reflects necessarily the materialization of the ideology that gave birth to it. It offers a more sophisticated sense of the text-history-audience-critic relationship and also the crucial relationship between texts and critical methodologies, namely how history and ideology shape readings and critical work . . . The ideal relationship between rhetorical studies and cultural studies is one of mutual critique and transformation. (Rosteck, 1999, p. 22)

This chapter describes salient aspects of rhetorical criticism and cultural criticism. As a critic of television, you can pick and choose various aspects from one or the other or from a blend of both. What is most important is what you ask about a television program or series. The tools to find the answers to those questions may then be sought out.

Rhetoric

Rhetoric is a twofold field of study: rhetorical criticism and rhetorical theory. Since this is a book about criticism, rhetorical criticism will be the main focus, although it is apparent that rhetorical criticism is grounded in theories.

Rhetoric is the study of symbols and how they are used to influence. Rhetorical criticism focuses on the conception, composition, presentation, and reception of messages that tend to be persuasive in nature, although they may also be informative. It is also a humane field of study of the choices made by persuaders, informers, and audiences as they work to co-create meaning and sustain human sociality. It is, thus, a cooperative art that brings senders and receivers of messages together in an attempt to bring about voluntary change or enlightenment. Classically conceived, rhetoric is concerned with systematic principles of idea development and reasoning, known as invention, organization, style, presentation, and ways to recall information, known as memory, all of which are phenomena that a critic can uncover and observe. It is believed that the success and significance of the messages are related to the methods used to develop and present them. A rhetorical critic identifies and explains how the methods of message development work to persuade or inform an audience.

Law & Order, a television series created by Dick Wolf that has been on the air since 1989, is about the police finding and arresting a criminal in the first half hour of the show, and lawyers prosecuting that criminal in the courtroom in the second half hour. When Assistant District Attorneys Alexandria Borgia (Annie Parisse) and Jack McCoy (Sam Waterston) make a persuasive speech to a jury, it is natural and appropriate to rhetorically analyze and criticize the arguments, evidence, and emotional pleas contained within the speech. When Cliff Huxtable (Bill Cosby) taught a moral lesson to one of his children on *The Cosby Show,* the persuasion in his words and deeds was readily apparent to most viewers. These persuasive messages of television programs can be rhetorically analyzed, for they are, in essence, discourse, that is, spoken or reported talk that sets forth ideas about a subject.

What, then, of television programs such as *CSI* or *The New Adventures of Old Christine* that have entertainment as the major focus for both their creators and their audience? Is it possible to use the concepts of rhetoric to analyze and criticize television programs when persuasion may not be so apparent? What about the background sounds (sound effects and music) and the images of television? Can they be analyzed according to principles of rhetoric as well? This chapter attempts to answer these questions, define television rhetoric, and introduce some aspects of rhetoric that can be used to analyze television.

First, it is necessary to understand what rhetoric is and how the rhetorical critic applies principles of rhetoric to a message. Rhetorical studies have been an important part of education since ancient Greece. Contemporary theories of rhetoric have been derived and adapted from the major treatises of classical writers such as Aristotle and Cicero. Throughout history, rhetorical theorists developed principles of rhetoric to try to understand the discourse of their own times—in assemblies, war councils, royal courts, elections, legal courts and councils, in the church, and in the marketplace. Mostly, they dealt with words because the messages were verbally conveyed, but many also dealt with the character of the speaker or treatise and presentational elements as well. Today, we communicate with images, sounds, and, of course, words, and we have adapted principles of rhetoric to understand the visual, aural, and verbal elements of messages.

Classical Rhetoric

Aristotle's definition of rhetoric has been an enduring one and, because of its extensive scope, has been used to justify rhetorical analysis of media. He defined rhetoric as "the faculty of discovering in the particular case what are the available means of persuasion" (Cooper, 1932, p. 7). Because the political and judicial systems placed prominence on oral persuasion in Aristotle's Greece, his theory of rhetoric was based upon observing persuasion in politics, in the courts, and in ceremonies. In *Rhetoric* (333 BCE), he laid out certain principles and classifications of persuasion in the context of occasions— courtroom proceedings, public ceremonies, and legislative and political activities. Aristotle viewed persuasion as an instrument of social adaptation, for it enabled people to live in society using strategically selected and stylized speech to influence one another. Rhetoric was very important in Greece, for people used it to debate internal problems as well as to decide which values were important in society. Through persuasive discourse, people attempted to reason together, to discuss ideas, and to make decisions regarding their lives. People such as Alexander the Great, who chose a career in public life, studied with teachers of rhetoric, including Aristotle, to learn how to choose message content (invention); how to arrange the content (arrangement); how to stylize the content into clear and impressive language (style); how to recall the content (memory); and how to present (delivery). These five categories were classified by Roman rhetoricians and are known as the canons of rhetoric: invention, arrangement, style, memory, and delivery.

Such a rhetorical system seems pragmatic and formulaic, but Aristotle's major contribution was invention, the development of ideas and the selection of content, namely proof. If one were to persuade, it was assumed that one had to prove an argument. Aristotle classified proof into two categories: *inartistic*, that which a persuader could refer to but not have to control— such as documents, wills, contracts, torture, situations, and even physical qualities—and *artistic*, that which a persuader could create or manipulate. Artistic proofs were of three major types: *ethos*, the speaker's character, integrity, and goodwill—known in contemporary terms as "source credibility"; *pathos*, the persuader's appeals to the emotions of the audience and the situation; and *logos*, the persuader's appeals to the rational side of the audience as well as their ability to process information.

Logos means "word" in Greek and probably comes closest to the contemporary meaning of communication as an interactive process during which the speaker and audience create and share intellectual meaning. Aristotle's two forms of *logos* were proof through examples and proof through enthymemes. Examples enabled the persuader to generalize and prove through citation of evidence that was meaningful to the audience, while enthymemes enabled the persuader and audience to co-create reasoning by interactively coming to a conclusion. The audience was an essential component of Aristotle's rhetoric, for the persuader not only appealed to an audience, but the audience completed the reasoning process by supplying missing elements.

Television advertising uses both forms of *logos,* especially enthymemes. A commercial for yogurt uses the song "Itsy-bitsy, teeny-weeny, yellow polka dot bikini" with an image of a yellow polka dot bikini hanging on the wall. A woman walks past the bikini while eating yogurt several times, wearing different outfits to suggest the passing of time. The commercial ends when she takes the bikini off the wall and gets into a convertible with a friend. The audience is expected to fill in the rest of the proof, namely that eating yogurt has enabled her to lose enough weight to fit into the bikini.

Aristotle's approach to rhetoric was pragmatic, but it also carried with it the cultural ideal of Greek society, that humanity should strive for excellence and to live life in a morally responsible way. The Greek work *telos,* meaning end or completion, stood for an optimal moral end. In ancient Greece, a person tried to achieve his or her *telos* by the end of life because by such an achievement, that person would experience moral excellence and contemplative happiness, and others would bestow virtue upon him or her. The Greeks considered rhetoric as the means that moved people toward a *telos* of moral excellence, for the end of rhetoric was the formation of public character in those with the potential for moral action.

Rhetoric Over the Ages

Many of Aristotle's principles and classifications were carried over and elaborated upon throughout history by a succession of rhetoricians such as St. Augustine (426) who developed the study of preaching for the clergy; Francis Bacon (1623) who incorporated scientific theory-building into the study of rhetoric; François Fenelon (1717) who stressed the social character of rhetoric and the use of communication to instruct and inform; and George Campbell (1776), a Scottish theologian who drew upon the works of early psychology to analyze audiences and developed four ends of speaking "to enlighten the understanding, to please the imagination, to move the passions, or to influence the will" (Golden & Corbett, 1968, p. 145).

These early forerunners of contemporary rhetoric offered rich and important ideas that may be adapted to the analysis and criticism of television. Although Aristotle limited his rhetoric to the discovery of the means of persuasion, later rhetoricians recognized information as a form of rhetoric. One way of describing the function of rhetoric without wedding it to persuasion or information was expressed by Donald C. Bryant, who wrote that the function of rhetoric is "adjusting ideas to people and people to ideas" (Bryant, 1953, p. 420).

Intentionality

Whether the desired purpose is persuasion or information, intentionality is often seen as the key focus of rhetoric, although not all rhetorical theorists agree. Aristotle laid the groundwork for the concept of intentionality with his teleological view of nature. Intentionality as activity is explicit in the work of contemporary philosopher John R. Searle (1979, 1984), who wrote that intentionality is "the feature by which our mental states are directed at, about, or refer to, or are of objects and states of affairs in the world other than themselves" (Searle, 1984, p. 16). Searle put it another way when he wrote quite simply, "If I have an intention, it must be an intention to do something" (Searle, 1984, p. 1). Rhetoricians note that intention carries with it the notion of consciousness because a person plans "for the purpose of obtaining some specifiable outcome" (Arnold & Bowers, 1984, pp. 875–876). In other words, intention is the purpose and end desired from an audience; however, it is not always possible to know the exact intention of a communicator. Thus, Arnold and Bowers modify the notion of intention to mean an *attributed* intention.

We assume that a scriptwriter for a situation comedy has the attributed intent to provoke laughter from an audience, or that a writer for a soap opera has the attributed intent to involve the viewer in a situation so he or she will tune in next time to find out what happens. In more obvious cases, we assume that a television commercial has the attributed intent to have the viewer remember the brand name, to have a positive attitude toward it, and to buy the product. There may be other more subtle attributed intentions in television fiction and nonfiction such as influencing attitudes and beliefs or reinforcing values and cultural norms. There may even be subconscious intentions that could be derived from a critic's interpretation.

The Symbolic Nature of Rhetoric

Rhetoric by its nature examines the symbolic, that is, symbols or words and images that stand for something else. As humans we generate symbols and expect others to know the meaning of the symbols. Symbols rely upon connections that are not necessarily causal. The word "cow" symbolizes a four-legged bovine mammal, but it is an arbitrary symbol that we have learned to mean a four-legged bovine mammal. The same animal is symbolized as *vache* in French and *Kuh* in German, neither of which resembles the English symbol "cow." The English language might have assigned a different symbol, for example, "ballerina," and that would have been the name that people learned to identify a four-legged bovine mammal.

Symbols stand for ideas and acts, that is, they stand in the place of ideas and acts, and, most significantly, symbols are created to signify something. The symbol © was created to signify "copyright," but one has to learn this meaning or it means nothing. Visual symbols such as a couple embracing or a father playing ball with his son may stand for a value such as love. It has been said that meanings lie in people, not in words, thus if a word or an image stimulates a recognition of something familiar in the audience's experience, then communication takes place. What symbols are attended to by an audience and how they are received is dependent upon a variety of factors—the perceptions, experiences, needs, and uses that an audience makes of television.

Television rhetoric works to shape audience expectations by conspicuously promoting programs and attempting to direct viewer perceptions through images and words. Although viewers choose what to treat as messages, television rhetoric actively attempts to shape those choices. It is, indeed, a circular situation, for television creators tap into cultural norms to attract an audience, and the audience in turn responds to them because they are agreeable, that is, some of the time. As we will see in the section on cultural studies, an audience can also choose to resist or negotiate meanings.

The Rhetoric of Kenneth Burke

A rhetorician who greatly influenced 20th-century rhetoric was Kenneth Burke. He defined rhetoric as "the use of words by human agents to form attitudes or induce actions in other human agents" (Burke, 1950, p. 41). He said that whatever form rhetoric takes, it is "the use of language as a symbolic means of inducing cooperation in beings that by nature respond to symbols" (Burke, 1950, p. 43). He contributed the idea of *identification* to rhetoric, that is, when people share a common substance or properties—citizenship, physical objects, occupations, friends, common enemies, activities, beliefs, and values—they unite by sharing a common substance, or in Burke's term, they become consubstantial, which means of the same substance. Burke added, however, that people share substance only momentarily because each person is unique. He wrote that identification was the key to persuasion: "You persuade a man only insofar as you can talk his language by speech, gesture, tonality, order, image, attitude, idea, *identifying* your ways with his" (Burke, 1950, p. 21). Identification can be on a conscious level. For example, Jennifer Aniston's hairstyle on *Friends* influenced a great many women to get their hair cut in the same style. On the other hand, Burke believed that identification can be subconscious or unconscious. For example, a person who buys a fancy bicycle may be subconsciously identifying with Lance Armstrong, seven-time winner of the Tour de France bicycle race, even though the bicycle was purchased to go back and forth to school.

Burke developed his concept of identification because he believed that people are basically divided or estranged from one another, therefore, they communicate in order to eliminate that division. Through identification with a common substance, people may transcend their differences and unite in a common attitude or behavior. As Robert Heath explained,

> By sharing common symbols—particularly those which relate to personal identity and role—individuals can be brought together. The key to using this strategy is to discover abstract terms high in the hierarchy of our vocabulary. The formula went this way: the higher, and therefore more abstract, the term [or symbol], the greater its appeal because it could encompass the identities of more people. (Heath, 1986, p. 17)

The Cosby Show, with its all–African American cast, was not only enormously popular in the United States but also in South Africa during *apartheid.* Perhaps the reason for its popularity in a country divided by racism was that the higher symbol that the show emphasized was family and not race. Dennis Ciesielski pointed out that Burke anticipated "the postmodern concept of the transcendent signifier in his observation that all action is symbolic of other action, all signs hold further implications" (Ciesielski, 1999, p. 244).

Although Burke stressed language, he included in rhetoric many other forms of discourse, including nonverbal activity, literature, and art. Art, he said, instructs people about their moral and social responsibilities. In a seminar that Burke taught when I was in graduate school, he told us that his definition of rhetoric included television. Identification between a viewer and a television program is usually a matter of preference for a certain character or the recognition of a situation in the program as being similar to the viewer's, but identification has the capability to influence the viewer to become involved to the point where he or she may adopt certain ways of speaking, clothing styles, mannerisms, or even attitudes and behaviors.

Burke described communication as a form of courtship whereby its form is an arousing and fulfillment of desires. He wrote, "A work has form insofar as one part of it leads a reader [viewer] to anticipate another part, to be gratified by the sequence" (Burke, 1931/1957, p. 124). This is exactly what television does, as stated in the desire/satisfaction formula in Chapter 1:

television executives and producers try to know what it is that the audience desires and then satisfy that desire in order to maintain an audience following. Burke's rhetoric is too complex to include its details in a single chapter. He offers a myriad of ways to examine rhetoric, many of which are suitable and useful for television criticism. There are several good books on Burke's theories of rhetoric and studies that use his various approaches to criticism such as the Dramatistic Pentad, cluster analysis, terministic screens, the representative anecdote, and the demonic trinity. The titles of these and other books on rhetorical criticism can be found at the end of this chapter.

There are other methods of rhetorical criticism that may be adapted to television. For example, rhetorical criticism can be used to critique belief systems that form interpretations of race, ethnicity, class, gender, religion, and sexual identity. Because these can also be analyzed with cultural studies approaches, they will be discussed later in the chapter. Because television is representational, these aspects are also discussed in Chapter 7, "Representation and Its Audience."

Television Rhetoric

Television informs, persuades, and represents the real and fictional worlds to its audience. Television utilizes conventional organization both in its scheduling and within the structure of programs. Both fiction and nonfiction television have the capability to elicit identification from viewers. Television relies on viewer memory to keep up with the plots and characters from day to day on soap operas and from week to week on prime-time series. Television has specific stylistic features that use both visual and aural symbols. The most rhetorical aspect of television is that viewers participate while they watch it and afterwards. They perceive, interpret, and accept or reject images as real or imaginary; they respond with laughter, shock, concern, relaxation, and reassurance; they talk about favorite shows with friends, fellow students, and coworkers. When my oldest son was a teenager, he and my mother would discuss at length the episodes of *All My Children.* Nancy Franklin, writing in *The New Yorker,* said that the people she knows talk about *24,* the series about counterterrorism agent Jack Bauer (Kiefer Sutherland), in which events unfold in real time over the course of one day. Franklin said that one woman calls her friend at the end of each show to discuss it; couples make dates to watch and discuss it together (Franklin, 2006). Television influences our language and what issues we consider important (the agenda-setting function of media). Agenda-setting is about the gatekeeping function of media news, whereby journalists tell viewers what issues are important. Research has shown that the news media have not told people what to think, but they have told them what to think about. Television also influences our perception of politicians and celebrities, fashion, hairstyles, fitness, and even what breed of dog to acquire. The outcome of the televised Westminster Kennel Club's annual dog show and the selection of "best in show" often results in an increase of popularity in certain breeds of dogs.

> Some examples of popular language expressions that were used on television programs are the following: "Awright, I'll tell ya what I'm gonna do!" (*Texaco Star Theater*), "Beam me up, Scotty." (*Star Trek*), "meathead and dingbat" (*All in the Family*), "The devil made me do it." (*The Flip Wilson Show*), "Yada Yada" (*Seinfeld*), "Wild and crazy guys" (*Saturday Night Live*), and ""Don't have a cow, man" and "D'oh!" (*The Simpsons*), "How you doin'?" (*Friends*), "Hey, Dummy!" (*My Name is Earl*), and advertising slogans: "Kodak moment," "Pepsi generation," "Where's the beef?" and "I can't believe I ate the whole thing."

While the sender's intent may be to entertain, there is always the possibility of influence whether it is direct or indirect. The intention of the sender is to capture a large share of the audience as measured by ratings, or it may be to get an audience to believe that what they see is really there as in news reporting or documentaries. Television commentators may influence our thinking by interpreting television speeches and events. Other examples of persuasion may be television's attempt to educate the public about a health hazard, to uphold law and order, to strengthen attitudes about diversity, to cherish family values, to foster competition, and so on. Verbal, visual, and aural symbols are chosen, arranged, and delivered to the audience. Which message symbols are attended to by an audience and how they are received is dependent upon a variety of factors—the perceptions, experiences, needs, and uses that an audience makes of television. Just as the senders may choose to treat television programming as messages, audiences also choose to treat television as a message.

Television rhetoric attempts to shape viewer expectations by conspicuously promoting programs and attempting to direct viewer perceptions. Media television critics tell viewers what they will and will not like on television. Internet blogs, sometimes written by television writers, tell viewers what to anticipate. What an audience attends to on television is, however, determined by many factors and individual preferences.

Rhetoric and Values

Television embodies the values of a culture, the values of the people who produce television programs, and the values of the people who watch them. Values are important to understanding the rhetoric of television because they are a crucial part of our belief systems. The accepted and affirmed cultural values of the mass audience are echoed in television situation comedies and dramas' resolutions of conflict as well as in the news and other nonfiction programming. A value is defined as an enduring belief that a specific mode of conduct or end-state of existence is personally or socially preferable. Specifically, a value is a prescriptive belief that judges whether or not a means or an end is desirable or undesirable. Conventional values are familiar standards of conduct as the rhetorician Karl Wallace pointed out in his essay "The Substance of Rhetoric: Good Reasons": "Some of them [the values] are compressed in concepts with which all of us are familiar: good and evil, pleasant-unpleasant, duty, obligation, self-interest, altruism, truth-telling, promise-keeping, honesty, fairness, courage, law-observance, utility, right and wrong, and the like. They appear typically in general statements called rules of conduct, regulations, laws, codes, principles, and moral maxims" (Wallace, 1971, p. 363). Values may, of course, be very personal and private, but they are public as well, for they are shared with and taught to others. Because values are important, they operate as measuring sticks against which behavior is measured and goals are obtained.

Television's fictional characters and their stories reinforce audience values, teach values to the audience, and use values as reasons for supporting resolutions of conflict. Television narratives frequently reflect values such as the work ethic, fair play, optimism, sensibility, justice, happiness, and good humor. Television stars such as Oprah Winfrey, Ray Romano, Mariska Hargitay, Ice-T, Edward James Olmos, Sam Waterston, Katie Couric, and Charles Gibson represent honesty, strength, goodness, fair-mindedness, and the vulnerability of the ideal American culture. News anchors like Walter Cronkite, Tom Brokaw, and Peter Jennings represented integrity and compassion. The creators of television programs are more likely to produce programs that reinforce values that relate to the nation's strengths and virtues. Television programs such as *Sesame Street* tend to be morality shapers, touching on themes of love, honesty, tolerance, and altruism. Family situation comedies tend to conclude each program with a mini-moral that reinforces family togetherness and parental authority. Values are inherent in reality shows that emphasize competition, victory, and rewards.

Every episode of *Frasier* illustrated strong values with which the audience could identify. The values were close family relationships, friendship, decency, compassion, and kindness. For example, in one episode, Frasier, pretentious as usual, wants to buy an educational toy for his son Frederick for Christmas, but he cannot decide whether to get a Junior Astronomer set or a Living Brain. Frasier's father Martin tells him that he should find out what Frederick really wants for Christmas. On Christmas morning, Frederick tells Frasier that he really wants an Outlaw Laser Robo-Geek. Martin has bought this toy to give to his grandson, but he gives it to Frasier to wrap and give to Frederick, thereby kindly teaching his son a lesson for living.

Values are also explicit in television news. Sociologist Herbert J. Gans analyzed values in network television news over 20 years. His findings were categorized into six types of values: (1) ethnocentrism—American news values its own nation above all, and foreign news is interpreted by the extent to which other nations live up to or imitate American values; (2) altruistic democracy—democracy is presented as superior to other forms of government; (3) responsible capitalism—competition is valued along with optimism and economic growth; (4) small-town pastoralism—small towns are perceived as friendly, cohesive, and slow-paced, all of which are desirable; (5) individualism—rugged individuals and self-made men and women are valued as heroes; (6) moderatism—groups that behave moderately are valued as opposed to extremists. Gans concluded that most news stories are about the violation of values, although the values themselves may not be explicitly articulated. He also noted that the values perceived by viewers tend to be the values that the viewers themselves believe in. He said that value-laden language reveals values: for example, a politician "arrives" in a city but a troublemaker "turns up" there. Rhetorical analysis of values attempts to uncover what Arnold and Bowers called "attributed intentions" because, as Gans wrote, the values underlying the news stories are implicit and subject to viewer recognition and interpretation (Gans, 1979, 2004).

Values are highly personal and enduring, therefore we defend them with great passion. This is what makes values effective as anchors for persuasion. A value is used as an anchor when audience belief is used as a foundation to create another belief. For example, if the audience believes in national security, then a related belief in support of luggage searches at airports can be derived from the first belief. As a consensus-building exercise in one of my classes, I asked the students to bring to class a list of values that were most important to them. The goal was to eventually compile a list of values that everyone in the class agreed upon in order to construct arguments such as "If you believe in good health, then you should stop smoking," or "If you value the environment, then you should recycle newspapers, plastic, and glass." The students put their values on the board for all to see. After we condensed duplicates—and there were many—I asked the students individually to walk up and erase any values that were not important to them. They erased "competition," "beauty," and "power," but much to my surprise, one person erased "equality." Then a student who is Hispanic-American walked to the board and erased everything. He said, "If you do not value equality, then I do not support *any* of your values." Needless to say, we had a strong class discussion that day, but the point of including this incident in this chapter is to remind us that not only are values extremely important to individuals, they are also not universally agreed upon.

Because television addresses a mass audience, the values that are inherent in its programs are collectively dominant in the culture. Values represent patterns of life in a culture, but marginalized people, whose life patterns differ from those of the mainstream, may or may not accept them. How, then, do they gain enjoyment from watching television? To answer that, we turn to cultural studies.

Cultural Studies

Because television is a major form of communication, a source of social understanding, and a connection to lifestyles other than our own, it is of major concern in cultural studies. Jeff Lewis (2002), whose book *Cultural Studies: The Basics* is a helpful guide to the subject, maintained that there are many forms of culture, for example, national culture, family culture, and television culture. Culture is defined as "actual practices and customs, languages, beliefs, forms of representation, and a system of formal and informal rules that tell people how to behave most of the time and enable people to make sense of their world through a certain amount of shared meanings and recognition of different meanings" (Jowett & O'Donnell, 2006, p. 193).

Meaning is a key concept in cultural studies, for meaning, as noted earlier, does not reside in a symbol, visual or verbal, but is in the relationship between a viewer of television and what is viewed. Meaning lies in the power of a symbol to signify something and in the viewer's potential to derive meaning from the symbol. In television, the viewer is the necessary other to be provoked into making meaning possible. The relationship between the viewer and the symbol is a complex one in which various elements interact and lead to an outcome that is dependent on culture and the cultural practices. Consequently, the possibility of multiple meanings, *polysemy*, exists because various view-ers incorporate their own experiences, lifestyles, values, and other cultural practices into their interpretations. The multiple meanings of various viewers cannot be reduced to a common mean or median, nor can derived meanings be fixed or stable across time.

For example, in an episode of *ER*, the television drama about a Chicago hospital emergency room, two African American surgeons, Dr. Peter Benton and Dr. Cleo Finch, are seen attending to a patient while nearby on the other side of the room, a group of five medical students, four men and one woman, are getting a tour of the emergency facilities. Dr. Finch, who is very light in color, says, "What is wrong with this picture?" Dr. Benton, who has much darker skin, is focusing on his patient and says, "Hmm?" Dr. Finch then says, "Those medical students—not a black face in the bunch." Getting no response from him, Dr. Finch says, "That doesn't concern you?" Dr. Benton looks up at the students and replies, "I see five. Not exactly a representative sample." She responds with, "I'm glad you take such an interest." He chuck-les and nothing else is said, but the look that is exchanged between these two doctors, who are also lovers, is probably meant to imply that Dr. Benton is not going to make an issue of racial diversity and that he can be quite patronizing when it comes to logic. This is consistent with how his charac-ter was portrayed on the series, for he was a brilliant, competent, and ambi-tious but arrogant surgeon.

A cultural studies critic would ask what meanings viewers could make of this brief scene. One viewer might agree with Dr. Finch that there should be better racial representation. Another might agree with Dr. Benton's logic, concluding that you cannot generalize from a small sample. Another might conclude that practicing good medicine is an African American doctor's only concern. Someone else might say that both positions are fairly represented and that is acceptable. There could be other meanings. For example, one could dispute the untypical representation of race in an elitist profession that requires years of study at great financial cost because such circumstances are unavailable to those without opportunity. Although Dr. Benton, profession-ally acted by Eriq La Salle, is an extremely competent surgeon, he is also very arrogant and moody, thus another viewer might say that he is "uppity" and erudite and no longer in touch with people of his race. Michael Michele, who played Dr. Finch, is tall, model-thin, and beautiful. Another viewer might see her as unrepresentative of women in general or African American women in particular and therefore be unable to identify with her or her atti-tude at all. For others, she could be a role model of what other women want to become. Someone else could observe that Dr. Finch did not say anything about the disproportionate ratio of men to women in the group of five medical students. Still another might note that because the chief of staff, Dr. Romano, and the chief attending emergency room doctor, Dr. Green, are white males, they represent white male dominance over the African American doctors.

These various meanings are some of the possible responses of several viewers upon seeing a brief scene on television; therefore the scene has the potential to be polysemous. Cultural studies critics understand that many meanings can be made from a single scene because viewers observe and interpret images and supporting dialogue through the lens of their own cultural experiences.

There are many ways to conduct a cultural studies critique, for there are many theoretical foundations ranging from writings by Karl Marx, Antonio Gramsci, Louis Althusser, Michel Foucault, Roland Barthes, Jacques Derrida, Raymond Williams, Stuart Hall, Lawrence Grossberg, and others. Also, as historical and political conditions change, cultural studies practitioners respond with relevant analyses. This chapter will not recount the history and various theories behind cultural studies, but rather this chapter offers a selection of some of the most influential ideas in contemporary cultural studies that can be constituted to develop critical approaches. (See Selected Readings in Cultural Studies at the end of this chapter.)

British Cultural Studies

Although cultural studies can be traced back to the 17th century, certain British academics were the first in the English-speaking world to address the making of meaning within culture. Thus, cultural studies, as we know it, grew out of the British Cultural Studies movement, primarily from the vision of Raymond Williams, a professor at Cambridge University, who said that there was no academic subject that enabled him to ask how culture and society and democracy and the individual voice could relate to one another. Williams believed that culture concerns everyone, for it is about the symbolic life of people. Williams was especially concerned with the customs of the working class. For example, in one of the programs that he made for the British Broadcasting Company, he talked about 18th-century paintings that depicted beautiful land and domestic animals. One painting had a very young girl, obviously of the upper class, dressed up in shepherd's clothes watching the sheep grazing on a meadow. Williams asked, "Where are the real shepherds?" His point was that the workers upon whom the running of the estate depended were invisible. Williams insisted on thinking about a painting or a novel or a television program from a much broader range of cultural practice. His writings encourage us to try to formulate meanings other than our own, ". . . in judging a culture, it is not enough to concentrate on habits which coincide with those of the observer" (Higgins, p. 59). He wrote: ". . . cultural texts should never be seen as isolated but always as part of a shared practice of making meaning involving everyone in a particular culture" (Couldry, 2000, p. 24). Williams asked how a work—any work—relates to the shared conditions of its time and what meanings a work has when it is absorbed into the lives of its audience. He believed that every person has the right to be seen and heard. This is the basic tenet of cultural studies.

Nick Couldry, whose book is a very helpful guide to cultural studies methodology as well as a critique of it, made the point that culture as it is actually practiced is a concentration of voices but not a dispersal of them. This prevents people from speaking in their own voices because they are represented by others (Couldry, 2000).

Williams also articulated his theory of "flow" on television as timed, sequential units that form a montage with confusing, overall meaning. For example, parts of television programs are melded to commercials, promotions, and public service announcements that flow into the news, and a talk show and then to a movie. These disparate items are assembled and placed within the same viewing experience.

Stuart Hall, professor emeritus at the Open University and a visiting professor at Goldsmiths College, University of London, is probably the most influential and prominent British cultural studies scholar. Whereas Williams was concerned with the laboring classes, Hall has used many examples of race and immigration in the United Kingdom in his writings and videos. (See Hall entries in the Bibliography.) Hall's contributions are many, but his model of the encoding and decoding of meaning is the most famous.

Power, Ideology, and Hegemony

First, however, it is necessary to explain Hall's view of power, a premise with which all cultural studies critics agree. Hall said that symbols are always associated with power relations, driven by economics, politics, or social discrimination, which determine who is represented and who is not, whose voice is heard and whose is not, what issues are important and what issues are not. Lewis defined power as that which is "considered to be something which enables one person or group to exert their [sic] will and interest over others"(Lewis, 2002, p. 25). Lewis wrote that cultural studies theory views power as attached to social structures such as class, ethnicity, and gender, or power is concerned with personal manifestations and experiences. He also maintained that power can be mobilized when a viewer chooses to watch a program or not and may also be activated when a person discusses a program with friends or partners.

Power is derived from the dominant ideology of a culture. *Ideology* is defined as:

> A set of beliefs, values, attitudes, and behaviors, as well as ways of perceiving and thinking that are agreed on to the point that they constitute a set of norms for a society that dictate what is desirable and what should be done . . . Ideology contains concepts about what the society in which it exists is actually like. It states or denies, for example, that there are classes and that certain conditions are desirable or more desirable than others. An ideology is also a form of consent to a particular kind of social order and conformity to the rules within a specific set of social, economic, and political structures. It often assigns roles of dominance or subordination to gender, race, sexuality, religion, age, and social groups. (Jowett & O'Donnell, 2006, p. 281)

Related to power is hegemony, defined as a way of life and thought that is dominant in society to the point that it seems natural. Williams wrote that hegemony "is lived at such a depth, which saturates the society to such an extent, and which . . . even constitutes the substance and limits of common sense for most people under its sway" (in Higgins, p. 113). Hegemony gives closure to meaning, for the meaning is intended to be a dominant one. Hegemony can give power or dominance to one group over another. People in the dominated group consent to be dominated, but the consent is negotiated with ongoing renegotiation and redefinition. The consensus may be broken when the ideologies of the subordinate groups cannot be accommodated.

For the producers of television, consumer satisfaction is important, thus focus groups are used in market research to determine what programs are likely to be successful based on ratings and thus economics. Victoria J. Gallagher wrote that hegemony occurs when "dominant groups control the flow of a cultural projection" (Gallagher, 2004, p. 152). Ideologies in place are presented on television as natural, especially since most creators of television come from a similar economic, social, and educational background. Yet, ideologies are subject to change as shown in television's growing openness to racial, ethnic, and sexual diversity. Hegemony is a fluid concept compared to coercion and control. Subordinate groups struggle for recognition and to have their voices heard. Some groups have a greater opportunity to do so than other groups. How groups are represented on television is constantly being redefined and understood. Explaining counterhegemony, Gallagher said that it occurs when "subordinates and their allies convert dominants to subordinate versions of the world. The result of counterhegemony is that many dominants gradually become more accepting of subordinates" (Gallagher, 2004, p. 153). Meanings perceived by viewers of a television program cannot always be predicted. Some may see a program as a reflection of the status quo, while others may perceive it as mockery and satire. Hall recognized that audience members are not passive but rather active consumers who decode symbols and representations and make their own meanings. Hall, in his encoding/decoding model, explains how viewers construct meanings.

Hall's Encoding/Decoding Model

Fundamental to Hall's work is the encoding process or message formulation in television, together with the social and economic conditions that explain why and how viewers decode or find meaning in a variety of ways. Hall's model of encoding/decoding is based on the premise that there is a correlation between a person's social situation and the meanings that person decodes from an encoded symbol (an image/discourse). In other words, there is no single meaning in the image/ discourse. If the meaning that the viewer decodes is the same as or similar to the meaning that the television image/ discourse encodes, then there would be perfect hegemony. However, if the image/discourse is representative of the dominant ideology and the viewer's social situation is not, then there is tension resulting in a negotiation between the viewer and image/discourse. In other words, the viewer does not necessarily passively accept the dominant meaning unless it is preferred by the viewer. By preferring a certain meaning, the viewer exercises power in interpreting the image/discourse.

For example, the female forensic scientists on *CSI* and *CSI: New York* are very slender and beautiful, have perfect hairstyles, and wear tight slacks and low-cut camisoles to work. There are a few African American and Hispanic women who work in the laboratories, but all the main female characters are white. *CSI: Miami* features an African American woman (Khandi Alexander) who portrays the coroner, Dr. Alexx Woods. In previous seasons, this show also featured actress Sofia Milos, who played Hispanic Detective Yelina Salas. *CSI: Miami* has had more diversity in its characters, but both these women are thin and gorgeous as well. If the viewer resists these images because their appearances are unrealistic and not very pragmatic in a work situation or because of the lack of diversity, then the viewer experiences a certain power in complaining about them. On the other hand, if the viewer believes these glamorous images are desirable, the viewer expresses a preference for them and the ideology that reinforces the image of idealized female bodies.

Hall believed that the image/discourse "hails" a person as if it were hailing a taxi. In other words, it calls to the person. To answer the call, the person must recognize that it is she or he, not someone else, who is being hailed. By responding to the call or "hail," a viewer recognizes the social position that has been constructed in encoding the image/discourse, and if the viewer's response is cooperative, the intended meaning is adopted, and the viewer has constituted herself or himself as a *subject*. A subject is a social construction wherein the viewer recognizes that she or he is being addressed or summoned by the hail and decodes the image/discourse accordingly. Thus, television viewers may be hailed as conformists or sexists or patriots or concerned citizens.

Hall named three social positions—dominant, oppositional, and negotiated—although he speculated that there could be multiple positions. The dominant position is decoded by the viewer who accepts the dominant or intended meaning. On the other hand, the oppositional position is in direct opposition to the dominant meaning, and an opposite point of view is decoded. The negotiated position is a completely open category for viewers who primarily fit into the dominant ideology but need to resist certain elements of it. Negotiated positions are popular with various social groups who tend to question their relationship to the dominant ideology. Negotiated meanings are what most people get out of television images/discourses most of the time. *CSI,* for example, consistently gets high ratings, but even faithful viewers question some aspects of the show. Cultural studies critics can interpret possible decoding positions from their own experience or derive multiple meanings by analysis. Hall said that we decode by interpreting "from the family in which you were brought up, the places of work, the institutions you belong to, the other practices you do" (Cruz & Lewis, p. 270). Another cultural studies practice is to interview viewers, often over time, to determine how people actively make sense of television images and discourses, social experience, and themselves.

Hall said that we can discover and play with identifications of ourselves, perhaps discovering something of ourselves for the first time. What is important to Hall is openness to understanding that what a person thinks one week may change the next. External events like new social movements and cultural differences can change the cultural context and thus both encoding and decoding processes (Morley & Chen, 1996). John Fiske, a professor at the University of Wisconsin, has praised Hall for making us aware that "people are neither cultural dupes nor silenced victims, but are vital, resilient, varied, contradictory, and as a source of constant contestations of dominance, are a vital social resource, the only one that can fuel social change" (Fiske, 1996, p. 220). Fiske has elaborated on Hall's model by breaking down the elements of the encoding process, specifically in television production, in his book *Television Culture* (1987), thus giving the television critic another set of categories to examine.

The Codes of Television Production

The term "code" comes from the study of semiotics. A code is a system of signs that is able to communicate meanings. Codes may be simple, as in the case of a STOP sign, or complex as in the case of a language. There are verbal, nonverbal, and representational codes, all of which can operate separately or together to encode meaning. In television studies, code refers to a range of audiovisual systems that have the capability to construct meaning (Casey, Casey, Calvert, French, & Lewis, 2002, p. 27). Fiske regards television as the bearer, provoker, and circulator of meanings and pleasure; echoing Hall, he believes that television is replete with potential meanings. Because a preferred meaning is intended in television production, the conventional codes of culture link the programs and the audience. Fiske defined *code* as "a rule-governed system of signs, whose rules and conventions are shared amongst members of a culture, and which is used to generate and circulate meanings in and for that culture" (Fiske, 1987, p. 4). Fiske organized categories of codes into three levels: reality, representation, and ideology.

1. Reality

Reality is encoded by certain *social codes* that relate to appearance, behavior, speech, sound, and setting. Appearance includes skin color, clothing, hair, makeup, speech, facial expressions, and gestures. Speech includes spoken language, accent, dialect, formal or vernacular style, and paralanguage, such as pitch, rate, and inarticulate utterances. Sound includes natural sounds, such as wind or rain, and artificial sounds, such as sirens or music. Indoor settings may denote place, such as a living room or a hospital. Objects in the place may denote taste or social class, and could promote certain feelings such as comfort or tension. Outdoor settings may suggest peace and tranquility or fear and danger.

Much depends on other codes to encode certain preferred meanings. Some physical behaviors, such as dancing, kissing, shaking hands, playing sports, fighting, and so on, may be easily recognized as such. Others require more contextual information and supplemental codes to provoke meaning.

Clothing can reveal certain personality characteristics such as formality, casualness, and sexuality. Once again, much depends on the other codes as they are put together to form a whole. Obviously, more information is necessary before one can draw conclusions about social codes, and furthermore, different people will interpret these codes in different ways. Social codes, once chosen for a television program, are encoded by representation.

2. Representation

Representation on television is encoded by technical codes with the camera, lighting, sound, music, and editing in order to transmit conventional representational codes, to convey the narrative, conflict, character, action, dialogue, setting, casting, and so forth. The following technical codes, as indicated by Fiske, have been discussed in Chapter 3, "Television Style." They are vital to representation on television and are suggested here as types of technical codes that function to encode meaning.

Camera use (placement angle, distance, movement, framing, and focus) like other technical codes can be specified by the director in order to achieve desired effects. A close-up, for example, may be used to represent intimacy on one hand or to reveal anxiety by emphasizing a person's furrowed brow or tears. *Lighting* changes the way we look at people by the way it is placed, for example, to create shadows across a person's face or to provide a certain color for special effect. *Editing* is a powerful way to provide continuity when none exists or to transform time, interaction, and other elements and rhythms. For example, I once appeared on a public television forum about television violence and children with eight other panelists. The moderator spoke at the beginning and then not again for two hours during which the nine panelists discussed the topic while being videotaped. When we finished, the moderator was videotaped, speaking into the camera for about 10 minutes. The final program was edited to appear as if the moderator would ask a question and two or three of the panelists would respond to it. The moderator appeared to be chairing a panel discussion. The responses had been carefully edited to fit the moderator's questions.

Sound and *music* create mood, attitude, and other various emotions. Music is also thematic and can suggest a program and various characters. It is important to recognize the role that technical codes play in encoding meaning.

Representational codes have to work together to encode a preferred meaning and to appear natural at the same time. A script provides the setting, narrative, conflict, action, dialogue, and characters, but the actors who are cast in various roles bring the characters and the plot to life. Casting of characters is complex because actors are real people whom viewers may know in other contexts, for example from films, talk shows, magazines, and so on. Certain actors bring with them other intertextual meanings from their very public lives.

The social codes (in *Reality*) play a large part in conveying conventional representational codes. Appearance, speech, sound, facial expressions, and gestures in a contemporary setting have to be consistent with what viewers know in their own culture. Narratives set in other cultures or time periods also have to convey a sense of naturalness, but even in these instances social codes are usually adapted to the culture of the present. For example, on American television, a program set in France will most likely have the dialogue spoken in English. The most striking example of adaptation to the present was on *M*A*S*H*, which had a narrative based on the Korean War, but because the show was on from 1972 to 1983, it had more to do with the Vietnam War than the Korean War. Other cultural codes may be more deeply embedded in representation. Fiske refers to these in level 3 as *Ideology*.

3. Ideology

Representational codes are organized into coherence and social acceptability by ideological codes, such as individualism, patriarchy, class, materialism, capitalism, and so on. All the codes come together to encode a preferred meaning that supports a certain ideology. Fiske maintains that a partriarchal code is embedded in the dialogue when a woman asks questions and a man answers them, seemingly because the man is supposed to be more knowledgeable than the woman. More broadly, on crime series when the criminal is caught and imprisoned, the ideology of law and order is coded. On the news, the stock market report is a code for the ideology of capitalism. Gans wrote that the daily reports of the Dow Jones Index are an indicator of the primacy of business, but there is no daily report of fluctuations in the prices of basic foods, and no one reports news about wages and salaries of workers (Gans, 2003). There is no guarantee that a different cultural analyst will make the same meanings or even find ideology at all. Viewers who occupy different social positions may interpret the representation as something altogether different. The process of interpretation and finding meaning gives the viewer a certain kind of pleasure in decoding.

Decoding and Pleasure

Fiske said that a viewer not only decodes meanings but also derives pleasure from the process. Pleasure can be derived from opposing the preferred meaning or negotiating an individual meaning or accepting the preferred or dominant meaning. Experiencing pleasure in one of these ways frees the viewers from ideological dominance and gives them a sense of control over the production of meanings. Fiske wrote:

> Pleasure for the subordinate is produced by the assertion of one's social iden-tity in resistance to, in independence of, or in negotiation with, the structure of domination. There is . . . real pleasure to be found in, for example, soap operas that assert the legitimacy of feminine meanings and identities within and against patriarchy. Pleasure results from the production of meanings of the world and of self that are felt to serve the interests of the viewer rather than those of the dominant . . . Pleasure requires a sense of control over meanings and an active participation in the cultural process. (Fiske, 1987, p. 19)

A viewer may experience pleasure in the validation of his or her social identity from accepting the dominant meaning. There may also be a form of pleasure in negotiating meaning in a person's own terms. Pleasure can even be derived from resisting the dominant meaning; as Fiske wrote, "By main-taining one's social identity in opposition to that proposed by the dominant ideology, there is a power in asserting one's own subcultural values against the dominant ones" (Fiske, 1987, p. 19).

The concept of pleasure is another indicator that viewers make active choices regarding the meanings they decode. People make their own sense out of what they see, and the sense they make is related to a pattern of choices about their own social identities. This is one of the reasons for tele-vision's popularity, said Fiske, because it offers "such a variety of pleasures to such a heterogeneity of viewers" (Fiske, 1987, pp. 19–20). This enables the viewers to actively participate in culture, which has a social system that can be held in place only by the meanings that people make of it.

To paraphrase Fiske regarding the pleasure of watching television, view-ers play a text the way a musician plays a score, by interpreting it, activat-ing it, and giving it a living presence. A television critic can do the same, and that gives much pleasure, too.

Summary

Both rhetoric and culture are interdisciplinary subjects based on various and complex ideas. This chapter has introduced some of the well-known aspects of both. Each of these subjects is worthy of an entire book or several books, and it would be unworthy reductionism to combine them. Rhetoric and cul-tural studies both have methodological fluidity and can be used in different forms to criticize television discourse. Rhetoric examines the available means of persuasion and information and how they work; cultural studies analyzes the production and exchange of strands of meanings and how they relate to social practices. There are areas where rhetoric and cultural studies intersect:

1. Rhetoric examines attributed intention; cultural studies analyzes the preferred meaning. These may not always be the same, but the preferred meaning can be an intentional one.

2. Rhetoric, as Rosteck has said, analyzes how discourse is produced, what it is, and what it does; cultural studies examines the codes of television involved in its production and generation of ideology.

3. Rhetoric is about the choices that the developer of discourse makes and the choices that a viewer makes in treating the discourse as a message; cultural studies is about the choices made in encoding and decoding meaning.

4. Rhetoric and cultural studies both link discourse to an audience, to society, and especially to context.

5. Cultural studies is about how ideology shapes a work; rhetoric is about how a work stems from and influences ideology.

6. Identification is a key factor in persuasion, and how one's identity is known through the decoding process is a key factor in cultural studies. The substance through which people rhetorically identify may be the same substance that marks identity in cultural studies, for example, nationality, class, gender, race, occupation, beliefs, and values.

7. Cultural studies examines polysemy, the multiple meanings that can be made by viewers from television discourse; rhetoric examines how a sender and receiver co-create meaning.

8. Both subjects focus on symbols and emphasize that meanings do not reside in the symbols themselves but in the people who encode them.

9. Values as foundations for persuasion may be studied in rhetoric; cultural studies analyze the ideology in discourse. Ideology is comprised in part of values.

10. Rhetoric is used to bring about change and enlightenment; cultural studies is about the lives of everyday people and how culture interacts with their lives.

Television rhetoric was defined as the study of technologically enhanced symbol systems and representations through which the senders (television producers, writers, directors, actors, cinematographers, set designers, and so on) attempt to shape perceptions, foster understanding, create identification, and influence the viewing behavior of the receivers (the television audience). Cultural studies has been presented as a way to demystify what attitudes, beliefs, values, preferred forms of conduct, and ideologies are embedded and reinforced in images and supporting discourse. Both approaches are of great value to the television critic and can be adapted as questions to ask when conducting a critique.

Exercises

1. Watch an episode of *CSI* and observe how the forensic scientists use evidence and artistic and inartistic proofs to locate the criminal.

2. Find and describe an enthymeme in a television commercial. What did you have to supply to complete the reasoning?

3. Is there anything on television that emphasizes *telos*, the movement toward moral excellence?

4. Find attributed intentionality in a television drama or situation comedy or in the news.

5. Select a television program that you frequently watch and describe the character with whom you identify. Analyze why you identify with this character.

6. Give an example of how a television program engages in courtship with you as a viewer. What desire does it arouse and satisfy?

7. Cite some examples from recent television shows and commercials that use language that has found its way into popular usage.

8. Select a scene from a television drama and analyze its polysemy.

9. Select a soap opera or a nighttime drama and tell how it relates to the shared conditions of our time.

10. Select a television show and examine the codes described by Fiske—reality, representation, and ideology.

11. Describe an instance in which a television show "hails" you and tell how you answer it.

12. Describe how hegemony has occurred for a disempowered group that has recently been represented on television.

13. By playing with meanings that you make from television, tell what you have learned about yourself in the process.

Suggested Readings in Rhetoric

Andrews, James R., Leff, Michael C., & Terrill, Robert. (1998). *Reading Rhetorical Texts: An Introduction to Criticism.* Boston: Houghton Mifflin.

Brock, Bernard L., Scott, Robert L., & Chesebro, James W. (1989). *Methods of Rhetorical Criticism* (3rd ed.). Detroit: Wayne State University Press.

Burgchardt, Carl R. (Ed.). (2005). *Readings in Rhetorical Criticism.* State College, PA: Strata Publishing.

Foss, Sonja K. (Ed.). (2004). *Rhetorical Criticism: Exploration and Practice* (3rd ed.). Prospect Heights, IL: Waveland Press.

Hart, Roderick P. & Daughton, Suzanne M. (2004). *Modern Rhetorical Criticism* (3rd ed.). Boston: Allyn & Bacon.

Heath, Robert L. (1986). *Realism and Relativism: A Perspective on Kenneth Burke.* Macon, GA: Mercer University Press.

Smith, Craig R. (1998). *Rhetoric and Human Consciousness: A History.* Prospect Heights, IL: Waveland Press.

Suggested Readings in Cultural Studies

Barker, Chris. (2000). *Cultural Studies: Theory and Practice.* Thousand Oaks, CA: Sage Publications.

Couldry, Nick. (2000). *Inside Culture: Re-imagining the Method of Cultural Studies.* London, UK: Sage Publications.

Evans, Jessica and Hall, Stuart, Eds. (1999) *Visual Culture: the reader.* London, UK: Sage Publications.

Fiske, John. (1987). *Television Culture.* London, UK: Methuen.

Hall, Stuart. (1997). *Representation.* Thousand Oaks, CA: Sage Publications.

Higgins, John. (1999). *Raymond Williams: Literature, Marxism, and Cultural Materialism.* London, UK: Routledge.

Lewis, Jeff. (2002). *Cultural Studies: the Basics.* London, UK: Sage Publications.

7

Representation and Its Audience

Mephistopheles to Faust: "Illusion holds you captive still."

—Goethe, *Faust*

Introduction

In Chapter 6, the concept of representation was presented as a television code, a range of audiovisual systems that has the capability to construct meanings. The concept of representation is central to the study of television. Television provides a continual flow of images and sounds that link viewers to the world. Television production shapes how an event unfolds and limits the meanings of what is seen. Television mediates reality by selecting and interpreting images in order to present them to the viewers. Representation of people and events is encoded by technical codes with the camera, lighting, sound, music, and editing in order to convey the narrative, conflict, character action, dialogue, setting, casting, and so on. Representational codes work together to encode a preferred meaning, yet at the same time to present the illusion of naturalness.

Because it is impossible to show everything on television, selection of images is necessary. The task of news is to represent the realities of daily life from all over the world. What we know about people in places such as Israel, Palestine, Iran, Iraq, China, Japan, Russia, Darfur, the Sudan, Kenya, and South Africa is very likely to come from television. Television drama and situation comedies have representations of women, men, husbands, wives, parents, children, race, ethnic groups, age, rich, poor, class, doctors, lawyers, police, firefighters, religious leaders, people from different parts of America and the world, and so forth. How do we know that what we see resembles the actual people and places? Furthermore, does it matter to us if they do or do not? Which groups are included and which are excluded? By understanding the concept of representation, the television critic can attempt to answer these questions. This chapter is an examination of representation, and explains what representation is, how it impacts a viewer, what role it plays in the depiction of gender, ethnicity, race, nationality, and class on television, and how it affects a society's collective memory.

What Is Representation?

Visual representation means to re-present, to project an image of someone or something. Even though the image will seldom be realistic in size because it depends upon the dimensions of the television screen, the viewer is expected to accept the image as realistic even though it is framed by a camera. As we saw in Chapter 6, verbal representation means that language stands in the place of someone or something, requiring that meaning to be learned. Verbal representation varies from language to language.

A common definition of representation is "a given which the act of representation duplicates in one way or another" (Iser in Krieger, 1987, p. 217). Stuart Hall, in his book *Representation: Cultural Representations and Signifying Practices,* emphasized meaning in the "language" of words, sounds, and images in his definition of representation: "The production of meaning through language . . . Any sound, word, image, or object which functions as a sign, and is organized with other signs into a system which is capable of carrying and expressing meaning is, from this point of view 'a language' " (Hall, 1997, pp. 16, 19). Representation was defined by W. J. T. Mitchell in his book *Picture Theory* as a fabricated stand-in for culture, suggesting the "constructed, artificial character of forms of life, in contrast to the organic biological connotations of 'culture' " (Mitchell, 1995, p. 423). Photographs, paintings, film, television, and computer images are forms of visual representation. They attempt to duplicate objects, places, or persons, but they are truly not duplicates. Rather they are substitutes that resemble what they attempt to duplicate or imitate. Skill in duplication, such as perspective in art to give a two-dimensional canvas the sense of a real three-dimensional view or knowledge of light and shadow to harness realism in photography and film, is as important to a sense of accuracy as it is to illusion in these media.

If the representation is a surrogate for the original, then it could be used as the original might function. This suggests that representation, although it is not the original, presents an illusion of the original and its function. Thus, a representative image *imitates* the real. It is an attempt to *substitute* a *resemblance* in order that a viewer may recognize it as real. An image is *constructed* to *re-present* someone or something. If it resembles the real, it has *verisimilitude*, an appearance of truth. In other words, it has to have credibility.

Television Representation

Television images are complex because they are based on visual representation. Television images are mediated images—three-dimensional places, people, and objects viewed on a two-dimensional plane—not life-size, and produced by technical means controlled by camera angles and movement, lighting, and computer manipulation. (High-definition TV has the capability of giving the illusion of three dimensions.) Acting, directing, camera work, lighting, and editing create a sense of intimacy, emotion, excitement, and other feelings. As we saw in Chapter 3, television employs art directors and set dressers to create realistic-appearing places, such as living rooms, restaurants, offices, hospitals, and other settings. When we see them in the frame of a television set, these images are reduced to the size of the screen— 20 inches up to 54 inches, depending on the screen's dimensions—none of which are as large as the actual studio sets. The actual sets in the television studio often have three walls with the fourth wall open to the cameras, directors, producers, writers, and, in the case of situation comedies, an audience. Because the person who watches a program on television cannot see the entire studio or stage, one could say that representation conceals as well as reveals. If a scene is outdoors, set in wintertime snow, for example, the material used to create the illusion of snow is artificial. Yet, the viewer can accept the image as a duplication of a given reality although what is real is represented by an imitation of it. Thus, that which is represented, is *re-presented* by a substitute, an imitation. Its effectiveness is dependent on the viewer's recognizing and accepting it. In order to achieve this kind of viewer response, the image must *resemble* that which is real.

Interpreting Representation

Ultimately, the viewer decides if an image resembles reality. As Kenneth Burke wrote, "A way of seeing is also a way of not seeing" (Burke, 1935/1984,

p. 49). The old adage "seeing is believing" can also be construed as "believing is seeing." How we perceive is influenced by our values, beliefs, and experiences, thus a representation on television is constructed via the perceptual filters of the television producers and seen through the perceptual lens of the viewer.

A television situation comedy uses a representation of a funny situation to provoke audience laughter, but the audience must be able to relate it to familiar experiences in order to comprehend the humor. David Marc wrote that the situation comedy is a representational form of American culture: "It dramatizes national types, styles, customs, issues, and language" (Marc, 1984, p. 13).

Television viewers may derive meaning from representations, and, because reality has multiple meanings to people, representations also constitute multiple meanings (polysemy). It is also quite possible that a representation may have no meaning to a viewer, or it may have a large range of meanings. The viewer interprets what is represented within a cultural context and locates meaning according to beliefs, values, and experience, thus an image does not have a fixed meaning. Images can touch levels of experience, according to Hall,

> . . . beyond the purely rational level of awareness, and disturb by the very way in which they exceed meaning. The cultural practices of looking and seeing, then, . . . rest on complex conditions of existence, some of which have psychic and unconscious dimensions of which the behavioral definition of meaning's 'effects' has only a very reductionist understanding. (Hall, 1999, pp. 311–312)

Reception of Televisual Images

Television and its viewers comprise a communication system of senders and receivers, messages, the transmission of the messages through a medium, and reception by viewers. The sender encodes through technologically enhanced representations and symbol systems comprised of words, sounds, and images. The receiver decodes meanings by selecting and interpreting images, sounds, and words, and assigning meanings to them. Viewers have certain expectations of established program conventions (as described in Chapter 5, "Television Genres") that color their responses. Producers of television have certain goals that they want to achieve, for example, to have viewers perceive images as credible, to provoke laughter, or to gain a faithful following for a series or a network, but because there is no immediate feedback from viewers, the producers' primary goal is to gain a large percentage of audience shares. Some television programs, mostly the competitive reality shows such as *American Idol* and *Dancing with the Stars,* give viewers feedback opportunities to call or e-mail responses and votes for contestants, and the Internet offers many opportunities for viewers to give their opinions of television programs. When the television comedy *Becker* celebrated its 100th show, a contest was held for viewers to spot how many times "100" was mentioned for a chance to win $100, an autographed script, a *Becker* jacket, or a 100-minute phone card. Yet, for the most part, the ratings system is still the primary means for television producers to gauge viewer responses in terms of numbers of people watching.

Viewer reception is dependent upon *perception* of mediated images. Perception is the process of extracting information from outside ourselves as well as from within ourselves. How we perceive is based on "complex psychological, philosophical, and practical habitual thought patterns that we carry over from past experiences" (Hayward, 1997, p. 73). Each individual has a perceptual field that is unique to that person and formed by the influences of values, roles, self-image, and cultural norms. Each of these shapes how a person perceives. The connection between perception and cognition leads to the cultural formation of meanings related to what is seen. Recognition of most meanings tends to be automatic because people have learned them. As Hall wrote, ". . . all sorts of objects, people, and events are correlated with a set of concepts or *mental representations* which we carry around in our heads. Without them, we could not interpret the world meaningfully at all" (Hall, 1997, p. 17). The concepts Hall referred to are organized, arranged, and classified into complex relations with one another. "Meaning," he wrote, "depends upon the relationship between things in the world—people, objects, and events, real or fictional—and the conceptual system, which can operate as *mental representations* of them" (Hall, 1997, p. 18). Because people broadly share conceptual systems and thus make sense of the world in roughly the same way, they can communicate with one another. "That," said Hall, "is indeed what it means when we say we 'belong to the same culture.' Because we interpret the world in roughly similar ways, we are able to build up a shared culture of meanings and thus construct a social world which we inhabit together. That is why 'culture' is sometimes defined in terms of 'shared meanings or shared conceptual maps'" (Hall, 1997, p. 18).

When a thing is different from the usual mental representation, confusion results in the attempt to recognize it. Harvard psychologist Jerome Bruner conducted experiments on perception wherein he had college students recognize playing cards. In one group he switched the colors, so the hearts and diamonds were black instead of red, and the spades and clubs were red instead of black. The students had difficulty recognizing the color-reversed cards. They tried to regularize what they saw by saying the red six of clubs was really a black six of clubs (Bruner, 1973). In extreme cases, if people have no familiarity with a thing, they may not perceive it at all. As we saw in the previous chapter, a wide variety of meanings (polysemy) can be made depending upon the viewer and the context.

Symbols

A symbol differs from an imitative representation, for it stands for something else but does not attempt to accurately duplicate it. A Valentine's Day card in the shape of a heart may symbolize love, or the empty boots in the stirrups of a saddle on a riderless horse may symbolize the death of a hero or heroine. Although both symbols and representations rely upon relationships or connections between the image and the receiver of the image, they are connections that are achieved in different ways. A connection between a symbol and its referent is not necessarily causal as is a visual representation of, for example, a living room on television. The heart-shaped symbol ♥ stands for love in our culture, but the connection between the symbol and its meaning had to be learned. In a culture where the heart-shaped symbol has no known meaning, it is unlikely to get a response, or it may get a different response. On the other hand, an anatomical drawing of a human heart should be a representation of a real human heart to anyone anywhere in the world who has adequate knowledge of human anatomy. We have learned to attach certain meanings to words, and when they are familiar enough, their presence stimulates a kind of recognition of something similar in our experience. We learn to attach meanings to visual symbols in the same manner that we have learned the meanings of words in our language.

The Illusion of Reality

Television images are both symbolic and representational. The camera records and/or transmits both live and filmed moving images that represent people, places, and events that symbolize ideas, values, activities, and other concepts. Although people may respond to television as if they are seeing something firsthand, they are not. What they see is an image of something that someone else has selected, created, or recorded. Images are constructed to perpetuate the illusion that what we see is natural and believable. Representation in television has come to be regarded, for the most part, as a realistic appropriation of the world. What viewers see on television are images demanding to be recognized as real.

Seeing something through a moving image camera is never the same as seeing it with the naked eye. All the facets inherent in the technology come into play to create a unique view. In addition to the production techniques used to transmit images, sound in the form of dialogue, music, and background elements is also important, for it assists in the interpretation of the image and has representative capability. A harsh musical chord in the context of a frightening event, for example, can represent danger. The dialogue that the actors speak conveys not just interaction but also attitude and intentions. Computer technology enables technicians to create elaborate illusions that appear to be real, but, in fact, are so far from reality that viewers can no longer assume that what they perceive was ever real. Computer technology can turn a group of five people into a crowd of 500 or place a deceased person like Frank Sinatra in a television commercial that appears to have him talking to a live actor about a product.

The Need for Images

Often a viewer responds to an image because there is a need for it. William Wordsworth, the early 19th-century poet, said that people *need* images because people want a sense of who their fellow human beings are in order to have a sense of identity. Raymond Williams agreed with Wordsworth, adding that we need representations of what life is like both in our own culture and in others. This is why we watch the National Geographic and Discovery channels in addition to programming that is set in our own country. Each semester when I teach television criticism, I ask my students why they watch television. Every semester they give me the same or equivalent response: "Because our lives are uninteresting, and the people's lives on television are more interesting than our own." For these students, television seems to fulfill the needs and fantasies that they do not attain in everyday life. Williams said that our society "has been dramatized by the inclusion of constant dramatic representation as a daily habit and need" (Williams, 1989, p. 7).

French psychiatrist Octave Mannoni claimed that people have "a persisting need to posit 'an other scene' of absolute, untroubled faith, whether that 'other scene' be primitive cultures, an epoch's own past, an individual's childhood" (Ray, 1985, p. 36). Further, Mannoni maintained that although people know that what they see is an illusion, they also want to believe it. Translated from the French, Mannoni's premise was "I know very well that this illusion is only an illusion, but nevertheless, some part of me still believes in it" (in Ray, 1985, p. 36). This double system of belief enables audience members who know that what they see on fictional television is not real to become absorbed in it as if it were real.

Thus, the impact of representation is that a need is fulfilled. Individuals may have specific needs that are satisfied from various kinds of representations of characters, plots, and action in television, but all television viewers have some kind of a need for representation.

Representation of the "Other"

The concept of the "other" stems from George Herbert Mead's (1934) social psychology and symbolic interaction. Initially it was defined as a symbolic unity located outside of the self and associated with one or more other individuals, real or fictional people (O'Sullivan et al., 1994). Cultural and feminist studies have appropriated the concept of the other to mean ". . . a person, persons, group, social class, community, race or nation who are not 'us' and who are defined by their difference from us; yet who by that difference contribute to our concept of self, as individuals, members of groups, etc." (Watson & Hill, 2003, p. 209). There is a generalized "other" as in "*Some people* watch reality shows on television, but I prefer drama." The "other" can also be a positive role model, a real or fictional person, someone who is respected and sets a good example to follow. In television studies, the "other" usually represents a group that people fear, dislike, or feel superior to, resulting in a "them and us" attitude. Dominant groups who have power over representation on television may endow subordinate groups with certain characteristics and habits turning them into the "other." When a group is the "other," individual differences tend to be lost, for the members of the group are homogenized into a collective "them." Such categories of identity are contrived to appear natural as if determined by biology or psychology. These categories also result in stereotypes that completely ignore individual personalities.

Film, radio, and television in the past were notorious for stereotyping gender, race, and ethnicity. Today one has to look carefully for notions of the "other" on television. Shows such as *Lost* and *Grey's Anatomy* feature diversity in their characters. The characters on *Lost* are African American, Korean, Iraqi, Hispanic, and whites from America and Australia. Daniel Dae Kim, a Korean-born actor who grew up in New York and Philadephia, who plays Jin on *Lost,* said,

> Nobody wants tokenism, and that's one of the reasons I'm so proud of this show. It shows America and television executives and movie producers that you don't have to have a lily-white cast of twentysomethings to have a successful project. The story lines speak to America regardless of color and can even be enhanced by mixtures of race and gender. (Fernandez, 2005, p. E30)

John Wells, whose company produced *The West Wing, Third Watch*, and *ER*, said that producers have a duty to develop interesting characters, not racial types:

> If racial identity is the only thing that's interesting about a character, that's extremely limiting and also insulting to how society works now. Sometimes in an attempt to diversify shows, the characters become stereotypical because they're there for the purpose of providing diversity and you're trying to write to that instead of trying to write human beings. (Fernandez, 2005, p. E30)

When Michael Crichton wrote the pilot for *ER*, he did not specify gender or race for any of the doctor characters on the show. The *ER* doctors are male, female, African American, Puerto Rican, Croatian, white, and disabled. The diverse results came from good casting.

Yet, there are many observers who insist that racial, ethnic, and gender "otherness" persists on television news reporting—where members of minority groups are frequently linked to crime and drugs—and that there is a small number of diverse characters on fiction television. Asian-Americans are particularly underrepresented in fiction television. Despite a growing Hispanic population in America, Hispanic actors are often relegated to servile roles. Lupe Ontiveros, whose parents were immigrants from Mexico, would love to play a Hispanic heroine, but for most of her 25 years as an actress she has played the role of a maid. Although she speaks perfect English, she has had to put on an accent to play a maid in television series such as *Veronica's Closet*, *Pasadena*, and *Leap of Faith*. Mireya Navarro, in a *New York Times* article about the role of the maid on television, said that it is a niche for Hispanic actresses, especially on prime-time television (Navarro, 2002, p. 1). Hispanic maids have made appearances on *Will & Grace* (Rosario), *Dharma & Greg* (Celia), and even on the animated *King of the Hill* (Lupino). The representation of Hispanics in leading roles has inched up by a small percentage with major roles by Jessica Alba on *Dark Angel*, Eva Longoria and Ricardo Antonio Chavira on *Desperate Housewives*, Sara Ramirez on *Grey's Anatomy*, and George Lopez on *The George Lopez Show*. PBS featured an all-Hispanic cast on its outstanding series, *American Family* (2002–2004) about a family living in Los Angeles.

It was not until *The Cosby Show* (1984–1992) came on the air that Donald Bogle, author of books about the representation of African Americans on television and in film, wrote that he saw on television families such as the ones he knew growing up in the suburbs. Bogle attributed the unique perspective of *The Cosby Show* to having an African American (Cosby) in control of the material (Bogle, 2001). When there is an absence of programs about African Americans, Bogle wrote, "Black viewers felt that

Photo 7.1   The Gonzalez family gathers for son Esteban's wedding to Ofelia, as *American Family: Journey of Dreams* begins. Pictured (l–r): Cisco (Parker Torres), Vangie (Rachel Ticotin), Esteban (Esai Morales), Ofelia (Kate del Castillo), Jess (Edward James Olmos), Nina (Constance Marie) and Conrado (Yancey Arias).

television was not fully and fairly representing them, not saying who they were and what their lives were like" (Bogle, 2001, p. 3). White viewers loved Cosby then as they now do Oprah, who has become an American icon. As Beretta Smith-Shomade wrote in her book *Shaded Lives,* Oprah Winfrey had "the potential to unite [the audience] across the [racial] difference" (Smith-Shomade, 2002, p. 176).

In 1999–2000, the National Association for the Advancement of Colored People (NAACP) urged the major television networks to improve their racial diversity or face a nationwide boycott. Network executives signed pledges to put more minorities on camera and behind it. Paul Farhi of *The Washington Post* claimed that

> television today is largely a paradise of racial equality and minority progress ... African Americans ... anchor the evening news, pitch products, announce and coach sports events, and are shown as doctors, surgeons, lawyers, business executives, military officers, teachers, reporters. Indeed, television has helped

change the social norm in America by denouncing racism and bigotry as
morally intolerable. Undoubtedly, exposure to people different than oneself, if
only through TV, helps shatter stereotypes and creates a foundation for understanding. (Farhi, 2000, p. 23)

Sexuality as portrayed on television also has changed with gay and lesbian
characters in recurring roles. *Ellen* had the first openly gay lead when Ellen
DeGeneres's character Ellen Morgan announced that she was gay on her
show three years after the show began in 1994. Will and Jack (Eric McCormack
and Sean Hayes) on *Will & Grace* are openly gay as are various other characters in minor and major roles. Fred Fejes pointed out that gays and lesbians
are attractive to advertisers because of their consumption habits. Although
gay and lesbian income is not greater than that of the general population, a
1994 study found that gays and lesbians were seen as far more likely to spend
their money on new products. "To advertisers," said Fejes, "they were a very
desirable group of innovative consumers" (Fejes, 2003, pp. 215–216).

Women's roles on television have progressed from the homemakers of the
1950s shows such as *Father Knows Best* and *Leave it to Beaver* where
women characters such as Margaret Anderson and June Cleaver represented
idealized and happy submersions into domestic life where they served others
and deferred to their husbands. Today women are featured protagonists in
television narratives as detectives, doctors, executives, lawyers, judges, and
action heroines. It would seem that there has been much progress given
women's absence in such roles in the past. However, as mentioned earlier in
this book, actresses who play women characters and women in nonfiction
roles such as news anchors and entertainment hosts are young, very beautiful, and have slender and firm bodies that are considered perfect. Youthful,
male bodies that are buff and perfect are often featured on dramatic television shows, but this is not always the case. Leading men do not necessarily
have ideal bodies. For example, James Gandolfini (*The Sopranos*) and Kevin
James (*The King of Queens*) are overweight. David Caruso (*CSI: Miami*)
and William Petersen (*CSI*) are older than their female costars. Men in nonfiction such as the news and magazine shows are often older with less-than-
idealized bodies, while their female costars are very attractive. Although
there are exceptions, there is still a double standard for women and men on
television as far as age and appearance are concerned.

Regarding ethnicity, some Italian Americans have chafed at the undignified
portrayal of Italians on *The Sopranos*. However, Regina Barreca's book *A
Sitdown with the Sopranos* (2002) has eight essays written by Italian Americans
about the show. Pronouncing Tony Soprano as Everyman rather than a
stereotype, each author has praise for *The Sopranos*, its writing, acting, and
production values.

What about the representation of middle-aged and senior citizen characters? Commercial television is sponsored by advertising that appeals to 18- to 49-year-olds, but courts the 18- to 34-year-olds more aggressively. That is why most of the lead characters in comedy or drama tend to be 20–30 years old. Parents on television used to be positively represented, but, according to Earl Pomerantz, former executive producer of *The Cosby Show* and writer for *The Mary Tyler Moore Show* and *Cheers,* parents on television today are represented as "monsters, maniacs, and morons" (Pomerantz, 2006, p. 42). Pomerantz cited the example of the "ego-crushing mother of *Two and a Half Men*" and the wimpy father on *Out of Practice.* He suggested that this may be because advertising discounts older consumers over 50 and that television writers tend to be young and may be getting revenge on their own parents by representing parents in a negative way.

What about the representation of class? Most television dramas feature middle- and upper-class groups. When lower classes are represented on situation comedies, they are often portrayed as unintelligent buffoons, especially lower-class men. What about the disabled? How often are people represented as wheelchair-bound or physically or mentally impaired? *Jericho,* a new show in the 2006–2007 season, includes a hearing-impaired young woman as the character Bonnie Richmond. In episodes, her family and friends communicate with her using sign language. Shoshannah Stern, the actress who portrays her, is deaf, thus she is authentic.

Advice for Television Critics

When we ask questions about representation of gender, sexuality, age, ethnicity, race, and class, we have to be careful that we are not representing these various groups as the "other." African American is a category used to describe people in America who are descendents of Africans, but what term do we use for people from Haiti or the Caribbean who have dark skin? Asian American is a large and meaningless compilation to represent Koreans, Chinese, Vietnamese, Cambodians, and so on. Darnell M. Hunt in his book *Channeling Blackness: Studies on Television and Race in America* explains that race does not exist in nature, but rather the idea of race was historically developed; it is social representation,

> a mental framework that works to order the way we see the world before us. We notice otherwise arbitrary differences on the surface of the human body and imbue these differences with social meaning . . . Key cultural forums like television today play a crucial role in this ongoing meaning-making process . . . Much of this meaning-making activity is wrapped up in our own

ongoing efforts to establish who we are, who we are not, and who we hope to be. (Hunt, 2005, p. 3)

As a television critic, pay attention to individual casting, the character's personality, and the narrative. Race, gender, age, and so on may not be the most important factors. For example, *Grey's Anatomy* features an interracial couple with the characters Preston Burke (Isaiah Washington, an African American), a top-notch surgeon, and Cristina Yang (Sandra Oh, a Korean American), an intern, but there is nothing in the show that emphasizes their racial backgrounds other than their appearances. The narrative stresses not that they are an interracial couple, but rather that they are like the "odd couple," for he is very neat and she is messy. She is also the most aggressive character on the show, a trait not often assigned to a woman.

Photo 7.2   Doctors Yang and Burke, the "odd couple" on *Grey's Anatomy*.

As a television critic, you will do more than count categories, although it is important to ask who is represented and who is not. Who is invisible? For example, how often are Native Americans represented on television? What about the deaf, the blind, the paraplegics?

It is important to see how a person is represented and scrutinize whether that representation is stereotypical, fixing the meanings that are given to groups. Are professional people in business and government represented as suspicious? Are Middle Easterners represented as terrorists? Even when groups are represented in quantity on television, such as women are today, many are cast in specific roles that visually focus attention upon their sexual attractiveness. Many female actresses playing professional women wear low-cut tank tops and tight slacks that accentuate their model-thinness. Male actors have to work out in strenuous fitness exercise to have toned bodies. Medical and empirical evidence indicates that the media play a strong role in conditioning women and men to adopt these idealized body shapes with possible harmful consequences (Wykes & Gunter, 2005).

As a television critic, you look for the visual encoding of men and women on television, whether they are in fiction or nonfiction roles. Also, you will examine the discourse to determine elements of power between and among group representations. As a critic of television, you will ask: What is at stake in a representation? How are we limited in our ways of seeing? Is there meaning that is different from what we expected to find in a representation?

Representation is a construction with a preferred meaning on the part of the encoder (the production staff), but, as we saw in Chapter 6, audience members can derive different meanings by negotiating or resisting the dominant meaning. As a television critic, you can play with meanings and discover what possibilities are there. It is important to remember that television production and distribution is a business, thus the representations may reinforce the identities of the consumer market. This is why representation is so complex. It has both artistic and economic goals.

Representation and Collective Memory

As anthropologist Gregory Bateson said, human memory is a social and cultural process: "We take image production to be the locus of heightened interplay of mnemonic process and cultural formation" (Kuchler and Mellion, 1991, p. 4). If memory is culturally constructed, then memory operates through representation. Certainly, our memory comes from our own nonmediated and mediated experiences, but there is also a continuum of representations and dramatic conventions that are included in our memories. Jefferson A. Singer and Peter Salovey, writing about how a person remembers the past, related past memories to present representations:

> Representative images crystallize characteristic interests, motives, or concerns of an individual into a shorthand moment . . . [Memories] have collapsed a sequence of associated experiences into a single one. By focusing on the one

representative memory, one gains access, whether implicitly or explicitly, to an extensive series of related memories. Individuals may open a memory bank with a snapshot, a song, a story, or a film. (Singer & Salovey, 1993, p. 63)

Collective memory is a memory that different persons, unknown to one another, remember of the same event. Societies share collective or public memories with ceremonies, rituals, and television images. Television delivers and creates history through representation in news and drama. Television is an external vessel of recollection, for it delivers and creates history as news. This creates a collective memory whereby we have shared representations of, for example, the Civil Rights Movement, Martin Luther King, Jr.'s "I Have a Dream" speech, the astronauts' walk on the moon, the assassination of John F. Kennedy, the Holocaust, the mushroom cloud of the atomic bomb, the dismantling of the Berlin Wall, the war in Vietnam (the first television war), the collapse of the Federal Building in Oklahoma City, the *Challenger* explosion, the Persian Gulf War, and the fall of the Twin Towers of the World Trade Center in New York City. This is a major means for new generations to "know" history. George Lipsitz wrote, "Time, history, and memory become qualitatively different concepts in a world where electronic mass communication is possible" (Lipsitz, 1990, p. 21). Television also creates history with docudramas, delivering historical events and persons through fictional representations of them.

On the other hand, people may have a memory but be unsure of its source. They may know it was not from direct experience but are unsure if it was from television news, a newspaper, magazine, or from another person. David Marc spoke of a shadow memory of "a continuing electronic paratext to experience [that] interacts with individual memory" (Marc, 1984, p. 135). Anthropologist Edmund Carpenter wrote that "television gives us a sense of reliving the past, of knowing the outcome even when we haven't seen the movie" (Carpenter, 1974, p. 16). Representation in its many forms provides us with memory, but it is important to remember that representation is dependent upon individual interpretation and assigned meaning to form memory.

Summary

This chapter has explored the meaning of the concept of representation. Representation cannot duplicate reality, only imitate it, attempt to substitute, or to provoke other stored representations that already reside in a person's memory. Recognition of this enables us to understand that representation is an imitation, never the real thing. Further, there are varying reasons why we need representation. Representations provide us with access to the past, satisfy our need to know what life is like for other people, enable us to live vicariously, fulfill a daily habit, and remind us that life may have been more or less complicated in another time. Finally, they are included in our individual and collective memories. These explanations help us understand the connections between encoded representations and the decoded reception of them. Sorting out these matters is important to you as a television critic, but it is also important for public consumers of representations to know what it is they are consuming, how it is that they are consumed, and how representations intermix with personal memories to create illusions that are a "real" part of our lives. Representation is not just about who is represented, but it is also about who is not represented. Representation is about how people, places, and objects are represented on television and the meaning that is endowed in them. Representation of people may be emblematic of a dominant meaning, but it is important to ask what is at stake in the representation. The more we understand about representations, their rationale, and their interpretations, the more we can effectively assess how they work and learn what their impact is on us.

Exercises

1. Select a television representation of a person from a country you have never visited or know little about. What is your impression of the person regarding national characteristics? Do you generalize that the person represents other citizens of the same country?

2. How might a representational image on television function as the real thing? Are you willing to accept the image as the real thing? If so, what function does it perform for you?

3. Watch a situation comedy and try to imagine the fourth wall. Describe what you think is there. In the same situation comedy, select a scene (indoors or outdoors) and ask if you accept it as a given reality. If so, why? If not, why?

4. Select your favorite situation comedy and ask if you relate it to your own familiar experiences. If not the entire situation comedy, how do you relate to a part of the narrative or to a character?

5. The term "polysemy" means many meanings. Watch a television show with a friend who has a different background and beliefs than your own. Afterward, discuss the meanings your friend made from the program and compare them with your own.

6. Select a favorite and familiar television show. Is it relevant to your culture as you know it? Does it project shared meanings for other people in your culture? Make a list of the shared meanings that you perceive.

7. Find an example of a visual symbol on television. Describe what it stands for and how you learned its meaning.

8. Select an example of background music or sound in a drama. Within the context of the narrative, describe what you think it means.

9. As an individual television viewer, do you *need* images? If so, what show satisfies that need and why?

10. Do you think that television characters have more interesting lives than you do?

11. What does the term "other" mean to you?

12. Describe some stereotypes that you observe on television. What shows do they appear on and what purpose do they serve?

13. Watch four hours of prime-time television on a weeknight (or daytime soap operas and talk shows) and identify the following:
    - Who are the African American characters and what are their roles or positions?
    - Who are the Hispanic Americans and what are their roles or positions?
    - Who are the Asian Americans and what are their roles or positions?
    - Next, ask if their country of origin is identified (for example, Korea in the case of Asian Americans or Mexico in the case of Hispanic Americans). Are there ways that their race or ethnicity is important to the narrative? If so, describe the ways.
    - What racial and ethnic group do you belong to? How is your group represented on television? Does it affect you and your sense of identity?

14. Examine the roles of women on fiction and nonfiction television. Are any of the women represented as subordinate in ability to men? Describe those who are. In work and/or romantic relationships, guess the relative ages of the women and the men. Describe the physical characteristics of the women and the men. Are there any differences in terms of cultural standards of attractiveness?

15. Look for the following groups as represented on television and ask (A) if the representation is positive or negative; and (B) if they are represented at all:
    - Italian Americans
    - Working-class people
    - Middle Easterners
    - Disabled people

- Russians
- Lawyers
- Irish
- Business professionals
- Middle-aged men and women
- Teachers
- Senior citizens
- Politicians

16. Select any other ethnic, age, or occupational group (farmers, musicians, children, and so on) that is represented that you wish to examine.

17. Select one of your collective memories that was represented on television before you were born. Do you have an image of it? If so, where did it come from?

Suggested Readings

Bogle, Donald. (2001). *Prime Time Blues: African Americans on Network Television.* New York: Farrar, Straus and Giroux.

Hall, Stuart. (1997). *Representation.* Thousand Oaks, CA: Sage Publications.

Hunt, Darnell M. (2005). *Channeling Blackness: Studies on Television and Race in America.* New York: Oxford University Press.

Lipsitz, George. (1990). *Time Passages: Collective Memory and American Popular Culture.* Minneapolis: University of Minnesota Press.

Wykes, Maggie & Gunter, Barrie. (2005). *The Media and Body Image: If Looks Could Kill.* Thousand Oaks, CA: Sage Publications.

8

Postmodernism

The case could be made that the people in this country who know the most about how postmodernism feels are all under the age of sixteen.

—N. Katherine Hayles, *Chaos Bound*

Introduction

Postmodernism is a controversial term that is often used to describe the style and aesthetics of contemporary television as well as architecture, the arts, and fashion. Postmodernism suggests that culture has undergone a transformation due in part to the proliferation of virtual reality–type images and discourses generated by technological developments—satellite and cable television, satellite radio, digital video recording devices, camera telephones, digital cameras, advances in computer use, and the Internet. These technologies have produced a surplus of images and discourses that demand our attention, but, of course, it is impossible to attend to all but a small percentage of them. Postmodern theorists claim that consumers of images and discourses on television have developed "strategies of absorption as they are worked over by popular texts [that] involves the manipulation of the array by an increasingly sophisticated knowledge of the conditions of their production, circulation, and eventual reception" (Collins, 1992, p. 332). Television critics argue over what postmodernism is and whether it is as prevalent as many writers contend. As a television critic, you will find it helpful to be acquainted with the term and to recognize the postmodern style if it exists in certain types of television programming. This chapter will define postmodernism, examine its roots and theories, and examine how it is manifested in television. Since most treatises on postmodernism emphasize the new technological developments in our culture, they are briefly discussed as follows.

The Emergence of New Technologies

The end of the 20th century and the beginning of the 21st century have witnessed an increase in wired and wireless transmission capacity so great that it is or will be

> ... possible to transmit any type of information (audio, video, or text) from any point in the network to any other point or points, and to do so in 'real time,' in other words quickly enough so that the receiver will see or record at least 24 frames of video per second with an accompanying audio frequency range of twenty to twenty thousand Hertz. (Poster, 2004, p. 583)

Mark Poster's statement about rapid transmission of information is given to support his thesis that "... electronic communications technologies significantly enhance these postmodern possibilities" (Poster, 2004, p. 582). There is no doubt that new communications technologies have changed our lives. Because of cellular phones, we not only can talk to our family and friends whenever we want to, but we also are often forced to hear other people's conversations and their phones ringing in the classroom, church, the movies, and other places where we do not want these disturbances. Camera phones enable us to send pictures to our friends but also create a nuisance as camera flashes go off at concerts and other events. Text messaging on cellular phones enables us to enter contests at live sports events, to vote on contestants in television reality shows, and to send and receive messages from others. Satellite radio expands our listening to regions that used to be out of range. E-mail lets us communicate with others all over the world, and the Internet gives us a constant flow of information and contacts with others. E-mail and the Internet also give us unwanted information and spam. We know that the new technologies are in our lives to stay and that we are quickly becoming dependent on them, but what do they have to do with postmodernism?

Poster maintains that the new technologies have implemented the creation of a simulated culture highlighted by "virtual reality." You no longer have to drive your car to an address to look at real estate because you can take a virtual walk through a house on the Internet. You do not have to go to a museum to enjoy art because you can see the paintings and sculptures online, and you can do so accompanied by another person who is not in the same place as you. As Poster wrote, "Virtual reality takes the imaginary of the word and the imaginary of the film or video image one step further by placing the individual 'inside' alternative worlds" (Poster, 2004, p. 586). These emerging systems of communication have created virtual communities, new identities and interactions, and new vocabulary, for example the weblog, or "blog." Blogs are, in effect, personal narratives, little stories that people share over the Internet with people whom they will probably never meet.

Postmodern theorists believe that the inundation of new technologies has influenced a postmodern society. Lili Berko wrote, "We find ourselves confronted with an image of a postmodern terrain whose geographic boundaries are less determined by physical structures than they are by the scope of the electronic signals emitted via the confluence of video and computational technologies" (Berko, 1994, p. 228). French theorists Jean Baudrillard and Jean-François Lyotard have claimed that the new media created by technology have produced a new social formation with an overload of information and images that have changed how we experience space and time. Certainly, the new technologies have enlarged our world. Postmodern theorists describe contemporary life as permeated with consumerism, materialism, and multinationalism. Lyotard wrote, "One listens to reggae, watches a western [movie], eats McDonald's for lunch and local cuisine for dinner, wears Paris perfume in Tokyo, and 'retro' clothes in Hong Kong" (Gitlin, 1998, p. 60). Lyotard and other postmodern theorists are discussed later in this chapter. The new social formation that these critics describe is encapsulated in the term "postmodern" that must now be defined, even though a common definition is almost impossible.

Postmodernism Defined

"Post" means after or beyond, thus postmodernism means beyond modernism. Therefore, let us first look at the definition of modernism. Modernism is characterized as a rejection of realist representation and was thus "a move away from the 19th century's 'objective' depiction of the world to various forms of abstraction and symbolism that emphasized subjective inward consciousness" (Collins, 1992, p. 329). Modernism can be traced back to the Middle Ages, according to philosophers Steven Best and Douglas Kellner, when philosophers such as René Descartes stated his preference for reason and thought as sources of knowledge and progress. Modernism was also associated with industrialization, with the "world view . . . that reality is ordered according to laws that the human intelligence can grasp" (Best & Kellner, 1991, p. 9).

> A postmodern joke: Descartes is on an airplane and the flight attendant asks if he would like something to drink. Descartes says, "I think not" and he disappears.

The "post" prefix, according to Best and Kellner:

> ... signifies an active rupture with what preceded it ... this rupture can be interpreted positively as a liberation from old constraining and oppressive conditions and as an affirmation of new developments, a moving into new terrains, a forging of new discourses and ideas ... On the other hand, the 'post' in postmodern also signifies a dependence on, a continuity with, that which it follows, leading some critics to conceptualize the postmodern as merely an intensification of the modern, ... a new 'face of modernity,' or a postmodern development within modernity ... The discourses of the postmodern therefore presuppose a sense of an ending, the advent of something new, and the demand that we must develop new categories, theories, and methods to explore and conceptualize this novum, this novel social and cultural situation. (Best & Kellner, 1991, pp. 29–30)

Modernism produced bold, new forms of expression in abstract art; functional, machine-inspired architecture; and stream of consciousness literature, but it was also characterized by feelings of hope and anxiety, skepticism, elitism, and the inevitability of human progress. Modernist values were seriousness, purity, reason, and individuality.

There are many definitions of postmodernism, a characteristic of postmodernism itself, but basically, as it relates to television, it refers to a stylistic and aesthetic change in the arts and culture (Casey, et al., 2002). Postmodernism breaks down the traditions of modernism, for it means that a body of work is nonlinear, playful, and assembled from various other forms, including modernism, that construct an eclectic pastiche, composed of parts borrowed from other works. Fredric Jameson described a pastiche as

> the imitation of a peculiar or unique style, the wearing of a stylistic mask, speech in a dead language; but it is a neutral practice of such mimicry, without parody's ulterior motive, without the satirical impulse, without laughter, without that still latent feeling that there exists something normal compared to that which is being imitated is rather comic. (Jameson, 1993, p. 16)

Boundaries of style and historical periods are blurred. Postmodernism plays with forms of the past, irony, cynicism, and commercialism. Words like *ephemeral, ambiguity, multiplicity, discontinuity, contradiction, unfinished, fragmentation, intertextuality,* and *irony* are used to describe postmodernism.

Postmodern architecture scorns traditional forms while copying and combining them. Charles Jencks, an architect whose book *What is Post-Modernism?* includes some of the clearest explanations, defined postmodernism as "double-coding: the combination of Modern techniques with something else (usually traditional building) in order for architecture to communicate with the public and a concerned minority, usually other architects" (Jencks, 1986, p. 14). Jencks emphasized that postmodern architecture is based on new techniques and old patterns, thus keeping some of the modern sensibility. The double-coding is the continuation of modernism and its transcendence. There is also an inherent intention in the work, such as irony, parody, displacement, complexity, eclecticism, or realism. Prominent examples of postmodern architecture combine steel and glass with curved and asymmetrical facades and mixed materials and often have forms copied from Classical Greek architecture or ancient Egyptian style. The form of the Acropolis, the Pantheon, or a pyramid may be copied but in contemporary materials. My favorite example of postmodern architecture is PPG (Pittsburgh Paint Glass) Place in Pittsburgh, Pennsylvania. It has a glass façade, but its spires mimic the neo-Gothic style. Its outline mirrors the Houses of Parliament in London. It is a blend of the past and present, the old and the new, that can be recognized by the public. Postmodernism embraces openness. Recognition by the public allows participation, and thus postmodernism bridges the gap between creator and audience. The postmodern style requires its audience to know what it mimics or parodies. This is also true in television.

Postmodern Television

Quite a few academic scholars believe that postmodernism exists on television. According to Jack Solomon,

> Postmodernism represents a new mode of perception: by radio, cinema, and most importantly, by TV. Viewing the world as a television camera views it, the postmodern eye reduces the length and breadth of experience to a two-dimensional spectacle, to a carnival of arresting images and seductive surfaces ... the postmodern experience is best described as a perceptual montage. (Solomon, 1998, p. 50)

Jonathan Bignell wrote that postmodernism is characterized in television as "self-conscious play with the conventions of television ... The pleasure of viewing programmes and advertisements ... derives from the viewer's recognition of this play" (Bignell, 2004, p. 162). Bignell quoted Robin Nelson, who suggested, "Postmodern texts might be summarily characterized by a formal openness, a strategic refusal to close down meaning. They create space for play between discourses, allegedly empowering the reader to nego-tiate or construct her own meanings" (Bignell, 2004, p. 163).

Postmodern television includes enjoyment derived from mixing up the conventions of various genres and programs. Hybrid genres (see Chapter 5, "Television Genres") such as the docudrama or the dramedy have become commonplace on television. Caren Deming wrote, television

> . . . flaunts its fluidity where genre is concerned. Although most individual episodes of any series are formulaic by design, television is determinedly recombinate at the series level. In part, television's generic hybridism is attrib-utable to the paradoxes built into its needs to be familiar and centrist while claiming to cut away at the edges—simultaneously exercising its penchants for recycling and topicality, nostalgia and immediacy . . . Stars appear as them-selves in narratives or in commercials and characters morph into hawkers with ease. Such fluidities combine with other postmodernist characteristics. (Deming, 2005, p. 133)

Intertextuality (references to other texts, genres, discourses, themes, or other media) is part of the play and thus the enjoyment. Viewer enjoyment of a particular text can be informed by recognition of experience with other texts. It is the interconnection of meanings across different media texts as well as connections between meanings.

Intertextuality, which includes allusions to other television programs, films from the past, actors, and news events, is a regular feature in many tele-vision programs. Perhaps the most popular example of intertextuality is found in *The Simpsons,* the animated situation comedy about a dysfunc-tional family, which has 15 to 20 intertextual references in each episode. The Simpson family watches a lot of television, thus there are many references to other television shows. On the episode, "Itchy & Scratchy & Marge," Marge Simpson crusaded against the "Itchy & Scratchy" show and was interviewed on "Smartline," a parody of *Nightline.* Characters from other television programs appear on *The Simpsons,* for example, Mulder and Scully from *The X-Files* and Captain Kirk from *Star Trek.* A character who is supposed to be Che Guevara—leader of Cuban revolutionaries in the late 1950s and early 1960s and an icon of revolutionary movements—has appeared on *The Simpsons* three times. (*The New Yorker* magazine had a cartoon with no caption with an image of Guevara wearing a T-shirt with the face of Bart Simpson on it.) Famous voices that are recognizable are used for recurring characters, such as Kelsey Grammer, who speaks the voice of Sideshow Bob. References to musicals constitute the narratives of individual programs, for example, "My Fair Laddy" and "The President Wore Pearls," a take-off of the musical *Evita* based on the life of Eva Peron of Argentina.

There is ample intertextuality on other television shows as well. Carol Burnett's wonderful parody of *Gone With the Wind* is a classic. Like Scarlett O'Hara, Carol Burnett wore a dress made from green velvet drapes, but hers included the drapery rods sticking out of her shoulders. Because the reference was easily recognized and because the drapery rods were so absurd, it was a perfect postmodern moment. Viewers of the television series *Lost* may recognize its roots in the 1950s film *Forbidden Planet*. Likewise, anyone who has seen the film *Invasion of the Body Snatchers* recognizes its plot elements in the television series *Invasion*. These intertextual references invite viewers to play with a television program through interactions that give them pleasure from their recognition of the referents.

The openness of postmodern television creates an opportunity for play between and among different texts. This has the potential to give the viewer pleasure, as defined in Chapter 6, and allows the viewer to negotiate or construct various meanings (polysemy) or perhaps no meaning at all. It also provides the viewer with knowledge of his or her own fragmented and fluid identity. Viewers may take a television program at face value, or they may attempt to make sense from the fragments of narrative, characterization, and intertextuality and enjoy the program's irony.

Cable and satellite television enable viewers to watch television programs made over the last six decades, but sometimes they are manipulated in the postmodern style. The Nickelodeon channel broadcasts television shows from the past with campy voice-overs, humorous graphics, and new editing, making new parodies out of old programs. *The Daily Show* parodies the news with commentaries on actual news footage that has been edited for the program.

Not all television is postmodern, for tight programming schedules and time allotted for commercials force timed segments. Situation comedies typically have some narrative resolution as do one-time dramas. However, dramatic series, soap operas, and reality shows that do not have immediate resolution hold the viewer in suspension in a style that could be considered somewhat postmodern. Viewers have to wait until next time—and that could be a different day and time, a lapse of a week or several weeks, or the next television season—to learn the outcome. Season finale cliffhangers make the viewers wait four to five months to find out who got shot or killed, who got elected, and who returned to a relationship. Yet, the viewers are able to resume with the program whenever it returns. Meanwhile, heavy promotions for these upcoming programs tantalize the viewers, urging them to come back to find out what happens next. Continuing episodes of *The Sopranos* were absent from television for a year, although reruns were frequent on HBO. Yet, after the year's absence, *The Sopranos* resumed with the story in 2006.

Not only do technological innovations bombard viewers with an overabundance of images and discourses, but technological developments also give viewers more control over what they watch on television. The remote control allows them to switch channels at will, creating their own juxtapositions. With digital video recorders such as TiVo, people are no longer bound to television schedules. They can watch what they want, when they want to, and they can zap the commercials, thus compressing the time it takes to watch a television show. If they want to review a scene, they can go back to it, or they can fast-forward through scenes they do not want to watch. DVD sales of entire seasons of television programs enable people to watch television in episodic fashion. Some people will watch an entire season of a television series in a single weekend.

MTV

Any treatment of postmodern television has to include MTV, for it has been the perfect example of visual disorder, exaggeration, and pastiche. John Fiske wrote that MTV is television's "only original art form . . . MTV at its most typical, most televisual [is a] mosaic of fragments: not sense but sensation. Energy, speed, image, youth, illusion, volume, vision, senses, not sense" (Fiske, 1998, pp. 167 & 171). Initially, MTV consisted of short music videos that sometimes told a story with multiple, flashing images enhanced by special effects and accompanied by a soundtrack. The term "video jockey," a person who conducts a television program of recorded music interspersed with chatter, jokes, and commercials, became a new word in our vocabulary. MTV blurs the boundaries between the videos and the advertising that provides 90 percent of its financing. The distinction between music video and advertising is broken down on MTV. According to Peter Wollen,

> Music videos are an advertising vehicle, promoting the sale of records. In fact, MTV is often credited with the resurgence of the fortunes of the music industry in the United States. In form, too, music videos have much in common with the more sophisticated ads and there has also been a rapid crossover between the two. (Wollen, 1997, p. 230)

MTV gave advertisers a place to be cool while reaching the desirable youth demographic. According to Beth Broday of Eastman Kodak, "Once MTV legitimized videos as programming with an inherent value, it became a business and an incomparable marketing tool for the record company" (The Art of the Music Video, 1997, p. 2).

MTV's signature style is compressed storytelling—if there is a narrative at all—rapid editing, extreme camera angles, slow motion, freeze-frame, repetition, and emphasis on images in a video style. MTV relies heavily on the breakdown of objective reality. The shape of a person or place may change several times within a single video clip. Animation and graphic images morph into shots of real people. It is eclectic and fragmented, appropriating images from old films, commercials, newsreels, modern art, fashion, and animation. It takes these intertextual images and reassembles them in nonlinear fashion with little regard for coherence. Liz Friedlander, a music video director, said that she and her colleagues in the industry are open to new insights and the unexpected. She offered a postmodern description for her work: "People in music video just want to mess things up and make them imperfect" (Art of the Music Video, 1997, p. 7). There are two MTV channels—MTV (music and lifestyle for teenagers) and MTV2 (rock, hip-hop, alternatives to dance music, and news about musicians). To attract an audience "too old for sister network MTV and too young for the History Channel," VH1 was developed for adults born after 1964. It is a 1970s and 1980s music channel with videos interspersed with celebrity news and pop culture (Poniewozik, 2004, p. 64).

Jack Solomon said, "In MTV video, the look is everything: character, the spirit that lives beneath the skin, is nothing. Images are put on and taken off at will, each new role unencumbered by the need for a coherent plot" (Solomon, 1998, p. 48). Solomon refers to pop celebrities who seem to have no self-identity but instead frequently change their identities, for example, Madonna, who has redefined herself over and over, and Michael Jackson, who not only went from being a Motown singer to pop music, but also drastically altered his physical appearance. Solomon quoted Pat Aufderheide's essay, "Music Videos: The Look of the Sound":

> Music videos have no heroes, because they do not feature individuals in the sense that plot-driven entertainment does. Music video offers unadulterated celebrity. The human beings do not play characters but bold and connotative icons. . . . [Rock-video stars play act as] sailors, thugs, gang members, gangsters, prostitutes, nightclub performers, goddesses, temptresses, and servants. [Their images are] drawn not from life or even myth, but from old movies, ads, and other pop culture clichés." (Solomon, 1998, pp. 48–49)

Kenneth J. Gergen, a professor of psychology, sees MTV as the ultimate breakdown of reason. In his book *The Saturated Self: Dilemmas of Identity in Contemporary Life,* he wrote that MTV

> . . . has carried the postmodern breakdown of narrative rationality to its furthest extreme. It relies heavily on the breakdown of objective reality. The shape or identity of an object or person may change several times within a given video clip, and what appears to be the reality of a photographed world may be revealed to be a drawing. (Gergen, 1991, p. 133)

Ann Kaplan, a prolific author on the subject of MTV, regards MTV as postmodern because rock videos "abandon the usual binary oppositions on which dominant culture depends . . . the oppositions that are abandoned are between high and low culture, masculine and feminine, past, present, and future, private and public, verbal and visual, realism and anti-realism" (Kaplan, 1998, pp. 35–36). She also wrote that the strategies of MTV must be considered within a profit-making institution. "Its mixture of texts, inclusion of ads, commentaries, displays; the central relationship of programming to the sponsors, whose own texts, the ads, are the real TV texts" (Kaplan, 1998, p. 34).

MTV's Influences

The MTV model has influenced the style of some television dramas that use handheld cameras to produce choppy images, rapid editing, contrasting images, and special effects. Characters in situation comedies sometimes talk into the camera, formerly a taboo in television fiction. Dramatic series often have multiple plots with a half dozen stories running at once and fragmented characters who come and go. Investigative news programs have elements of tabloid newspapers. Docudramas blur fact and fiction. David Letterman throws pencils at the camera, walks around backstage during his show *Late Night with David Letterman,* and on the set, the directors and the camera operators and their equipment are often visible. Popular songs are used as musical accents in *Grey's Anatomy, Rescue Me, Men in Trees,* and *CSI.* Many television commercials have postmodern features with multiple images crammed into 15 or 30 seconds, lack of continuity, partial stories, and tangential scenes interspersed and interwoven together.

Solomon described a Calvin Klein advertisement on television for the perfume Obsession:

> It's virtually impossible to tell just what is going on. A tormented woman seems to be torn between a young boy and an older man—or does the young boy represent a flashback to the older man's youth? Maybe it's her kid brother? Her son? She touches his face for an instant but refuses to be touched and glides away. Tears run down her glacial Art Deco face, but it isn't clear what she's crying about. She speaks a few words, but their meaning is obscure. A surrealistic dream vision rather than a coherent narrative, the Obsession commercial substitutes eccentric imagery for narrative significance. What matters is the 'look,' the inscrutable aura of postmodern chic. (Solomon, 1998, pp. 49–50)

Not all television programs or commercials have postmodern traits, but as a television critic you will recognize them when they are present.

Postmodern Theories

Kaplan regards postmodernism as a theoretical and critical concept (Kaplan,1998, p. 32). She wrote ". . . the postmodern moment is a break initiated by modernism . . . The break that modernism initiated is at once fulfilled with the development of recent electronic technologies and, at the same time, drastically altered in the process so as to become 'postmodern'" (Kaplan, 1993, p. 1).

Best and Kellner (1991) traced the development of the use of the term "postmodern" to the 1940s and 1950s when it was used to describe new forms of poetry and architecture. They said that the term was not used to describe that which opposed or came after modernism until the 1960s and 1970s. The 1960s was a time in which new art forms emerged—light shows, mixed media, rock concerts, and Andy Warhol's pop art. (Andy Warhol is best known for painting a Campbell's soup can and multiple images of Marilyn Monroe and Jackie Kennedy. His work reflects the overpowering influence of the many images in society.) The boundaries of low and high culture began to be broken down. In the 1970s, books about the postmodern condition began to appear. Postmodern theorists criticized modernism for its rationalism, causality, and the search for universal themes. These theorists preferred micro or localized theories, fragmentation, multiplicity, and ambiguity. In 1976, sociologist Daniel Bell wrote *The Cultural Contradictions of Capitalism* in which he developed the theme that the modern era was coming to an end. His view of a postmodern age was:

> . . . the unleashing of instinct, impulse, and will . . . an extension of the rebellious, anti-bourgeois, antinomic and hedonistic impulses . . . [It] is thus a product of the application of modernist revolts to everyday life, the extension and living out of a rebellious, hyperindividualist, hedonist lifestyle . . . a radical assault on tradition which is fuelled by an aggressive narcissism that is in profound contradiction with the bureaucratic, technocratic, and organizational imperatives of the capitalist economy and democratic polity. (Best & Kellner, 1991, p. 13)

As rapid changes in social and economic life occurred, they were paralleled by dramatic changes in social theory, especially in France. Political upheavals such as the student strikes in France in 1968, according to Best and Kellner, called for a break from the institutions and politics of the past and brought about developments of postmodern theory. The students in France had called for a change in the university system, its bureaucracy, conformity, and disciplines that they said had no relevance to reality. As a result, Michel Foucault and others generated theories that joined the connections between power and knowledge. Foucault's critique of modernism and humanism made him a major source of postmodern thought. He developed the theme that power and knowledge created new forms of domination. Yet, Foucault was not a postmodernist; rather his work reflects premodern, modern, and postmodern perspectives (Best & Kellner, 1991). His hostility to modernism is the most obvious postmodern feature of his work. He championed "the amazing efficacy of discontinuous, particular and local criticism" (Best & Kellner, 1991, p. 38).

Other theorists resisted the idea of unified theories, thus many of the postmodern theories that emerged were conflicting and diverse. Because of political upheavals around the world, postmodern theorists were attracted to such political movements as feminism, gay rights, and environmentalism. Their theories tended to

> . . . map in fragments and to ignore the more systemic features and relations of social structure that were the focus of modern social theory . . . Postmodern theorists do not do social theory *per se*, but rather eclectically combine fragments of sociological analysis, literary and cultural readings, historical theorizations, and philosophical critiques. (Best & Kellner, p. 259)

Berko wrote that postmodern theories converge around three major philosophical categories: subjectivity, representation, and the transcendental. The subject is seen as unclear, conflicted, and moving about like a nomad. Identity is confused and goes through many changes. Representation, regarded as standing in for reality, has been replaced by simulation and digitizing. Narratives that transcend difficulties and provide culture with a framework for comprehending the world have been rejected. In fact, many postmodern theorists claim there are no narratives anymore. Berko wrote, "The differences among the theorists of the postmodern become manifest in their attitudes toward these philosophical categories; one either celebrates or laments the 'supposed' death of the subject, of representation and/or the transcendental" (Berko, 1994, p. 229). She quoted Hal Foster who adds another position on postmodernism: "In cultural politics today, a basic opposition exists between a postmodernism which seeks to deconstruct modernism and resist the status quo and a postmodernism which repudiates the former to celebrate the latter: a postmodernism of resistance and a postmodernism of reaction" (Berko, 1994, p. 229).

Lyotard, in an article that he wrote for the *Postmodern Reader,* explained his position on postmodernism as a state that can be recognized only after the event because "being postmodern is a momentary condition that lasts for a short time. The postmodern is not an epoch or period but it is a characteristic of how cultural products are perceived" (Bignell, pp. 167–168). Lyotard approved of postmodernism, according to Bignell, because "he values things which are hard to categorise and hard to judge. Once something can be explained, judged and categorized Lyotard believes that its creative challenge and artistic interest are lost" (Bignell, 2004, p. 168). Lyotard rejected narrative because it can be controlled and ordered by criteria for judgment. He preferred abstract art because it presents something that is unpresentable.

Jean Baudrillard, a French sociologist, is considered one of the most high-profile postmodern theorists (Best & Kellner, 1991). His work is complex and far-reaching, but essentially Baudrillard claims that modernism, dominated by production, industrial capitalism, and a political economy, is dead and that a new era of postmodernism dominated by simulations and new forms of technology, culture, and society has emerged. The simulations take on a life of their own in this new epoch. Baudrillard wrote about television, in which he said the image of the doctor (the simulated doctor) is sometimes taken for the real doctor, and the image of the lawyer on television is taken for the real lawyer. This he calls "hyperreality," a blurring of distinctions between the real and the unreal. The prefix "hyper" means that it is more real than real. He said that the lifestyle described in magazines has replaced the actual lifestyles of people. In other words, the image becomes that which determines the real. In his postmodern landscape, the boundaries between entertainment and information, between politics and images, implode. This is Baudrillard's theory of implosion—images have replaced reality. (See Best & Kellner, 1991, pp. 111–122). Yet, Baudrillard described television as a

> . . . pure noise and a black hole where all meaning and messages are absorbed in the whirlpool and kaleidoscope of the incessant dissemination of images and information to the point of total saturation, where meaning is dissolved and only the fascination of discrete images glow and flicker in a mediascape within which no image any longer has any discernible effects. (Kellner, 2005, p. 42)

Kellner summarized,

> On the Baudrillardian view, the proliferating velocity and quantity of images produces a mindscreen where images fly by with such rapidity that they lose any signifying function, referring only to other images ad infinitum, and where eventually the multiplication of images produces such saturation, apathy, and indifference that the tele-spectator is lost forever in a fragmentary fun house of mirrors in the infinite play of superfluous, meaningless images. (Kellner, 2005, p. 42)

After devoting an entire book to postmodern theory, Best and Kellner concluded that postmodern theory is too abstract and lacks concrete, empirical and sociohistorical analysis (Best & Kellner, 1991). They did, however, recognize three different responses to the claim that we are living in a post-modern era: (1) there has been a rupture with modernism and we are in a totally new era that requires new theories; (2) there is no rupture with modernism, for there are continuities between the modern and the present time; and (3) there is an argument for a dialogue between continuity and discontinuity with theories to explain the breaks between them (Best & Kellner, 1991).

With regard to television, the third option is probably the most accept-able. Television certainly has continuity, but it also has discontinuity. That is why Stuart Cunningham wrote that television is both modern and postmodern.

> Television in its traditional broadcast form achieves effective cross-demographic communication because of its continuing modernist role. It is also a major postmodern form, embodying disjunctive aesthetics, clashes of the superficial and the serious, and pervasive image construction that "threatens" to become constitutive of reality rather than merely reflective of it. Within the accepted understanding of television's role as a provider of information and entertainment, is its postmodern provision of contemporary cultural and DIY [do-it-yourself] citizenship—the construction of selves, semiotic self-determination and functional media literacy. (Cunningham, 2005, pp. 205–206)

Postmodern theories essentially deal with the surface, the immediate, and the abstract. They tend to contradict one another, thus perplexing us as we try to understand them. Yet, they have provided us with different ways of thinking about culture and about television. Although postmodern theorists reject the notion of critiquing television with a set of standards, they have, perhaps inadvertently, given us a set of categories to look for if an instance of television is to be called postmodern.

Summary

There are many "posts" in the literature of culture, for example, post-structuralism, post-colonialism, post-Communism, post-industrialism, post-Marxism, post-humanism, and post-feminism, but the "post" that has been most often applied to television is postmodernism. It has come to mean a sense of rupture, the passing of the old and the advent of the new.

We live in an age of high technology with multiple electronic devices that have enabled us to experience wider communications and alternate realities. The way in which we view and use television has changed accordingly.

Basically, postmodernism is about the stylistic and aesthetic changes in the arts and culture and is notable in some television programs. A television program or commercial that is nonlinear, playful, and assembled from various other forms, including modernism, and constructs an eclectic pastiche can be considered postmodern. These features are especially prevalent on the MTV and VH1 channels. MTV style has influenced other programming and advertising.

Not only is postmodernism *in* television programs, but it also manifests itself in the way viewers *watch* television using remote controls and recording devices to create their own programming at convenient times. Yet, it should be recognized that only some television is postmodern. Many programs have linear, straightforward narratives and many viewers watch programs at the time they are scheduled and see all the commercials. It is important, however, that you as a television critic not only recognize the differences between the modern and postmodern on television but also how they overlap.

Exercises

1. How many electronic devices do you own? In what ways have they changed your life? Do you watch television differently than you did two or three years ago? Do you think that the programming on television has changed in the past two or three years? If so, how?

2. Take a tour of an alternate reality on the Internet. Some television Web pages—for example, the page for *CSI*—let you virtually walk through the show's sets. Describe the experience.

3. Do you "blog"? If so, do you regard your blog as narrative? If you do not blog, then read someone else's blog and determine if it is a narrative.

4. Watch an episode of *The Simpsons* and count and describe the number of intertextual references. Then watch some television commercials to see if you notice intertextual references in them. Do any of them reference other television programs?

5. Using a VCR or a recordable DVD, record some television programs and then construct a postmodern pastiche from parts of the recording. Can you do this without constructing a narrative?

6. To what extent do you rely on reason and universal theories? To what extent have you found reason and general theories prevalent in your education?

7. Other than television, what experiences in your life could be considered postmodern?

8. Watch a television event that has no meaning at all. Describe your reaction to it. Does it give you pleasure? If so, explain.

9. Locate an example of a television program that has an overlap of the modern and the postmodern. Describe it in your own words.

10. Watch some music videos on MTV for an hour. Describe what you have gained from the experience.

11. Look for influences of MTV in another television program or commercial and describe it.

12. How does the remote control or recording device such as a VCR or DVR give you control over television?

Suggested Readings

Berger, Arthur A. (Ed.). (1998). *The Postmodern Presence: Readings on Post-modernism in American Culture and Society.* Walnut Creek, CA: Altamira Press.

Best, Steven & Kellner, Douglas. (1991). *Postmodern Theory: Critical Interrogations.* New York: Guilford Press.

Brooker, Peter & Brooker, Will (Eds.). (1997). *Postmodern After-Images: A Reader in Film, Television and Video.* London, UK: Arnold.

Jencks, Charles. (1989). *What is Post-Modernism?* (3rd ed.). London, UK: St. Martin's Press.

Kaplan, E. Ann. (1993). *Postmodernism and Its Discontents.* London, UK: Verso.

PART IV

Critical Applications

9

Guidelines for Television Criticism

Introduction

Now that you understand the various aspects of television as a business, production procedures, television style, narrative, genre, elements of rhetoric and cultural studies, representation, and postmodernism, you are ready to do an in-depth analysis of a television program or an episode from a series. Whether you select fiction or nonfiction programming is entirely up to you. Select a program that you can record and will not mind viewing several times because you will need to examine several aspects of it. Select a program that you want to question or one with which you are familiar. As stated in Chapter 1, it is perfectly acceptable to analyze a favorite program or one that suits your interests and tastes. Your goals are to understand the various elements of a television program, to analyze it, to interpret possible meanings, to judge the quality of the program, and to communicate your assessment in writing.

This chapter brings together the elements of the previous chapters into eight sections: (1) critical orientation; (2) story and genre; (3) organization; (4) demographics; (5) context; (6) the look of the program and its codes; (7) analysis; and (8) judgment. Each category includes questions that you can ask about a television program. Depending on what you want to know about the program, you can select a few or all of the categories. Not all the questions will be relevant to the program you have selected, so you can choose the questions that are most pertinent. The questions are necessarily general, thus you can tailor them to fit the elements of the program you have chosen and the intent of your criticism.

To use the eight categories of questions in this chapter, the television critic needs to be familiar with the contents of the previous eight chapters of this book. I have used the ideas, theories, and methods of the previous chapters to develop questions for analysis and criticism. Rather than repeat unnecessarily, I have assumed that you have read the previous chapters and have participated in the exercises at the end of each chapter.

You will not want to use all the questions in this chapter nor do you need to. I hope that you will pick and choose the questions that will be most useful to you as you conduct your analysis. The more you watch the program you have selected to critique, the more you will see.

Critical Orientation

After you have selected the television program you want to analyze, ask initially what you want to know about it. Assess how you react to it and make a list of those reactions, for example, laughter, fright, shock, anger, empathy, relaxation, boredom, tension, curiosity, and so on. If it is an episodic program, try to be aware of other episodes. You can check the program's Web site for episode summaries, the names of the characters, the cast, the characters' back stories, the production staff, and possibly blogs by the writers, which may give you some insight into the motivation behind the script. The easiest way to locate television programs' Web sites is to use a search engine such as Google or Yahoo. If it is a series or specialty programming, you can check the Nielsen ratings on the Web. Also, you can purchase or check out books about the program from the library, bookstore, or online booksellers. Check to see if the book is unauthorized or is the official companion to the show. Unauthorized books may not be accurate although they may contain useful information. In the authorized books, you are likely to find interviews with the creators, the writers, the producers, the cast, and the consultants. You also may find episode summaries with names of guest actors, writers of particular episodes, and directors. Books such as *CSI: Crime Scene Investigation Companion* (2004) and *Behind the Scenes at ER* (1995) include glossaries of scientific terms used in the programs. *This Thing of Ours: Investigating The Sopranos* (2002) includes 10 pages of intertextual references from the first two seasons of *The Sopranos*. Sources such as these can save you time in searching for background details.

Here are some questions to ask for critical orientation.

1. What attracted you to this program?

2. Do you identify with any of the characters?

3. Does the program have a personality or an actor whom you enjoy watching?

4. Are there relationships in the program that you find intriguing?

5. What interests you about the story or the contents of the program?

6. Is the program novel in some way, especially in comparison to other television programs?

7. Is this a program that you are willing to take seriously and spend a lot of time with?

8. Do you talk to your friends about the program?

Story and Genre

Now that you have selected a program to analyze, watch it in its entirety and identify its genre. A very important question to ask at this stage is "How is the story told?" For most television narratives, there is deferred gratification and viewer anticipation. The critic asks how these factors occur.

For example, the television series *Monk* on USA Network could be considered a hybrid genre, for although it is mostly about solving crime, it also has some comedy in it. As a crime show, it features San Francisco police officers and a special detective named Adrian Monk. It is 60 minutes in length and has an ensemble cast. It features a new crime and its solution each week. As a comedy, it sometimes provokes laughter in a workplace setting. The comedy comes mainly from the character of Monk, expertly played by Emmy award–winning Tony Shalhoub, who suffers from the obsessive-compulsive disorder brought on by the murder of his wife. Monk is afraid of germs, crowds, and disorder. He is constantly putting things back in order, in straight lines. Although obsessive-compulsive disorder is a very serious condition, the comedy comes about because Monk constantly gets himself into situations that put him in crowds, get him dirty, and create disorder. The ensemble cast includes a detective named Randy who is always saying and doing dumb things. There is also an upbeat, jazzy song (*It's a Jungle Out There*) with the opening credits that suggests lightheartedness. The show, however, centers on Monk's uncanny ability to solve a crime. He is perceptive, very intelligent, and determined to track down the criminals. Thus, as an audience, we can expect to see how the clues come together to solve a crime, but we can also expect to be exposed to humor.

As a narrative, *Monk* follows the disequilibrium (lack)/equilibrium or enigma, delay, and resolution formula in linear fashion in four acts. In the episode "Mr. Monk Can't See," a fireman is killed in the fire station where Monk has brought 30 fire alarms to be tested, which is symptomatic of his obsessive-compulsiveness, for he uses all of them in just five rooms. The other firemen have gone to a five-alarm fire, thus the hero Monk is alone with the killer (the villain) who throws a chemical solution in his eyes and escapes. The lack is that Monk cannot see and consequently becomes very depressed. The enigma is twofold: Will the killer be caught? and Will Monk regain his eyesight? The delay is Monk's reluctance to work. To keep him active, the police captain, Leland Stottlemeyer, persuades Monk to help solve the crime. At the fire station, Monk touches the coat rack and discovers that there are five coats—but there were six when he was there earlier. His obsessive-compulsiveness reveals the first clue: the killer stole a fireman's coat so he could go back to the burning house to retrieve something he left there that would identify him. This leads the detectives to connect the five-alarm fire that killed a young woman to the murder of the fireman. In a filthy alley where the coat was thrown in a dumpster, Monk discovers that if he cannot see dirt, he is not afraid of it, and he is elated. This helps him regain his confidence and eventually solve the crime, creating a resolution. However, Monk realizes that the fireman's killer was also hired by another villain, Peter Breen, to kill the woman in the fire—thus another enigma is created with a delay while Monk tries to connect Breen to the killer. He does so and regains his sight in time to shoot Breen who has gone after him with a knife. The murders are solved; Monk's lack is removed; equilibrium is restored. The epilogue depicts a relaxed Monk reading a book in his living room. He looks at the picture of his departed wife and smiles, thus there is closure until the next episode.

As a hero, Monk has superior abilities that he uses to complete his task. Others cannot solve the crime without his help. His obsessive-compulsive disorder gives him insight into things that the other detectives do not have. Because he obsessively counts things, he discovers the missing coat. As an injured hero, he cannot see, but resourcefully uses his intelligence and per-ceptiveness to track down the villains. Although blinded, Monk is not a mythical prophet like the Greek Tiresias who prophesized the future; Monk is, however, modeled after the archetypal hero who faces obstruction (blind-ness) but overcomes it to complete a task.

Here are some questions that the critic can ask about the story and genre.

1. What are the conventions that make up the genre?

2. If the program appears to be a hybrid genre, what are the conventions of the genres that have been combined to make it a hybrid?

3. What are audience expectations of that particular genre?

4. What is the narrative progression? Describe the events.

5. How is time presented? Are the events successive? Do they go back and forth in time, or do events occur simultaneously?

6. What is the lack or disequilibrium, and how is the lack removed to restore equilibrium?

7. Is there a hero or heroine and a villain or villainy? How is the hero or villain represented? What are their actions, and how can their personalities be derived from their actions? Does the hero or villain have superior abilities?

8. How does conflict play out? Are there oppositions such as good and evil, legal and illegal, work and home, and/or masculine and feminine?

9. Is there closure or delay until the next episode? How is this presented?

10. Identify the stages of the hermeneutic code—enigma, delay, and resolution— that move the narrative forward. (The enigma engages viewer interest by presenting a riddle such as "who committed the crime?" and teases the viewer to guess what happens next. The delay stalls or postpones the solution to the enigma. A resolution to the enigma is finally found, but it may create another enigma.) Can you identify the enigma, delay, and resolution or several of them in the narrative?

11. Are there elements of older stories that are retold in the narrative?

12. Can you identify myths? Do the myths give lessons for social order?

13. Are there archetypes and rituals in the narrative? If so, how do they relate to the myths?

Organization

Examine the parts of the program—the lead-in, the acts, the scenes, and the ending.

Opening Segment

An example from *ER* illustrates what you can look for in the opening. After five rapid-paced scenes from previous episodes, the lead-in consisted of two different events that created tension: the first was in Dr. Luka Kovac's apartment where he and nurse Sam Taggert talked about a separation; the second is at the L-train station where two twenty-something women in fashionable suits and high-heeled shoes did not acknowledge Dr. Abby Lockhart's request to hold the door for her as she rushed to get on the train. She managed to squeeze in the door as it was closing and sat with Dr. Neela Rasgotra, while the other two women whispered and stared at Abby and Neela who were dressed casually in jeans and flat, homely shoes. Abby confronted the two women about their whispering, whereupon one said with giggles and sarcasm, "Your shoes look comfortable." When they got off of the train, one of the women in high heels twisted her ankle and sat on a bench. Neela went to help her, telling her that her ankle might have been broken, but the woman snobbishly said, "I want a second opinion." Abby turned around and said, "I'm Dr. Lockhart and my opinion is that your ankle is broken, and you are a bitch!" whereupon Abby and Neela walked away. The mood in these two events shifted from the sadness that Luka felt to an angry confrontation between two different types of women. Abby and Neela were established as unconcerned about their appearance, while the two fashionable women were established as superficial. Despite their snobbish treatment of Neela and Abby, Neela tried to help the woman with the injury, while Abby was acerbic in her dismissal of the woman. Both these events created tension that would be heightened in the acts to follow and created the question, "What happens next?" Following the lead-in, the signature music and credits were presented. The familiar percussion beats and electronic musical notes that signify *ER* were heard while "ER" appeared in two different-sized fonts, "ER" and "ER." Then in very quick succession, the eight leading actors were pictured in muted shades of gray in the context of emergency room cases with their names at the bottom of the frame as each one was shown aiding a patient. Finally, a large "er" in lowercase letters was shown in the middle of the screen as the music faded. The mood that was evoked by the credits included rushing, urgency, and stress. The mood of the characters that was established by the lead-in was that Luka was sad and Abby and Neela were angry because they were regarded as "others" by the fashionably dressed women. The viewer knows, however, that these women are truly the "others" because they are superficial.

Here are some questions to ask about the opening of the program.

1. Does the program have a collage of scenes from former shows at the beginning? ("Previously on . . .) If so, do they create a sense of tension and curiosity about what will happen next?

2. What happens in the lead-in, the beginning of the narrative that sets the scene? How does it entice the viewer to stay with the program?

3. Look and listen to the opening credits. What mood does the music create? Are there other sounds? Are the characters introduced to you in some context? Are the titles symbolic in their appearance, color, or placement?

4. What mood is evoked by the lead-in and by the credits?

The Structure of the Program

After the opening sequence, look at the structure of the show. If it is a 30-minute show, there should be two acts; if it is a 60-minute show, there should be four acts. Examine the acts and scenes for their structure. If there are commercials, note how the scenes before and after the commercials accommodate them. Here are some questions to ask about structure.

1. How do the scenes build on one another?

2. Does the show have a beginning, a middle, and an end?

3. Are there connectives between the scenes and between the acts?

4. If there are commercial breaks, how does the scene before the commercial end? How does the scene after the commercial begin? What gives the scenes continuity?

5. When the show comes to an end, is there closure or is the plot left open until next time?

6. What happens during the closing credits?

7. How are the previews for the next show presented? Are they immediately after the end of the program or after the commercials?

Demographics

Demographics—the description of groups of people according to gender, age, race, ethnicity, occupation, income, educational level, and shared values—identify target audiences for television programs, sponsors, and advertisers. There are different ways to determine the demographics for a television program. The story line and the ways in which the contents and characters are incorporated into the program should offer strong hints about the potential audience. The day and time that the program is scheduled reveal general information about the intended audience. Information found on the Internet and in books about the program may include demographics. If there are commercials, the intended audience can be interpreted from them. Product placement within the narrative provides clues about the audience as well. Some of the questions you can ask to interpret demographics follow.

1. Whom does the program "hail"? In order to be a subject of the program, what is the expected social position of the audience?

2. To what demographic group is the subject of the program likely to appeal?

3. Are the characters and the actors who portray them young adults, children, middle-aged, or seniors? Are the characters supposed to be single, members of families, lower, middle, or upper class?

4. What are their domestic arrangements? Are the domestic arrangements traditional or nontraditional? What are their domestic surroundings like?

5. If there is product placement embedded in the program, what do the products tell you about the intended audience?

6. If there are commercials between the acts and scenes, at whom are the advertisements aimed?

7. Are the advertised products low, average, or high priced?

8. Are the advertised products for young or older adults, children, or pets?

9. Are the advertisements aimed at singles or couples, male or female, parents or grandparents?

10. Are food advertisements for home cooking, fast foods, or restaurants?

11. To what age groups are medical advertisements targeted?

12. Do the commercials specify certain interests or hobbies?

13. What lifestyles do the advertisements suggest?

Context

Context refers to what is happening in the world. Context embraces the concept of "ripped from the headlines," television stories that reflect actual events. Events can be serious such as threats of terrorism to places and people or they can be more lighthearted as in situation comedies. An episode of the situation comedy *The King of Queens*, which aired one week before the 2006 Academy Awards show, included two contextual references. The lead character Doug's buddy Spence had enough frequent flyer miles for two trips and tried to talk Doug into going with him on an archeological dig. Doug said he did not want to go. When Spence asked him where they could go, Doug replied, "Not *Brokeback Mountain*," mentioning the name of a highly regarded film nominated for several Academy Awards. Because the film is about the love affair of two men, Doug's remark suggested his reluctance to go on a trip with a male friend. The main plot of the show dealt with an infestation of bedbugs in Doug's house, which had been brought in by an uncle who previously had gone to a resort. Not long before the show aired, there had been warnings in newspapers and news magazines about people carrying bedbugs from hotels into their homes. Thus, you can expect the plots of situation comedies also to be "ripped from the headlines."

Context also includes cultural values, social issues, trends, and fads. Intertextuality means that the television program contains references to other events, real or imagined, fiction or nonfiction. Here are some questions to ask about context.

1. How do the characters and events in the program reflect real people and events?

2. What societal and cultural values are represented in the television images and discourse?

3. Does the program reinforce or challenge mainstream societal and cultural values?

4. Are contextual and social issues clearly referenced or are they embedded in the plot?

5. What ordinary personal issues and attributes are recognizable?

6. Can viewers recognize their own fallibility in the characters in the program?

7. What evidence of fads and trends can be detected in the images and discourse?

8. Are there intertextual references to real events and people?

9. Is it possible to specify an attributed intent or a message to the program?

10. What do you think is the expected reaction from the audience?

The Look of the Program and Its Codes

How a program looks contributes to its believability and to the emotions that are conveyed, thus it has to do with the sets, the casting of characters, costumes, makeup, dialogue, physical movement, music, and sound effects. The look of a program is accomplished by camera work, lighting, editing, and direction. Here are some questions to ask about the look of a program and the reality and representation codes.

1. Are the events located in an indoor studio dressed to look like a home, an office, a hospital, coffee shop, bar, restaurant, or another place? Do events take place outdoors in a city, suburb, or rural area?

2. If you are looking at an indoor set, what makes it look realistic and natural? What objects, furniture, and other articles contribute to the look?

3. Are the colors bright or subdued? How do the colors contribute to the overall look of the set? Do the colors create mood?

4. How do the objects, furniture, and other articles reflect the characters in the set?

5. Are the objects, furniture, and other articles consistent with the time period of the program?

6. What elements provide an authentic look to outdoor scenes? Is there ambient sound?

7. Is there symbolism in the outdoor scenes?

8. Do the actors who were cast for the parts seem right for the characters they play? What personal and physical attributes of the actors contribute to the personalities of their characters on the program?

9. Do the characters have depth or just a few characteristics? Are there repetitive characteristics that reinforce a character's personality? Are any of the characters social types (easily recognizable people such as hippies, hillbillies, yuppies, Southern belles, gangsters, cowboys, maids, and so on)?

10. Do the costumes the actors wear seem realistic? How do the costumes reflect the characters' personalities?

11. Is the makeup natural? Does the makeup convey something about the character?

12. How do the physical actions of the characters reveal their personalities and/or motives?

13. Do the actors express their feelings through facial expressions? Can you observe what the character is feeling but not saying in the subtexts of facial expressions and physical movements? Does sound reinforce the subtext?

14. Does the dialogue sound realistic? What is included and what is left out in the dialogue that could engage the viewer to fill in information or speculation?

15. Is there music in the program other than in the opening credits? If so, what do you think is its intended purpose?

16. If there are sound effects, do they complement the dialogue and action? Can you attach meaning to the sound effects?

17. How does the camera work—the shots (close, medium, or long), movement, and angles—convey the characters' emotions, reactions, and personality characteristics?

18. When there are different shot lengths, how do they move the narrative forward?

19. Do you see "elbows" shots? How do they enhance the story or character?

20. How are reaction shots used to play off characters against one another? Does the silent reaction of a character reveal a subtext?

21. How do the camera work and editing convey continuity or discontinuity in the narrative?

22. Is the lighting bright or dark? What effect does the lighting have on the mood of the program?

23. Are certain actors given special lighting? How can you tell this?

24. If you were the director, would you change any of the shots, lighting, or sound?

25. If you classify the program as postmodern, how would you justify this? In other words, what are the characteristics of the program that make it postmodern?

26. Does the program have a signature look? If so, describe it.

27. How do the producers of the program get the viewer to believe that what is seen is really there?

Analysis

To analyze means to take something apart; synthesis means to put it back together. As a television critic, you are taking a television program apart in order to understand and evaluate it. Your insights are developed from your knowledge of the critical process. Your interpretation will have given you a deeper understanding of a television program, and your readers will benefit from your work by seeing a television program in a different way. How you approach your analysis of the television program depends upon the questions that you ask of it. Because a television program is made for an audience, questions of analysis focus on audience involvement in the program and how that is accomplished. You will not want to use all the questions for analysis that follow, but they are listed here for your selection.

1. How are ideas developed in the program? How are the ideas adjusted to people and people to ideas?

2. Can you hear laughter from the studio audience? If so, is it likely to provoke laughter from the viewer? Is there any evidence of "canned" laughter from a laugh track?

3. What personal, cultural, and national values are inherent in the program or in certain characters and issues? How are the values communicated?

4. Are there moral lessons? How are they developed? Is the concept of *telos*—a life of moral excellence—evident in the program?

5. Are evidence and reasoning used to support a conclusion? Does the program ask the viewer to participate in the co-creation of reasoning?

6. What emotional appeals are present? How are they conveyed?

7. What shared substances can you detect that may lead the audience to identify with the program's characters, ideas, and lessons?

8. What are the qualities of the characters or real people such as news anchors, game show hosts, and participants on reality shows that are likely to create positive identification for audience members?

9. Can you attribute an intention to the program? If so, is it to persuade or inform?

10. How do you think the program may influence certain types of viewers? Does the program have the capability to influence attitudes, beliefs, values, and behaviors? Could it influence fashion, hairstyles, or body image?

11. How does the program relate to the shared conditions of its time—the culture?

12. Who or what has power or domination over others in the program? Whose voice is heard and whose is not? Who asks questions and who supplies the answers? What issues are given importance and which ones are not?

13. Is there an ideology that assigns roles to certain people or that advocates a set of norms for all to follow? Is there hegemony, where the subordinates are led to consent to the system that subordinates them? Have the subordinates "consented" to accept the social system as natural? Have the subordinates reversed the power structure causing the subordinates to become powerful and the dominant ones to become weak?

14. What is present and what is absent? How is the viewer limited in ways of seeing?

15. Could the viewer place oneself inside the image, identifying with it? If so, what does the viewer get out of the image through the identification?

16. How does the program position the viewer as a subject? How does the program "hail" the viewer?

17. What meanings are preferred by the program? In other words, what are the dominant meanings? What meanings (polysemy) can different viewers make from the program? What meanings can be derived from resisting the dominant meaning? What meanings can be derived from negotiating with the dominant meaning?

18. How might the decoded meanings give the viewer a sense of power or pleasure? How is this related to the viewer's sense of identity?

19. How could the program help the viewer as subject make sense of social experience?

20. Does the program have the potential to be absorbed into the lives of the viewers? Might they take on new meanings, new identities, and/or new knowledge?

21. As a television critic examining the polysemous meanings, do you discover anything about yourself?

22. Does the representation of characters, places, and events seem natural? Is it possible for the viewer to recognize these characters, places, and events through the representations?

23. How are people represented in categories of gender, race, ethnicity, age, occupation, and physical capabilities?

24. Who is represented and who is not? Is anyone represented as the "other"? Is anyone classified with a loss of individual differences? Are there stereotypes?

25. If there are symbols, how can they be recognized and how do they function? What is the frame of reference for symbolization?

26. Does identification of intertextuality heighten the pleasure derived from the program?

Judgment

While recognizing the limitations of the medium of television, the time allotted, and the business constraints of the television industry, you are ready to evaluate what has been created and how it is presented. Incorporate your answers to the questions you chose to ask in making your judgment. Your judgment is an original contribution and, as such, your conclusions should be substantiated with clear analysis and description. Your evaluation of the program should be based on critical standards such as these:

1. A television program should accomplish what it sets out to do and do it well.

2. A television program should provide entertainment or information.

3. A television program should be well written, engage and respect its audience, and allow for audience involvement and identification.

4. A television program should be professionally produced in such a way that the audience can accept what it sees and hears.

5. You can design your own criteria developed from your questions for analysis.

Writing Television Criticism

To communicate your evaluation in writing, you will have the following six topic areas in your paper, (1) an introduction with a thesis sentence, a statement of the purpose of your critique, and material that orients the reader to your topic; (2) a description of the television show and a summary of the narrative; (3) production information about the show's creators, cast, and popularity; (4) a description of your critical approach to the program and the questions you chose to ask; (5) your interpretation of the categories you have chosen with examples from the program that describe and clarify what you found; and (6) your overall evaluation and your contribution to understanding the program. Topic 5, your interpretation, will constitute the bulk of your written evaluation.

When you write television criticism, use the vocabulary of criticism; for example, when you discuss narrative, use specialized terms such as "enigma," "delay," and "resolution," and when you talk about allusions to other media, use the term "intertextuality." It is not sufficient, however, to merely use the vocabulary, for you must explain what it means and how it is presented in the television program.

Always proofread your writing, and use a dictionary and thesaurus for accuracy and variety. Write to your readers; that is, keep in mind that you have an audience. Remember that your goal is to offer insights to the reader in order to help him or her see television in a new way.

Summary

With guidelines, television criticism can be rewarding and fun to do. Although you are using specific questions for analysis, your work is subjective criticism, dependent on your ability to closely examine the elements of a television program. If you want to check your own objectivity, you can try the same approach on a different program or episode to measure how reliable your interpretations are. It is also possible to work with a coauthor to get different perceptions and points of view.

If at all possible, try to get tickets to a television show in production. It does not matter whether it is a local or national studio; either way, it will enhance your understanding of the creative process to visit a studio and watch either a run-through or a filming of a program.

As a television critic, you will have gained insights that are educational and useful to you. These insights will change the way you watch television, making it more enjoyable. If you plan to produce television, you will have a greater awareness of what television is and what it can accomplish. Overall, you will have become a more discerning consumer of television.

10

Sample Criticism of a Television Program: *CSI: Crime Scene Investigation*

Season 4, Episode 17, "XX"

Introduction

Television crime dramas often feature police officers or detectives solving crimes by means of the interrogation of suspects or shoot-outs with criminals. In 2000, a different crime drama began that emphasizes brainpower over gun power. It went into its seventh season in the fall of 2006. Inspired by Barry Scheck's testimony in the O. J. Simpson trial in 1995, actual crimes that occurred in Las Vegas and elsewhere, and the writers' imaginations, *CSI: Crime Scene Investigation* features the examination of scientific evidence by forensic scientists to solve crimes. The scripts focus viewer attention on evidence with lines like "Concentrate on only one thing—the evidence—what cannot lie," "There is always a clue. I follow evidence until it leads to the truth," and "There is no room for subjectivity in this department. We handle each case objectively."

Thesis

CSI has a distinctive visual style, tells a compelling story with moral undertones, and represents different genders and ethnic groups as professional, competent, and powerful. It also invites viewer participation in examining evidence and following the reasoning used to resolve the crimes. *CSI* also includes dialogue, music, and colors to remind the viewer that it is, after all, entertainment.

Purpose

The purpose of this analysis is to critically examine the television program *CSI: Crime Scene Investigation* for its visual style, its story and substance, the representation of forensic science and scientists, and the ways that it encourages viewer involvement in examination of the evidence and the solution to crimes. In addition, production information about the show has been included to provide insight into its origins and the producers' motives.

Description of CSI

CSI: Crime Scene Investigation is broadcast on Thursday nights on CBS. It has been ranked as number 1 in the Nielsen ratings for three years, slipping to third place in the 2005–2006 after Fox's Tuesday and Wednesday night broadcasts of *American Idol* (Levin, 25 May 2006, p. 3D). It has enjoyed worldwide popularity from the United States to Asia. *CSI* features forensic scientists who work in the Las Vegas Police Department Crime Scene Investigations Bureau using the latest scientific and technical methods to examine criminal evidence and solve crimes. As a crime drama, it is not necessarily a "whodunit," but rather it functions as a "howdunnit." It has been described as "a mixture of Sherlock Holmes and Viva Las Vegas" (Willam C. Paley Television Festival, 2001).

CSI is popular with young people and has had tremendous influence on their career choices. For example, in 2001 West Virginia University's forensic science program had three students, but in 2005 it had 400. Since *CSI* went on the air, there have been 10,000 applications for forensic science positions in the Las Vegas Police Department (Tomashoff, 2005, p. 29).

CSI has inspired two spin-off programs, *CSI: Miami* and *CSI: New York* as well as book-length novelizations of the episodes. Each episode features one or two crimes, starting at point A and ending with a complete resolution at point B. (There was an exception when a two-part episode, "A Bullet Runs Through It" extended over two weeks in the fourth season of the show.) It has been mostly consistent in its format, production values, and ensemble cast since its inception in 2000.

Because Las Vegas is a city of entertainment and gambling, there is a constant influx of criminals and their victims. The fictional Las Vegas Police Department's night shift ("graveyard shift") Crime Scene Investigations Bureau is led by Gil Grissom, senior forensics officer and former coroner, and his elite team of investigators who use their scientific skills and state-of-the-art equipment to examine evidence, often from unlikely sources. The team members are Catherine Willows, a single mother trying to juggle her job and being a parent; Nick Stokes and Warrick Brown, who often compete to see who can solve a case; Sara Sidle, an intelligent, young scientist; and Captain Jim Brass, a homicide captain who used to work in forensics. Assisting them are lab technician Greg Sanders, who moved up to the investigation team in the 2005–2006 season, Dr. Al Robbins, the medical examiner, Dr. David Phillips, the assistant coroner, and various laboratory technicians.

Description of the Episode

The episode that is criticized here is entitled "XX" and aired on March 4, 2004. Two unrelated events occur: (1) body parts are found on a car windshield and under a bus that was transporting women inmates from a prison to a work-release program; and (2) a man is found stabbed to death in his brother's apartment. Catherine Willows and Nick Stokes work the body parts case while Gil Grissom and Warrick Brown investigate the stabbing death. Greg Sanders and Wallace Langham assist with the laboratory duties. Although Catherine, Nick, and Captain Brass believe that the woman whose body parts were found was trying to escape from prison by tying herself beneath the bus, they discover that she was murdered by another inmate. Gil and Warrick examine the evidence to determine that the man stabbed himself to commit suicide after losing all of his brother's money in a gambling scheme. This episode was directed by Deran Sarafian and written by Ethlie Ann Vare, who also wrote three other episodes.

Production Information

The Museum of Television and Radio, with locations in Los Angeles and New York City, holds seminars with producers, directors, writers, and actors of television shows. The production information presented here is from two of their seminars, which can be viewed on tape in either of the museum's facilities (The William S. Paley Television Festival, 2001, 3 March, and The Shooting of the Dead: The Look of CSI, 2001, 3 October). The following quotations about the production of *CSI* are from the seminars, unless otherwise noted. The members of the panels included Anthony Zuiker, the creator and executive producer of *CSI*; Carol Mendelsohn, co-executive producer; Ann Donahue, executive producer; Jonathan Littman, consulting producer; Danny Cannon, director and production consultant; Michael Barrett, director of photography; Alex Smight, editor; Bruce Golin, postproduction supervisor; Richard Berg, production designer; and actors William Petersen (Gil Grissom); Marg Helgenberger (Catherine Willows); George Eads (Nick Stokes); Jorja Fox (Sara Sidle); and Paul Guilfoyle (Jim Brass).

Anthony Zuiker traveled with the Las Vegas Police during the graveyard shift for five weeks, observing their work. He said, "When I did the research for the show at the crime lab in Las Vegas, the first thing I noticed was that they will go to five or six crime scenes a night. [Thus], the use of multiple story lines is intentional and an attempt at verisimilitude" (Flaherty, 2004, p. 15). As a result Zuiker wrote a script, his first, and Jonathan Littman pitched it to CBS twice before they bought it. The writers are Zuiker, Mendelsohn, Donahue, and others. They base their scripts on real crime stories and on their imagination. Before *CSI,* Zuiker drove a tram at the Mirage Hotel where he saw "all kinds of people, many crazy, authentic characters in Las Vegas" on which he bases some of the characters in his scripts. They also consulted a former CSI forensic pathologist, Liz Devine, who joined the staff full time to help with the forensic science and the actors' pronunciation of scientific terms. Everyone connected with the show reads a lot of science, including anatomy books. The writers also discuss science in production meetings. Donahue said they often break writing rules because "We try to tell our stories visually." She also said, "It used to be you never wrote a flashback, but Anthony wrote flashbacks, and they worked."

The show is produced near Los Angeles, but the cast and crew go to Las Vegas for every four or five shows to get a better feel for the city. All the equipment in the laboratory set, which is in Santa Clarita, California, is real, including a $50,000 microscope. Joel Stein, in an article about *CSI* for *Time* magazine, wrote, "The *CSI* set could serve as one of the country's best crime labs, since it boasts cutting-edge equipment donated by publicity-seeking manufacturers" (Stein, 2003, p. 72).

CSI has a unique visual look, carefully designed by the production staff. Danny Cannon, the director, said, "We wanted a different visual style [to take the viewers inside a world they have never seen]. I always ask, 'Can I see it?'" As a result, the show uses extreme close-ups, explained Cannon. "We really show you forensics—large enough so you can see what a hair follicle looks like. There are snap-zooms—snap into a body or zoom into a piece of evidence." Jonathan Littman said, "We go into the body, making it almost three-dimensional. We have made TV director-centric. TV is moving toward high definition. We'd all better develop a more visual attitude." The production staff said that they give the show a "heightened look," more like film than television. They use color to convey emotions. Two cameras are used to film the action, which they described as "creeping cameras to keep people guessing." Great care is taken for each scene. The production team may spend two hours with a setup for one line in a scene. Flashbacks are filmed with an 8-millimeter camera to make them look like home movies.

The audience is included in the examination of evidence along with the characters. All the members of the staff and the cast credited the audience for being able to follow the trail of the evidence. They said they wanted to make the audience work, to make them reach. William Petersen said, "We supply 30 percent and expect the audience to supply 70 percent of the subtext. We hope to challenge people cerebrally as they watch the show."

The wardrobe choices for Gil include monochromatic colors, whereas Catherine's clothes may be more flamboyant. Marg Helgenberger, who plays Catherine, said that she is interested in Catherine's back story, for she used to be an exotic dancer. Helgenberger said, "She treats evidence the way she treated males in the audience." She said the style of acting is very different because "you look at the evidence without speaking and the audience knows what you're feeling."

Postproduction work supplies the special effects that are developed by the movie staff who made the film *Black Hawk Down*. *CSI* is a Jerry Bruckheimer production, thus the directors, set designers, costumers, and makeup artists are Hollywood film people. Bruckheimer, who reads every outline and script and watches the "dailies" and editing, said, according to Cannon, that they should push the limits of their creativity. He told Cannon, "Push it—go darker."

Zuiker claims the audience base for *CSI* ranges from 6 to 60. He said that the show has influenced many young people to go into forensic science. He said there has been a 5,000-fold increase in students wanting to major in the field.

Questions for Analysis

I chose the following questions for analysis to achieve the purpose stated at the beginning of this chapter. I then clustered the questions into four headings: Visual Style, Story and Substance, Representation, and Viewer Involvement. The emphasis for this critique is on rhetorical and cultural analysis, especially audience involvement, and the ways in which the visual style contributes to the overall effect.

1. Visual Style
   A. How does the camera work—the shots (close, medium, or long), movement, and angles—convey the characters' emotions, reactions, and personality characteristics?
   B. Is the lighting bright or dark? What effect does the lighting have on the mood of the program?
   C. Are the colors bright or subdued? How do the colors contribute to the overall look of the set? Do the colors create mood?
   D. What elements provide an authentic look to outdoor scenes?
   E. Do the costumes the actors wear seem realistic? How do the costumes reflect the characters' personalities?
   F. Do the actors express their feelings through facial expressions? Can you observe what the character is feeling but not saying in the subtexts of facial expressions and physical movements?

2. Story and Substance
   A. Identify the stages of the hermeneutic code—enigma, delay, and resolution—that move the narrative forward.
   B. What happens in the lead-in, the beginning of the narrative that sets the scene? How does it entice the viewer to stay with the program?
   C. Look and listen to the opening credits. What mood does the music create: Are the characters introduced in some context? What mood is evoked by the lead-in and credits?
   D. How are ideas developed in the program? How are the ideas adjusted to people and people to ideas?
   E. Are there moral lessons? How are they developed?
   F. Are evidence and reasoning used to support a conclusion? Does the program ask the viewer to participate in the co-creation of reasoning?
   G. What emotional appeals are present? How are they conveyed?
   H. Who or what has power or domination over others in the program? Whose voice is heard and whose is not? Who asks questions and who supplies the answers?
   I. Is there an ideology that assigns roles to certain people or that advocates a set of norms for all to follow?
   J. What meanings are preferred by the program?

3. Representation
   A. Does the representation of characters, places, and events seem natural?
   B. Do the characters have depth or just a few characteristics? Are the characters and actors who portray them young adults, children, middle-aged, or seniors? Are the characters supposed to be single, members of families, lower, middle, or upper class?
   C. How are people represented in categories of gender, race, ethnicity, age, occupation, and physical capabilities?

4. Viewer Involvement
   A. To what demographic group is the subject of the program likely to appeal? At whom are the commercials aimed? What lifestyles do the advertisements suggest?
   B. How do you think the program may influence certain types of viewers?
   C. How does the program position the viewer as a subject? How does the program "hail" the viewer?

Analysis and Interpretation

Visual Style

The overall look of *CSI* is dark. The characters tend to be in dark spaces; subdued lighting creates shadows over parts of their faces. For example, as Gil and Warrick examine the dark room where a man named Adanto Adams lies dead from stab wounds, their faces in close-up shots are half-lit as they photograph the body. When Sara and Nick go to the women's prison during the day, the cell that they examine is quite dark. Nick uses a blue light to look for blood under the cot. Presumably, it needs to be dark to use a blue light. Using flashlights, Nick and Sara examine the back of the prison bus— it is dark in the bus even though it is daylight outside. Their faces are also half-lit in close-up. In the autopsy room where Gil and Dr. Robbins examine Adanto's body, the lighting is blue to suggest objectivity; Gil and Robbins have dark shadows on their faces. The darkness and the shadows on their faces, however, do not suggest that the characters are sinister. Rather the mood is very serious and the characters appear to be very intensely focused on the evidence. The camera lingers in close-ups on the evidence—body parts, stab wounds, the dead woman's skull. When Warrick and a lab technician examine handwriting samples, the camera moves in for extreme close-ups of the written letters as the technician explains what they mean. The bloody, mangled body parts are also filmed in lingering close-up shots as Catherine picks up each one, putting a number card beside it as she photographs them. One brightly lit close-up shot is of one of the victim's feet. It suggests a sense of sadness rather than gore or repulsiveness.

The establishing shot of the women's prison is a low-angle shot looking up at the barbed wire and light pole. It is brightly lit with lots of yellow, as are the aerial shots of the desert that follow. This tells us that the prison is in the desert, in a desolate, dry locale where the sun beats down on it. In this episode, each act begins with an establishing shot. There are three high-angle, aerial long shots of the Las Vegas hotels and casinos at night and one at dusk. Basically, these shots function to tell the viewer the time of day and location.

Visual Credits

The credits begin with an aerial long shot of Las Vegas at night, and the subsequent shots are very dark. There are a lot of neon green and blue colors against black backgrounds as the cast is introduced in close-ups. The signature "snap-zoom" shots are prevalent as a blood splatter is grossly magnified to individual platelets that change from red to green. Images that appear to be DNA spirals change colors from neon green to red. A single blue-lit eye fills the frame; then the camera zooms into the pupil with the lights turning it from yellow to blue. Danny Cannon developed a way to use a periscope lens to create the illusion of going inside a body. Zuiker said, "We wanted to create a point of view that we'd never seen before in television—to see what a bullet looks like when it goes into a body" (Flaherty, 2004, p. 15). There are several abstract images in black, blue, and red. A red cylinder turns to blood splatter. Hands covered in surgical gloves holding a test tube are lit in neon green. The colors add visual interest suggesting something surreal. The moods that the visual images create are those of urgency, discovery, and curiosity. The viewer is being led to understand that this is a show about evidence and laboratory analysis used to solve crimes.

The "XX" episode has 10 grainy, gritty flashbacks related to the two deaths. Cannon said, "When we want to really kick everyone's teeth in with the flashbacks, it's hard and grainy and gritty" (Flaherty, 2004, p. 87). Zuiker explained their use. "You see tiny alterations in every flashback until the final piece of evidence is put into place in Act 4, and then that flashback contains an alteration that makes you go 'Ah, that's what happened!' " (Flaherty, 2004, p. 15).

The sets have a realistic look about them. The apartment where Adanto was stabbed is sparsely furnished and the hallway outside appears to be old and rundown. The overall impression is that this is a cheap apartment house. In one scene, Warrick goes to a casino at The Palms Hotel to check on Adanto's gambling. The prevalence of gambling machines with colored lights and gaming tables, the variety of colors of clothing on the customers, and the ambient sounds of bells and clattering coins seem natural for the setting. The cells in the women's prison are small, stark, and furnished only with the bare necessities. These cells give the impression of cramped space and unpleasantness. The sets that are the laboratories are spacious, clean, and appear to have the latest equipment. Interestingly, the laboratories are not brightly lit; rather there is ambient light from the equipment, but the background is shaded in subdued colors. One would expect a laboratory to be brightly lit, but perhaps the darkened background suggests that the characters are dealing with death and murder.

Photo 10.1   Warrick and the laboratory's handwriting analyst examine the
evidence on *CSI*.

The wardrobe for the actors consists of dark jackets and pants. Greg, the laboratory technician, was the only character who wore a light color in this episode. In the fourth season, Greg is considered to be a somewhat goofy character with a choppy haircut highlighted in toffee-colored streaks. (In Season 6, Greg became an investigator with a conservative haircut and darker clothing.) The dark clothing of the characters matches the mood of the dark interior shots, again suggesting intensity and seriousness. At the beginning of this episode, Catherine wears dark slacks, a jacket, and a cap. She is dressed for being outdoors in cool weather. In Act 2, Catherine appears in the lab in a very low-cut and revealing black top. This suggests her past as an exotic dancer and that she is a sexy woman. Presumably, her appearance also holds some viewers' interest.

Subtexts are revealed in Catherine's facial expressions. In the opening teaser, as she and Nick discuss the woman whose body parts are on the road and under the bus, Nick says that the bus must have spit the body parts down the road. Catherine says, "If the bus is going 65 miles per hour, what's the distance from the tip of her nose to the tip of her toes?" The expression on her face is almost one of amusement. It suggests that she is hardened to the horror of death or that she copes with it by using humor. In another scene with Dr. Robbins, Catherine watches while he performs a pregnancy test on the corpse. (He has assembled her body parts.) When he tells Catherine that the test is positive, the camera moves in close to Catherine's face as she says, "Who's your daddy?" Although there is some humor in the way she says it, it also suggests that this is a clue to the woman's murder. In a later scene, Catherine has a triumphant look on her face when she discovers the murder weapon and says, "A lock in a sock." Catherine is a mother, so she may be mimicking Dr. Seuss, the popular children's book author who makes those kinds of rhymes. Ann Donahue, who enjoys writing for the Catherine character, said, "I am in love with the way that Marg does a scene. She knows how to throw lines away better than anybody since Lauren Bacall. She plays text, subtext, and sub-subtext, and when she's in a scene you cannot take your eyes off her" (Flaherty, 2004, p. 87).

Gary Dourdan, who plays Warrick, also has strong facial expressions that suggest subtexts. When he returns from the casino and watches the casino's surveillance tapes that show Adanto losing all of his mentally disabled brother's inheritance at the blackjack table, the expression on Warrick's face is one of sympathy. The definite impression is that he knows how it feels to lose all your money when gambling. (It helps the viewer to know that Warrick used to have a gambling problem. This is his back story and also the subject of previous episodes.) When Gil asks him what he thinks Adanto's state of mind was, Warrick answers with one word, "Desperate," while his face takes on a desolate expression. Warrick then returns to the crime scene, the brother's apartment, where he imagines Adanto killing himself. When the viewer sees in the flashback that it was indeed suicide, it is anticipated because Warrick has indicated as much with his facial expressions.

The visual style and acting of the "XX" episode reveal a dark world of death and sadness without being frightening or righteous. The characters are intensely dedicated to their work, but they also exhibit a strong sense of humanity.

Story and Substance

The lead-in does not include scenes from previous episodes. It opens with a couple driving behind a bus; the driver of the car keeps honking at the bus to go faster while the woman in the passenger seat says, "Just pass him." Suddenly a disembodied arm lands on the windshield. It is a shocking image. Next there is an elbows shot of Brass who is approached by Catherine and Nick asking if there is a dead body. Brass tells them that the driver of the car saw the arm shoot out from under the bus that was taking women prisoners to a work-release site. Catherine looks under the bus and sees body parts tied to the undercarriage. She and Nick discuss it, assuming that the dead woman was trying to escape from prison. The lead-in ends there, enticing the viewer to stay with the program to find out what happened and to whom the body parts belong. Because the lead-in to the story began immediately after the previous program, the viewers are not likely to change the channel once they are hooked.

The visual credits were discussed under the "Visual Style" heading. Here the credits are considered as a way to introduce the characters and set the mood. The credits begin with an aerial shot of Las Vegas at night as a musical note begins the *CSI* theme song, *Who Are You?* sung by The Who, a famous rock group. White letters—"CSI"—are superimposed on blue and green; the next shot is the same but spells out "CRIME SCENE INVESTI-GATION" at the bottom in case the viewers do not know what *CSI* stands for. The next shot is of the backs of five people in silhouette. It is possible to make out William Petersen and possibly Marg Helgenberger, but it is hard to make out their identities. The figures stand tall, feet firmly planted on the ground, indicating confidence and authority. The camera then moves into a close-up of an unidentified male in surgical gloves holding a magnifying glass. The top of the screen has a commercial slogan "and Volkswagen—On the Road of Life" that reminds us of one of the sponsors. The cast is introduced with Petersen first, wearing gloves and shining a flashlight on something and then using a fingerprint duster. His credit says "starring William Petersen" as he is shown in close-up. It is clear that he is the star of the show even though it is an ensemble cast. At the top of the next screen it says, "There are passengers and there are drivers," another Volkswagen slogan that also suggests that the CSI team has power for they are the drivers. Next there is a long corridor that looks like the walls of a subway. Blood spatters appear, magnified to fill the screen. The Who sings *Who Are You?* as we see a person who appears to be a doctor looking at an x-ray of a human torso. Marg Helgenberger is the second cast member shown as the camera moves into a close-up of her face—she is looking at a corpse. The next shot is a neon green-lit hand in gloves holding a test tube as the song continues, "Who, who, who." Then there appears to be a blood vessel magnified many times over as the camera zooms in on it while the music goes "Who, who, who, who." The screen is filled with what appear to be green blood platelets; then the camera zooms in on what look like DNA spirals. The third cast member who is introduced is Gary Dourdan looking into a closet with a flashlight. Then there is a close-up of an eye, turning from yellow to blue. Is this supposed to be Dourdan's eye? George Eads is introduced next in a close-up as the song continues, "Who are you?" He smiles with bright, white, and perfect teeth. The next scene shows Petersen once again with smoke surrounding his body but with no caption. Then Jorja Fox is shown shining a flashlight on a mattress, and then her face is seen in close-up as the music continues, "I really wanna know." Eric Szmanda, who plays Greg, appears next looking into a microscope. Then Robert David Hall, the actor who plays Dr. Robbins, is seen with a scalpel in his hand as the song continues, "Oh, Oh, Oh, Who." Last there is a medium long shot of Paul Guilfoyle, cast as Captain Jim Brass. He walks into a room and begins firing a gun. He is the only one of the cast in the credits with a visible gun. This demonstrates that he is a police officer, not a forensic scientist. The song finishes "Come on, tell me who are you, you, you," as the image fades to a blue and black abstraction. Then there is a skull, lit in green, x-rays, and finally, the screen says "Created by Anthony E. Zuiker." All of this happens in two minutes.

The opening credits accomplish two things: (1) They introduce the cast in a hierarchy of importance. They are viewed in the context of their various work roles that indicates that they are professional criminal investigators. There is nothing in the credits to indicate anything about their personal lives. (2) The credits set a mood that suggests a serious consideration of microscopic evidence viewed with laboratory equipment.

The song, *Who Are You?* suggests that the crime scene scientists are trying to identify their victims, but the song also reminds us that the show is provided for entertainment. Furthermore, the song is a signature musical brand for *CSI*.

Hermeneutic Code

In "XX," there are two enigmas that create disequilibrium in the narrative: (1) Was the young woman (Antoinette Stella, whose prison name was Baby Girl), whose body parts were found, murdered, and, if so, by whom? and (2) Who stabbed Adanto? There are several delays—first, Catherine and Nick believed that Baby Girl died while trying to escape, and second, Gil and Warrick surmise that Adanto was murdered. As they examine the many pieces of evidence and eliminate suspects, they prove that Baby Girl was murdered by her cellmate, who tied her body beneath the bus, and that Adanto stabbed himself in a suicide because he had lost all of his brother's money. One major delay in the case of Baby Girl was the strong suspicion that the bus driver killed her. When Sara interviewed him, he made crude remarks about the women prisoners and indicated that he used a woman prisoner named Juana to clean out his bus and his own personal vehicle. Another delay had to do with the five equally placed stab wounds on

Adanto's body. The narrative progresses in a straightforward fashion, interrupted only by the flashbacks, as the crime scene analysts use evidence and reasoning to support their conclusions. The story does, however, move back and forth between the two investigations, suggesting real time.

Photo 10.2   Sara and Nick interview the prison bus driver.

Warrick's evidence included the surveillance tape that showed Adanto losing all his money and the marks in the apartment door that Warrick deduced were made by Adanto to hold the knife that he rammed his body against. His reasoning was based on his past experiences as a gambler because he understood desperation. There was also a strong moral lesson in the gambling incident because the casino manager said that every loser has a system. Adanto's naïve belief in his gambling system caused him to lose his brother's inheritance. His brother and guardian were questioned but ruled out as suspects. The brother, named Zero, was described as "a nine-year old in a man's body," thus he was left without the means to live alone and attend a special school.

Catherine examined the records of Baby Girl's commissary purchases to determine that the girl was pregnant. This was confirmed by a pregnancy test performed by Dr. Robbins. Greg tested the DNA to prove that the bus driver was the father. Nick and Wallace, the lab technician, tried to identify the tattoo on Baby Girl's arm, but were mystified by it. They also could not understand how she could get a tattoo in a prison that is set in a desert miles from any businesses. Sara came to their rescue when she recognized the tattoo as half a heart and told them that the dye came from a desert insect known as a cochineal. They asked Sara how she knew that, and her reply was that Gil had given her an entomology book for Christmas. Nick and Wallace exchanged looks, remarking, "Gil didn't give me anything for Christmas." This is a vague allusion to the implied attraction between Gil and Sara in previous episodes.

When Catherine interrogated Juana, she saw the other half of the heart tattooed on her arm and realized that she was the killer, but first she had to find the weapon. First she looked through Juana's laundry and, not finding anything, asked to see her socks. A combination lock from her locker had been placed inside Juana's bloody sock, and Catherine surmised that it was used to bash in Baby Girl's head. This is when she said, "A lock in a sock." As all the clues fall into place, the viewer can reason along with the characters, anticipating and therefore accepting the resolutions. This is also referred to as an "action code" (see Barthes's narrative theory in Chapter 4), which makes complex ideas immediately recognizable to the audience, while at the same time, the significance becomes apparent in the narrative. The audience thus becomes the coauthor of the story.

This episode focuses on the power that the police force has over suspects and criminals. When the prison warden protests Catherine's DNA tests on the prison staff members, Catherine produces a warrant that immediately gives her the power to conduct the tests. The bus driver is taken into custody and interrogated even though he protested that he did not kill Baby Girl. Although Gil is the team leader, he does not exert any authority over his team members in this episode, nor do the men act superior to the women in any way. The two women investigators have knowledge power, for it is Sara who tells the men what Baby Girl's tattoo means when they are unable to figure it out, and it is Catherine who solves the crime.

The women prisoners are surface characters, for they constitute "the other," the powerless outcasts from society. The bus driver tells Sara that he cannot care about them because "they will return to their pimp boyfriends when they get out." Juana's character, however, has depth that can elicit sympathy from the audience. Catherine talks to Juana who tells her how lonely it is in prison. Catherine recognizes that Juana had been used by a man who let her take the rap for drugs. Catherine discloses that her "ex" cleaned out the savings she had hoped to use for a house for her and her daughter. Thus, although Juana is identified as the murderer, it appears that Catherine handles her with empathy, or else Catherine is clever in extracting a confession from Juana by attempting to identify with her. As the murderer and a prisoner, Juana is also the "other."

Zero, Adanto's mentally disabled brother, is also an "other." His name was given to him by playmates, according to his guardian. His dialogue and facial expressions are simplistic, although he is able to articulate his previous conversation with his brother, and he attends school. Yet, he is different, powerless, and thus an "other."

The explicit meanings in this episode are: (1) crime does not pay; (2) casino gambling is a no-win situation that hurts people; and (3) smart and dedicated forensic scientists gather evidence to solve crimes. Yet, Catherine extracted a confession by appearing to bond with Juana, and Warrick relied on intuition and his past gambling experiences to realize that Adanto committed suicide. Although evidence was used in each case to get to the point, emotional reasoning was used to resolve the enigmas and restore equilibrium.

Implicit meanings in the episode are: (1) Juana and Baby Girl were lovers, although Juana said, "I'm not like that." Yet Juana killed Baby Girl because she had sex with the bus driver after she had promised Juana that she would end her involvement with him. Also, the half a heart on each woman's arm symbolized love, although this was never articulated in the episode. (2) Greg's gambling past is never spoken about, yet it is apparent that he understands the desperation of losing a lot of money. (3) Sara's mention of a Christmas gift from Gil suggests that they may have a personal relationship.

What does the title, "XX," mean? There are no clues to its meaning in the episode. "XX" is never used in the dialogue. Does it mean the Roman numeral 20? If so, why? Does it mean "to wipe something out"? Perhaps. There is no information about the meaning of the title on the *CSI* Web pages. It is an unresolved enigma, not in the narrative but to this critic.

The ideology is that justice is on the side of the law. Adanto's brother and guardian and the bus driver are found innocent following interrogation and examination of the evidence. The last scene is a very high-angle shot looking down on Juana being put into a cell where she lies on her bed and looks up with despair. We know that she will stay in prison for a long time.

Representation

Catherine, Sara, and the prison warden are slender, beautiful women. Zuiker said he wanted to create flawed characters to make them more human, but this does not apply to the women's appearances. We see them as beautiful actresses rather than real people although we can accept their characters. The actors who portray the characters range in age from the late 20s to late 40s, which is realistic. Nick and Warrick are young and handsome, while Gil and Dr. Robbins are somewhat overweight and middle-aged. Each character has depth and a recognizable personality. In this episode, there is no mention of the characters' personal lives other than the slight hint about Sara and Gil and Catherine's disclosure about her ex-husband.

The principals in the ensemble cast consist of two women and five men, one of whom (Gary Dourdan) is an African American. Archie Kao, a laboratory technician, appears to be a Korean-American, but he has a small role. The prison warden is an African American woman with power and authority; however, the close-up shots of her face reveal expert makeup that emphasizes her beauty. She is both beautiful and powerful in her job, but she must yield to Catherine's power of having an official warrant to test the prison staff for DNA. Juana is a young Hispanic actress, who is also very attractive, but as a prisoner, she is the "other." Robert David Hall, who plays Dr. Robbins, is a double-leg amputee, but this is never referred to in any of the episodes and is known only because of his biography on the Internet. In other episodes of *CSI*, more women and African Americans have been represented. "XX," however, has a majority of white males.

Viewer Involvement

Although Zuiker said that the audience for *CSI* ranges from 6 to 60, the commercials are aimed at young, affluent men and women. The commercials are for high-priced cars, power drinks, cosmetics, credit cards, toothbrushes, mouthwash, motor oil, hand sanitizers, cell phones, a fitness studio, and a movie that opens the following day. These products suggest an active lifestyle for people who can afford it and who care about their appearance, hygiene, fancy cars, and entertainment.

Because the viewers are invited to examine the evidence and the clues, and follow the development of the resolution, they are expected to be intelligent and willing to learn about forensic science. Also because some of the anatomical shots are gruesome, the viewers are expected to be strong enough to look at them. Thus, as subjects, the viewers are hailed as intelligent, curious, youthful, and interested in crime stories.

Summary

CSI ranks high in the ratings, thus it has attracted a very large audience. It is a different kind of crime show, in both its visuals and narrative. Although the characters are well drawn and have become very familiar, science is the star of the show.

I think that *CSI* fulfils the criteria for a good television show outlined in Chapter 9. It accomplishes what it sets out to do. It provides entertainment *and* information. It is generally well written, engages and respects its audience, and certainly allows for audience involvement. It is professionally produced in such a way that the audience can accept what it sees and hears.

Suggested Readings

Flaherty, Mike. (2004). *CSI: Crime Scene Investigation Companion.* New York: Pocket Books.

Ramsland, Katherine. (2001). *The Forensic Science of C. S. I.* New York: Berkley Boulevard Books.

References

Abelman, R. (1998). *Reaching a critical mass: A critical analysis of television entertainment.* Mahwah, NJ: Lawrence Erlbaum.

Adler, R. B. (Ed.). (1981). *Understanding television: Essays on television as a social and cultural force.* New York: Praeger.

Akass, K. & McCabe, J. (Eds.). (2004). *Reading Sex and the City.* London, UK: I. B. Tauris.

Allan, M. D. (2005). The late, late comer. *Los Angeles Times Magazine,* 18 December (pp. 14–17, 32).

Allen, R. C. (Ed.). (1992). *Channels of discourse, reassembled* (2nd ed.). Chapel Hill, NC: University of North Carolina Press.

Allen, R. C. & Hill, A. (Eds.). (2004). *The television studies reader.* London, UK: Routledge.

American Playhouse. (1992). [seminar on videotape], 16 December. Beverly Hills: Museum of Television and Radio.

Andrejevic, M. (2004). *Reality TV: The work of being watched.* Lanham, MD: Rowman and Littlefield.

Andrews, J. R., Leff, M. C., & Terrill, R. (1998). *Reading rhetorical texts: An introduction to criticism.* Boston: Houghton Mifflin.

Ang, I. (1990). Melodramatic identifications: Television fiction and women's fantasy. In M. E. Brown (Ed.), *Television and women's culture.* Newbury Park, CA: Sage Publications.

Aristotle. (333 BCE). (trans. Lane Cooper) (1932). *The rhetoric of Aristotle.* New York: Appleton-Century-Crofts.

Arnold, C. C. & Bowers, J. W. (1984). *Handbook of rhetorical and communication theory.* Boston: Allyn & Bacon.

The Art of the Music Video. (1997). Rochester, NY: Eastman Kodak Company.

Associated Press. (2001). Morning TV shows busy promoting parent companies. *Bozeman Daily Chronicle,* 23 November (p. C3).

Associated Press. (2003). Tuning into television. *Bozeman Daily Chronicle,* 31 August (p. A7).

Associated Press. (2004). Super Bowl ads. *Bozeman Daily Chronicle*, 1 February (p. C4).

Associated Press (2005). 'Stealth ads' infiltrate TV programming. *Bozeman Daily Chronicle*, 22 July (p. TW21).

Auto pilot, it's not, as fall season nears (1998). *USA Today*, 30 June (p. D3).

Avins, M. (2005). The high life without airs. *Los Angeles Times*, 25 May (pp. F1, 10).

Barker, C. (2000). *Cultural studies: Theory and practice*. Thousand Oaks, CA: Sage Publications.

Barnouw, E. (1978). *Sponsor: Note on a modern potentate*. Oxford, UK: Oxford University Press.

Barreca, R., Ed. (2002). *A sitdown with the Sopranos: Watching Italian American culture on TV's most talked-about series*. New York: Palgrave Macmillan.

Barthes, R. (1974). *S/Z: An essay* (trans. Richard Miller). New York: Hill and Wang.

Battaglio, S. (2001). Late-night time is still the right time. *The New York Times*, 23 September (pp. 21 & 27).

Bauder, D. (2005). Lacking, perhaps, help from above, 'Joan' is gone. *Orange County Register*, 30 May (p. Life 6).

Bauder, D. (2005). Nielsen enters DVR generation. *Bozeman Daily Chronicle*, Dec. 19 (p. A2).

Bauder, D. (2006). NBC cancels West Wing after 7 seasons. ABC News, 22 January. Retrieved January 22, 2006 from http://abcnews.go.com.

Bellafante, G. (1996). Makeover mania: network series old and new are getting radical—and often last minute—revamps. *Time*, 16 September (p. 78).

Bellamy, R. V., Jr. & Walker, J. R. (1996). *Television and the remote control: Grazing on a vast wasteland*. New York: The Guilford Press.

Berg, A. (2005). *The Writers Grotto*, 9 November. Retrieved October 6, 2006 from http://www.cbs.com/primetime/threshold/blog.php.

Berger, A. A. (1997). *Narratives in popular culture, media, and everyday life*. Thousand Oaks, CA: Sage Publications.

Berger, A. A., Ed. (1998). *The postmodern presence: Readings on postmodernism in American culture and society*. Walnut Creek, CA: Altamira Press.

Berko, L. (1994). Surveilled: Video, space, and subjectivity. In N. Browne (Ed.), *American television: New directions in history and theory* (pp. 223–254). Langhorne, PA: Harwood.

Best, S. & Kellner, D. (1991). *Postmodern theory: Critical interrogations*. New York: Guilford Press.

Bianco, R. (2000). Producers went back to Ohio to find show's humor. *USA Today*, 1 November (p. D5).

Bianco, R. (2003). Building a better sitcom. *USA Today*, 11 April (p. E1, E4).

Bianco, R. (2004). The family is back, and life is good. *USA Today*, 17 February (p. E2).

Bignell, J. (2004). *An introduction to television studies*. London, UK: Routledge.

Bobbin, J. (2005). Networks stagger start and ending times. *LA Times TV Schedule*, 4 April (p. 17).

Bogle, D. (2001). *Prime time blues: African Americans on network television.* New York: Farrar, Straus and Giroux.

Boxer, S. (2003). McLuhan's messages, echoing in Iraq coverage. *The New York Times,* 3 April. Retrieved April 3, 2003 from http://www.nytimes.com.

Brock, B. L., Ed. (1999). *Kenneth Burke and the 21st century.* Albany, NY: State University of New York Press.

Brock, B. L., Scott, R. L., & Chesebro, J. W. (1989). *Methods of rhetorical criticism: A twentieth-century perspective.* Detroit: Wayne State University Press.

Brooker, P. & Brooker, W., Ed. (1997). *Postmodern after-images: A reader in film, television and video.* London, UK: Arnold.

Brown, J. A. (1997). "Television Criticism (Journalistic)". In H. Newcomb (Ed.), *Encyclopedia of Television,* Vol. 3 (pp. 1643–1644). Chicago: Fitzroy Dearborn.

Brown, M. E. (1990). *Television and women's culture.* Newbury Park, CA: Sage Publications.

Browne, N. (1994). *American television: New directions in history and theory.* Langhorne, PA: Harwood.

Bruner, J. (1973). The course of cognitive growth. In J. Angin (Ed.). *Beyond the information given: Studies in the psychology of knowing.* New York: W. W. Norton.

Bryant, D. C. (1953). Rhetoric: Its function and scope. *Quarterly Journal of Speech, 39,* 401–424.

Burke, K. (1931/1957). *Counter-statement.* Chicago: University of Chicago Press.

Burke, K. (1935/1984). *Permanence and change: An anatomy of purpose.* Berkeley, CA: University of California Press.

Burke, K. (1950/1969). *A rhetoric of motives* (reprint). Berkeley, CA: University of California Press.

Burns, G. & Thompson, R. J. (Eds.). (1989) *Television studies: Textual analysis.* New York: Praeger.

Butler, J. G. (2002). *Television: Critical methods and applications.* Mahwah, NJ: Lawrence Erlbaum.

Buzzard, K. S. (1990) *Chains of gold: Marketing the ratings and rating the markets* (p. 137). Metuchen, NJ: Scarecrow Press.

Byrne, B. (2002). "Friends" turns 200. *Eonline,* 7 November. Retrieved April 3, 2003 from http://netscape.eonline.com.

Caldwell, J. T. (1995). *Televisuality: Style, crisis, and authority in American television.* New Brunswick, NJ: Rutgers University Press.

Campbell, J. (1972). *Myths to live by.* New York: Bantam Books.

Campbell, J. (1988). *The power of myth.* New York: Anchor Books.

Carpenter, E. (1974). *Oh, what a blow the phantom gave me.* New York: Bantam.

Carter, B. & Rutenberg, J. (2003). ABC and WB unveil fall lineups. *The New York Times.* Retrieved May 14, 2003 from http://www.nytimes.com.

Carter, B. (2004). "Friends" finale's audience is fourth biggest ever. *The New York Times.* Retrieved May 8, 2004 from www.nytimes.com

Carter, C. (2001). Lecture at Montana State University. (23 April).

Casey, B., Casey, N., Calvert, B., French, L., & Lewis, J. (2002). *Television studies: The key concepts.* London, UK: Routledge.

Carvell, T. (1997). Why sweeps matter! Film at 11! *Fortune, V. 135,* January 13. (p. 22).

Cavanaugh, T. (2006). Happy 40th birthday Star Trek. *Reason,* August/September. (pp. 57–64).

Chocano, C. (2004). Heartless hit. *Los Angeles Times,* 4 June. (pp. E1 and E25).

Ciesielski, D. "Secular Pragmatism": Kenneth Burke and the [Re]socialization of literature and theory. In B. L. Brock (Ed.). (1999). *Kenneth Burke and the 21st century* (pp. 243–267). Albany, NY: State University of New York Press.

Collins, J. (1992). Postmodernism and television. In R. C. Allen (Ed.), *Channels of discourse* (pp. 327–353). Chapel Hill: The University of North Carolina Press.

Congress to audit Nielsen system (2004). *USA Today,* 14 May on line. Retrieved October 6, 2004 from www.usatoday.com/life/television/news/2005-05-13-nielsen-system-debate_x.htm

Cooper, M. (1989). *Analyzing public discourse.* Prospect Heights, IL: Waveland Press.

Couldry, N. (2000). *Inside culture: Re-imagining the method of cultural studies.* London, UK: Sage Publications.

Creating prime-time drama: *Law & Order* (11 November 1997). [University satellite seminar]. Beverly Hills: Museum of Television and Radio.

Creating prime-time comedy: *The Simpsons* (12 February 2003). [brochure] Beverly Hills: Museum of Television and Radio.

The creative process (1997). [Seminar on videotape], October 8. Beverly Hills: Museum of Television and Radio.

Creeber, G. (Ed.). (2001). *The television genre book.* Berkeley, CA: University of California Press.

Cruz, J. & Lewis, J. (Eds.). (1999). *Viewing, reading, listening: Audiences and cultural reception.* Boulder, CO: Westview Press.

Cunningham, S. (2005). Culture, services, knowledge: Television between policy regimes. In J. Wasko (Ed.). *A companion to television* (pp. 199–215.) Malden, MA: Blackwell.

Della Femina, J. (2001). The final score: Beer 21, dot coms 0. *The Wall Street Journal,* 26 January (p. A14).

Deming, C. J. (1990). For television-centered television criticism: Lessons from feminism. In M. E. Brown (Ed.), *Television and women's culture.* Newbury Park, CA: Sage Publications.

Deming, C. (2005). Locating the televisual in Golden Age television. In J. Wasko (Ed.), *A companion to television.* Malden, MA: Blackwell.

DiMaggio, M. (1990). *How to write for television.* New York: Fireside.

Dines, G. & Humez, J. M. (Eds.) (2003). *Gender, race, and class in media.* Thousand Oaks, CA: Sage Publications.

Dintrone, C. V. (2003). *Television program master index* (2nd ed.). Jefferson, NC: McFarland.

Donnelly, W. J. (1996). *Planning media: Strategy and imagination* (p. 184). Upper Saddle River, NJ: Prentice Hall.

Dow, B. J. (1996). *Prime-time feminism: Television, media culture, and the women's movement since 1970.* Philadelphia: University of Pennsylvania Press.

Dow, B. J. (2001). Television and the politics of gay and lesbian visibility. *Critical Studies in Media Communication, 18*(June), 123–140.

Early, F. & Kennedy, K. (Eds.). (2003). *Athena's daughters: Television's new women warriors.* Syracuse, NY: Syracuse University Press.

Edgerton, G. R. & Rose, B. G. (2005). *Thinking outside the box: A contemporary genre reader.* Lexington, KY: University Press of Kentucky.

Elliott, S. (2003). Altered reality: ABC's new show "All American Girl" will work in products of sponsors. *The New York Times,* 12 March. (p. C7).

Ellis, J. (1982). *Visible fictions: Cinema, television, video.* London, UK: Routledge & Kegan Paul.

Evans, J. & Hall, S. (Eds.). (1999). *Visual culture: The reader.* London, UK: Sage Publications.

Farhi, P. (1997). The eye that never blinks. *The Washington Post National Weekly Edition,* 12 May (p. 21).

Farhi, P. (1998). TV violence: it's not all on the same wavelength. *The Washington Post National Weekly Edition,* 22 June (p. 21).

Farhi, P. (2000). TV's skin-deep approach to race. *The Washington Post National Weekly Edition,* 21 February (p. 23).

Fejes, F. (2003). Advertising and the political economy of lesbian/gay identity. In G. Dines & J. M. Humez (Eds.), *Gender, race, and class in media* (pp. 212–222). Thousand Oaks, CA: Sage Publications.

Fernandez, M. E. (2005). *Lost* takes an odd path to diversity. *Los Angeles Times,* 13 February (pp. E1, E30).

Fernandez, M. E. (2005). *Raymond*'s writers get ideas from their families. *Los Angeles Times,* 11 May (p. E7).

Fisher, W. R. (1989). *Human communication as narration: Toward a philosophy of reason, value, and action.* Columbia, SC: University of South Carolina Press.

Fiske, J. (1987). *Television culture.* London, UK: Methuen.

Fiske, J. (1996). Opening the hallway: Some remarks on the fertility of Stuart Hall's contribution to critical theory. In D. Morley & K. Chen (Eds.), *Stuart Hall: Critical dialogues in cultural studies* (pp. 212–220). London, UK: Routledge.

Fiske, J. (1998). MTV: Post-structural, post-modern. In A. A. Berger (Ed.), *The postmodern presence: Readings on postmodernism in American culture and society* (pp. 166–179). Walnut Creek, CA: Altamira Press.

Flaherty, M. (2004). *CSI: Crime scene investigation companion.* New York: Pocket Books.

Foote, J. S. (Ed.). (1998). *Live from the trenches: The changing role of the television news correspondent.* Carbondale. IL: Southern Illinois University Press.

Foss, K. A. (2002). *Readings in contemporary rhetoric.* Long Grove, IL: Waveland.

Foss, S. K. (2004). *Rhetorical criticism: Exploration and practice* (3rd ed.). Long Grove, IL: Waveland.

Fox, NBC, CBS face indecency sanctions from FCC. Retrieved February 24, 2006 from http://www.museum.tv/archives/etv/F/htmlF/federalcommu.htm

Franklin, N. (2006). Bauer power: a new day dawns on 24. *The New Yorker,* 20 February (p. 174).

From Pitch to Polish: The Collaborative Process (1996). [seminar on videotape], 16 January. Beverly Hills: Museum of Television and Radio.

The Future, [3d of three seminars with Joshua Brand and John Falsey] (11 February 1993). [seminar on videotape] Beverly Hills: Museum of Television and Radio.

Gallagher, V. (2004). Memory as social action: Cultural projection and generic form in civil rights memorials. In P. A. Sullivan & S. R. Goldzwig (Eds.), *New approaches to rhetoric* (pp. 149–172). Thousand Oaks, CA: Sage Publications.

Gans, H. J. (2004, 1979). *Deciding what's news: A study of CBS Evening News, NBC Nightly News, Newsweek, and Time.* Evanston, IL: Northwestern University Press.

Gans, H. J. (2003). *Democracy and the news.* New York: Oxford University Press.

Gerbner, G., Gross, L., Signorelli, N., Morgan, M., & Jackson-Beeke, M. (1979, Summer). The demonstration of power: Violence profile no. 10. *Journal of Communication, 29,* 177–196.

Gergen, K. J. (1991). *The saturated self: Dilemmas of identity in contemporary life.* New York: Basic Books.

Gitlin, T. (1983). *Inside prime time.* New York: Pantheon Books.

Gitlin, T. (1998). Postmodernism: What are they talking about? In A. A. Berger (Ed.), *The postmodern presence: Readings on postmodernism in American culture and society* (pp. 58–73). Walnut Creek, CA: Altamira Press.

Gliatto, T. (2002). The dead zone. *People,* 14 October (pp. 113–115).

Golden, J. L. & Corbett, P. J. (1968). *The rhetoric of Blair, Campbell, and Whately.* New York: Holt, Rinehart and Winston.

Gomery, D. (2006). Cable News Network. Museum of Broadcast Communications. Retrieved January 21, 2006 from http://www.museum.tv/archives.

Grossberg, L. (1996). On postmodernism and articulation: An interview with Stuart Hall. In D. Morley & K. Chen (Eds.), *Stuart Hall: Critical dialogues in cultural studies* (pp. 131–150). London, UK: Routledge.

Grover, R. (1997). The art of the TV deal. *Business Week,* 2 June (p. 121).

Haigh, R. W., Gerbner, G., & Byrne, R. B. (1981). *Communications in the 21st century.* New York: John Wiley.

Hall, S. (1973). Encoding and decoding in the television discourse. Centre for Contemporary Cultural Studies Working Paper. Birmingham, UK: University of Birmingham.

Hall, S. (1997). *Representation.* Thousand Oaks, CA: Sage Publications.

Hall, S. (1999). Introduction to looking and subjectivity. In J. Evans & S. Hall (Eds.), *Visual culture: The reader.* London, UK: Sage Publications.

Hart, R. P. (1989). *Modern rhetorical criticism.* Glenview, IL: Scott, Foresman/Little Brown.

Hartsfield, R. (1990). TV, seriously. *Sky Magazine,* 84–90.

Harwood, R. (1998). The Brinkley transformation. *The Washington Post National Weekly Edition*, 26 January.

Hayles, N. K. (1990). *Chaos bound: Orderly disorder in contemporary literature and science*. Ithaca, NY: Cornell University Press.

Haynes Johnson delivers the Annenberg lecture (1994). *Newslink*, 4(1), 5.

Hayward, J. W. (1997). *Letters to Vanessa: On love, science, and awareness in an enchanted world*. Boston: Shambhala Publications.

Heath, R. L. (1986). *Realism and relativism: A perspective on Kenneth Burke*. Macon, GA: Mercer.

Helford, E. Rae (Ed.). (2000). *Fantasy girls: Gender in the new universe of science fiction and fantasy television*. Lanham, MD: Rowman and Littlefield.

Higgins, J. (1999). *Raymond Williams: Literature, Marxism, and cultural materialism*. London, UK: Routledge.

Hill, C. A. & Helmers, M., Eds. (2004). *Defining visual rhetorics*. Mahwah, NJ: Lawrence Erlbaum.

Hilliard, R. L. (1991). *Writing for television and radio*. Belmont, CA: Wadsworth.

Hinson, H. (2003). The show that doesn't start with a dead body. *The New York Times*, 9 March, Arts and Leisure, Section 2 (p. 10 AR).

Hirsch, E. (1999). *How to read a poem and fall in love with poetry*. New York: Harcourt Brace.

Hollywood in wartime: National mood guides filmmakers in times of crisis. (2001). *Bozeman Daily Chronicle*, 21 October (p. A6).

How Roy Wagner reveals the souls of characters on *House*. (2005). *In Camera*, October 3.

Hunt, D. M. (2005). *Channeling blackness: Studies on television and race in America*. New York: Oxford University Press.

Jameson, F. (1993). Postmodernism and the consumer society. In E. A. Kaplan (Ed.). *Postmodernism and its discontents: Theories, practices* (pp. 13–29). New York: Verso.

Jasinski, J. (2001). *Sourcebook on rhetoric: Key concepts in contemporary rhetorical studies*. Thousand Oaks, CA: Sage Publications.

Jencks, C. (1989). *What is post-modernism?* (3rd ed.). London, UK: St. Martin's Press.

Jeopardy! star Jennings gives show a boost (25 July 2004). *Bozeman Daily Chronicle*, p. A2.

Johannesen, R. L. (Ed.). (1971). *Contemporary theories of rhetoric: Selected readings*. New York: Harper and Row.

Jones, L. (1996). "'Last week we had an omen:' The mythological X-Files." In D. Lavery, A. Hague, & M. Cartwright, (Eds.), (1996). *Deny all knowledge: Reading The X-Files*. Syracuse, NY: Syracuse University Press.

Jowett, G. S. & O'Donnell, V. (2006). *Propaganda and persuasion*. Thousand Oaks, CA: Sage Publications.

Jung, C. G. (1971). (trans. R.F.C. Hull). *The portable Jung*. New York: Viking Press.

Jung, C. G. (1969). *Four archetypes: Mother/rebirth/spirit/trickster*. Princeton, NJ: Princeton University Press.

Justice on the small screen. (2005). *Los Angeles Times,* 17 December (p. B20).

Kaminsky, S. M. (1985). *American television genres.* Chicago: Nelson-Hall.

Kaplan, A. E. (Ed.), (1993). *Postmodernism and its discontents: Theories, practices.* New York: Verso.

Kaplan, A. E. (1998). Feminism/Oedipus/postmodernism: The Case of MTV. In A. A. Berger (Ed.), *The postmodern presence: Readings on postmodernism in American culture and society* (pp. 30–44). Walnut Creek, CA: Altamira Press.

Kellner, D. (2005). Critical perspectives on television from the Frankfurt School to postmodernism. In J. Wasko (Ed.), *A companion to television* (pp. 29–50). Malden, MA: Blackwell.

Kingston ends ER shift. (2004). *USA Today,* 8 June (p. D1).

Kolbert, E. (1994). Finding the absolutely perfect actor: The high-stress business of casting. *The New York Times,* 6 April (pp. C13 & C18).

Krieger, M. (Ed.). (1987). *The aims of pepresentation: Subject/text/history.* New York: Columbia University Press.

Kubey, R. (2004). *Creating television: Conversations with the people behind 50 years of American TV.* Mahwah, NJ: Lawrence Erlbaum.

Kubey, R. & Csikzentmihalyi, M. (1990). *Television and the quality of life: How viewing shapes everyday experience.* Mahwah, NJ: Lawrence Erlbaum.

Kuchler, S. & Mellion, W. (1991). *Images of memory: On remembering and representation.* Washington, DC: Smithsonian Institution Press.

Kuney, J. (1990). *Take one: Television directors on directing.* New York: Praeger.

Lavery, D. (Ed.). (2002). *This thing of ours: Investigating The Sopranos.* New York: Columbia University Press.

Lavery, D., Hague, A., & Cartwright, M. (Eds.). (1996). *Deny all knowledge: Reading The X-Files.* Syracuse, NY: Syracuse University Press.

Lévi-Strauss, C. (1963). *Structural anthropology* (trans. Jacobson, C. & Schoepf, B.). New York: Basic Books.

Lévi-Strauss, C. (1969). *The raw and the cooked* (trans. Weightman, J. & D.). New York: Harper and Row.

Levin, G. (1999). NBC tries to fix errors of comedy. *USA Today,* 21 June (p. D3).

Levin, G. (2006). Numbers add up for no. 1 CBS. *USA Today,* 25 May (p. D3).

Lewis, J. (2002). *Cultural studies: The basics.* London, UK: Sage Publications.

Lieberman, D. (1996). Static over TV ratings system. *USA Today,* 20 Feb. (p. 3B).

Lipsitz, G. (1990). *Time passages: Collective memory and American popular culture.* Minneapolis: University of Minnesota Press.

Lometti, G. E. (1997). Audience research: Industry and market analysis. In H. Newcomb (Ed.), *Encyclopedia of television,* Vol. 1 (p. 112). Chicago: Fitzroy Dearborn.

Longworth, J. L., Jr. (2002). *TV creators: Conversations with America's top producers of television drama* (vol. 2). Syracuse, NY: Syracuse University Press.

Loory, S. H. (2005). CNN today: A young giant stumbles. *Critical Studies in Mass Communication* 22(4), 340–343.

Lule, J. (October 2005). CNN at 25. *Critical Studies in Mass Communication* 22(4), 339.

MacNeil/Lehrer News Hour (1989). [seminar on videotape] Beverly Hills: Museum of Television and Radio.

The making of a prime-time schedule (1997). (University satellite seminar). Beverly Hills: Museum of Television and Radio. 15 October.

Malinowski, B. (1961). *Sex, culture, and myth*. New York: Harcourt, Brace, and World.

Marc, D. (1984). *Demographic vistas: Television in American culture*. Philadelphia: University of Pennsylvania Press.

Marc, D. (1989). *Comic visions: Television comedy and American culture*. Boston: Unwin Hyman.

Marc, D. (1995). *Bonfire of the humanities: Television, subliteracy, and long-term memory* (pp. 53–56). Syracuse, NY: Syracuse University Press.

Marc, D & Thompson, R. J. (1995). *Prime time, prime movers* (p. 223). Syracuse, NY: Syracuse University Press.

May, R. (1991). *The cry for myth*. New York: W. W. Norton.

McCarthy, M. (2004). Ad buyers bet on what will hit for new TV season. *USA Today*, 27 May, p. 6B.

McDowell, J. (2003). Gone in 60 seconds. *Time*, 29 September (p. 20).

McDowell, J. & Ressner, J. (2006). Brave new TV land. *Time Bonus Section*, April (pp. A1–A6).

Mead, G. H. (1934). *Mind, self, and society*. Chicago: University of Chicago Press.

Meehan, E. R. (2005). *Why TV is not our fault*. Lanham, MD: Rowman and Littlefield.

Metzler, K. (1979). *Newsgathering*. Englewood Cliffs, NJ: Prentice-Hall.

Meyers, R. (2004). Bad company. *Direct TV: The Guide*, March (pp. 15–19).

Meyrowitz, J. (1985). *No sense of place*. Oxford, UK: Oxford University Press.

Mitchell, P. (2002). TV's pandering to youth squanders media's power. *USA Today*, 12 June (p. A13).

Mitchell, W. J. T. (1995). *Picture theory: Essays on verbal and visual representation*. Chicago: University of Chicago Press.

Mittell, J. (2004). *Genre and television: From cop shows to cartoons in American culture*. New York: Routledge.

Monaco, P. (1998). *Understanding society, culture, and television*. Westport, CT: Praeger.

Morley, D. (1988). *Family television: Cultural power and domestic leisure*. London, UK: Routledge.

Morley, D. & Chen, K. (Eds.). (1996). *Stuart Hall: Critical dialogues in cultural studies*. London, UK: Routledge.

Munson, W. (1993). *All talk: The talkshow in media culture*. Philadelphia: Temple University Press.

Navarro, M. (16 May, 2002). Trying to get beyond the role of the maid. *The New York Times*. Retrieved May 16, 2002 from http://www.nytimes.com.

Nehamas, A. (1990). Serious Watching. *South Atlantic Quarterly*, 89(1), 157–180.

Newcomb, H. (Ed.). (1997) *Encyclopedia of television*. 3 vols. (p. 1482) Chicago: Fitzroy Dearborn.

Newcomb, H. (2005). Reflections on *TV: The Most Popular Art*. In G. R. Edgerton & B. G. Rose (Eds.), *Thinking outside the box: A contemporary genre reader* (pp. 17–36). Lexington, KY: University Press of Kentucky.

Newcomb, H. & Alley, R. S. (1983). *The producer's medium: Conversations with creators of American TV*. New York: Oxford University Press.

Newcomb, H., Ed. (2000). *Television: The critical view* (6th ed.). New York: Oxford University Press.

O'Connor, A., Ed. (1989). *Raymond Williams on television*. London, UK: Routledge.

O'Donnell, V. (1996). Interview with James Burrows, August 13, Hollywood, CA.

O'Donnell, V. (2004). Interview with Jeff Meyer, 15 May. Los Angeles, CA.

O'Donnell, V. (2006). Telephone interview with Jeff Meyer, 15 March.

O'Donnell, V. & Kable, J. (1982). *Persuasion: An interactive-dependence approach*. New York: Random House.

Ostrow, J. (2001). Hybrids old but different. *Denver Post*, 22 July, (pp. 1E and 7E).

O'Sullivan, T., Hartley, J., Saunders, D., Montgomery, M., & Fiske, J. (Eds.) (1994). *Key concepts in communication and cultural studies* (2nd ed.). London, UK: Routledge.

Ott, B. & Walter, C. (2000). Intertextuality: Interpretative practice and textual strategy. *Critical Studies in Mass Communication, 17*(4), 429–446.

Pecora, N. (2005). The changing face of children's television. In G. R. Edgerton & B. G. Rose (Eds.), *Thinking outside the box: A contemporary genre reader* (pp. 91–110). Lexington, KY: University Press of Kentucky.

Pomerantz, E. (2006). Why do advertisers still covet the 18–49s? *Television Quarterly, 36*(3&4), 40–44.

Poniewozik, J. (2004). Reheat and serve. *Time*, 2 February (pp. 64–65).

Porter M. (1998). The structure of television narratives. In L. R. Vande Berg, L. A.Wenner, & B. E. Gronbeck (Eds.), *Critical approaches to television*. Boston: Houghton Mifflin.

Poster, M. (2004). Postmodern virtualities. In R. C. Allen & A. Hill (Eds.), *The television studies reader* (pp. 581–595). London, UK: Routledge.

Pourray, J. (1995). *Behind the scenes at ER*. New York: Ballantine Books.

Priest, P. J. & Dominick, J. R. (1994). Pulp pulpits: Self-disclosure on *Donahue*. *Journal of Communication 44*(4), 74–97.

Prince, G. (1989). *Narrative, international encyclopedia of communications*, Vol. 3 (pp. 161–164). New York: Oxford University Press.

Ray, R. B. (1985). *A certain tendency of the Hollywood cinema: 1930–1980*. Princeton, NJ: Princeton University Press.

Rayner, P., Wall, P., & Kruger, S. (2004). *Media studies: The essential resource*. London, UK: Routledge.

Reed, J. S. (1986). *Southern folk, plain & fancy: Native white social types*. Athens, GA: University of Georgia Press.

Reuters, S. G. (2001). School violence replayed in TV dramas. Britannica.com .Retrieved June 1, 2001 from www.britannica....ews/reuters/article?story_id= 163923

Richter, D. H. (1989). *The critical tradition: Classic texts and contemporary trends.* New York: St. Martin's Press.

Robinson, P. (2005). The CNN effect revisited. *Critical Studies in Mass Communication, 22*(4), 344–349.

Rose, B. G. (Ed.). (1985). *TV genres: A handbook and reference guide.* Westport, CT: Greenwood Press.

Rosteck, T. (Ed.). (1999). *At the intersection: Cultural studies and rhetorical studies.* New York: Guilford Press.

Rubin, A. M. & Step, M. M. (1997). Viewing television talk shows. *Communication Research Reports, 14*(1), 106–115.

Russell, J. T. & Lane, W. R. (2002). *Kleppner's advertising procedure,* 15th ed. Upper Saddle River, NJ: Prentice Hall.

Samuels, A., Shorter, B., & Plaut, F. (1986). *A critical dictionary of Jungian analysis* (pp. 152–153). New York: Routledge.

Sandell, J. (1998). I'll be there for you: *Friends* and the fantasy of alternative families. *American Studies, 39*(2) (summer), 141–155.

Scholes, R. & Kellogg, R. (1966). *The nature of narrative.* London, UK: Oxford University Press.

Searle, J. R. (1979). *Expression and meaning: Studies in the theory of speech acts.* Cambridge, UK: Cambridge University Press.

Searle, J. R. (1984). *Minds, brains, and science.* Cambridge, MA: Harvard University Press.

Seiter, E. & Wilson, M. J. (2005). Soap opera survival tactics. In G. R. Edgerton & B. G. Rose (Eds.), *Thinking outside the box: A contemporary genre reader* (pp. 136–155). Lexington, KY: University Press of Kentucky.

The shooting of the dead: The look of *CSI* (2001). [seminar on video], 3 October. Beverly Hills: Museum of Television and Radio.

Silverstone, R. (1999). *Why study the media?* London, UK: Sage Publications.

Simon, R. (2005). The changing definition of reality television. In G. R. Edgerton & B. G. Rose (Eds.), *Thinking outside the box: A contemporary genre reader* (pp. 179–200). Lexington, KY: University Press of Kentucky.

Singer, J. A. & Salovey, P. (1993). *The remembered self: Emotion and memory in personality.* New York: Free Press.

Singhania, L. (2002). TV losing touch with Boomers. *Bozeman Daily Chronicle,* January 20, p. C3.

Smith, C. R. (1998). *Rhetoric and human consciousness: A history.* Prospect Heights, IL: Waveland Press.

Smith, R. R. (1976). *Beyond the wasteland: The criticism of broadcasting.* Falls Church, VA: National Communication Association.

Smith-Shomade, B. E. (2002). *Shaded lives: African-American women and television.* New Brunswick, NJ: Rutgers University Press.

Solomon, J. (1998). Our decentered culture: The postmodern world view. In A. A. Berger (Ed.), *The postmodern presence: Readings on postmodernism in American culture and society.* Walnut Creek, CA: Altamira Press.

Spigel, L. & Olsson, J. (Eds.). (2004). *Television after TV: Essays on a medium in transition*. Durham, NC: Duke University Press.

Stark, S. D. (1997). *Glued to the set: The 60 television shows and events that made us who we are today*. New York: Free Press.

Stein, J. (2003). TV's top gun. *Time*, 5 May (pp. 71–72).

Stempel, T. (1996). *Storytellers to the nation: A history of American television writing* (p. 237). Syracuse, NY: Syracuse University Press.

Sullivan, P. A. and Goldzwig, S. R. (Eds.). (2004). *New approaches to rhetoric*. Thousand Oaks, CA: Sage Publications.

Television and the mind, the infinite mind. (2002). New York: Lichtenstein Creative Media. Broadcast on National Public Radio, 2 October.

The Thursday factor (2005). *TV Guide*, 5 June, p. 10.

Timberg, B. (2000). The unspoken rules of television talk. In H. Newcomb (Ed.), *Television: The critical view* (6th ed.). New York: Oxford University Press.

Tomashoff, C. (2005). Does CSI make people smarter? *TV Guide*, 25 September–1 October (p. 29).

Torres, S. (2003). *Black. white. and in color: Television and black civil rights*. Princeton: Princeton University Press.

Turner, C. R. (2002). Product placement of medical products. Presented at the conference of the National Communication Association, New Orleans, November 23, 2002.

Unger, A. (1997). It's the writing, stupid. *Television Quarterly, 4*, 10–23.

Vande Berg, L. R., Wenner, L. A., & Gronbeck, B. E. (1998). *Critical approaches to television*. Boston: Houghton Mifflin.

Vedantam, S. (2001). A hit to our psyche. *The Washington Post National Weekly Edition*, 19–25 November (p. 34).

Viewer reaction saves Cagney and Lacey (1984). *Dallas Morning News*, 17 February (p. C11).

Wallace, K. (1971). The substance of rhetoric: Good reasons. In R. L. Johannesen (Ed.), *Contemporary theories of rhetoric: Selected readings*. New York: Harper and Row.

Wasko, J., Ed. (2005). *A companion to television*. Malden, MA: Blackwell.

Watson, J. & Hill, A. (2003). *Dictionary of media and communication studies* (6th ed.). London, UK: Arnold.

Webster, J. G., Phalen, P. F., & Lichty, L. W. (2000). *Ratings analysis: The theory and practice of audience research* (2nd ed). Mahwah, NJ: Lawrence Erlbaum.

Wells, W., Burnett, J., & Moriarty, S. (2003). *Advertising: Principles and practices* (6th ed.). (p. 271). Upper Saddle River, NJ: Prentice Hall.

Wilkins, L. & Patterson, P. (1987). Risk analysis and the construction of news. *Journal of Communication, 37*(3), Summer, pp. 80–92.

The William S. Paley Television Festival. (2001). *CSI: Crime scene*. #63602, 3 March. [seminar on videotape] Beverly Hills: Museum of Television and Radio.

Williams, R. (1974). *Television: Technology and cultural form*. London, UK: Fontana.

Williams, R. (1989). Drama in a dramatised society. In A. O'Connor (Ed.), *Raymond Williams on television* (pp. 3–13). London, UK: Routledge.

Wollen, P. (1997). Ways of thinking about music video (and postmodernism). In P. Brooker & W. Brooker (Eds.), *Postmodern after-images: A reader in film, television and video* (pp. 229–232). London, UK: Arnold.

Writers Guild of the East (n.d.) The Late Show with David Letterman. Museum of Television and Radio, New York.

Wykes, M. & Gunter, B. (2005). *The media and body image: If looks could kill.* Thousand Oaks, CA: Sage Publications.

Index

20/20, 119
24, 12, 37, 45,122-123
24-hour news, 103 (table),
      115,117, 122–123
48 Hours, 104 (table),119
60 Minutes, 104 (table), 118

ABC Family channel, 123
Academic critics, xvii
A.C. Nielsen Company, 23
Actors, 66, 81, 122. *See also*
      CSI, actors; Female actors
Advertising:
   actors and, 29
   appeal to gays and lesbians, 173
   as entertainment, 29–30
   cost of, 25–26
   demographics. *See* Demographics
   logos in, 140-141
   MTV and, 188
   postmodernist, 190
   scheduling, 32
   Super Bowl, 25–26
African Americans, 8, 150–151, 154,
      171–172, 174
Age:
   of actors, 122
   of characters, 174
   of viewers. *See* Demographics
agenda-setting, 145
Airports, xiv
All My Children, 126, *145*

Allen, R. C., 126
Allen, S., 112
Alley, R. S., 37
Allusions, 79, 111–112, 186
Amanpour, C., 117
American culture. *See also* Values,
      147, 148, 166
*American Family: Journey of
      Dreams,* 171–172
American Idol, 31,128, 167, 216
American Playhouse, 40
An American Family, 127
Analysis, 88–92, 199–200,
      209–211, 219–221. *See also*
      Television criticism
Anchors, 115, 116, 147
Angels In America, 63–64, 82–83, 125
Animal Planet, xiv, 9, 32
Animated shows, 39, 101 (table),
      110–111. *See also The Simpsons*
Aniston, J., 143
Antigone, 77
Apple Computer, 25–26
Apprentice, The, 128
AQRI rule, 29
Arbitron Company, 23
Archetypes, 83-85, 202
Aristotle, 74, 140–141
Armstrong, L., 144
Arnold, C. C., 148
Art direction, 62–63
Arthur (the Aardvark), 72, 129

Asian-Americans, 170–171, 174
Assistant directors, 41
At the Intersection: Cultural Studies and Rhetorical Studies (Rosteck), 137
Athletes, as heroes, 85, 88
Audience research, 8, 22
Audience. *See* Viewers, Live audience
Auerback, L., 42
Aufderheide, P., 189
Avins, M., 37

Baby Boomers, 23
Bachelor, The, 76, 128
Bacon, F., 141
Baker, R., 124
Balto, 72
Barbaro, 88
Barnouw, E., 30
Barrecca, R., 173
Barthes, R., 75–76
Bateson, G., 176
Battlestar Galactica, 36
Bauder, D., 27
Baudrillard, J., 183, 193
Becker, 167
Bell, D., 191
Berko, L., 183, 192
Berman, G., 98
Best, S., 183–184, 191, 193–194
Bianco, R., 5, 123
Biggest Loser, The, 78
Bignell, J., 128, 185–186, 192–193
Black and white television, 63
Blocking, 66
Blogs, 39, 183
Bochco, S., 38–39
Bogle, D., 171–172
Brand, J., 42
Brand identity, 9
Braun, L., 27
Briggs A., xv
British cultural studies, 151–152
British television, 17, 119, 124
Broday, B., 188

Brown, J. A., 5
Brown, N., xv
Bruckheimer, J., 11–12, 219. See also *CSI: Crime Scene Investigation*
Bruner, J., 167–168
Bryant, D. C., 142
Buffy, the Vampire Slayer, 45, 129
Burke, K., 143–145, 165–166
Burnett, R., 112
Burrows, J., 110
Business of television, 15, 21–48, 79, 176. *See also* Advertising

Cable channels:
    advertising, 22, 37
    business, 15
    censorship absence, 16
    eroding network viewership, 31
    executives, xvii
    news. *See* Cable News Network, Fox News
    pitches to, 35
    postmodernism on, 187
    ratings, 24
    scheduling, 34
    target audiences, 32–33, 129
    See also Technologies
Cable News Network (CNN), 32, 103, 115, 117
Caesar, S., 38, 112
Cagney and Lacey, 27
Camera shots, 45, 52–54, 60–61, 57, 209
Campbell, G., 141
Campbell, J., 86, 88
Cancelled shows, 27
Cancer, 44,110
Candid Camera, 127
Cannon, D., 41, 218, 222
Capitalism. *See also* Business, 148, 191
Carol Burnett Show, The, 112, 187
Carpenter, E., 177
Carson, J., 112
Caruso, D., 173

Carter, C., 15
Cartoon Network, 129
Casey, P, 39
Casting, 42-43, 157–158
Categories. *See* Genres
Celebrity news, 104, 119
Cellular phones, xiv, 182
Censorship, 15, 34, 44, 123
Channel One, xiv
Challenger, xvi, 85
*Channeling Blackness: Studies
    on Television and Race in
    America* (Hunt), 174
Characters, 80–83, 86, 101–109, 208
Charlie Rose, 64, 114
Chase, D., 123
Chicago Hope, 31
Chiklis, M., 120
Children's television, 97, 109, 129
Children's Television Act, 129
Chocano, C., 77
Ciesielski, D., 144
Civil Rights Movement, 177
Class, social, 151, 174
Clifford the Big Red Dog, 72,129
Close to Home, 120
Close-up shot, 52
CNN. *See* Cable News Network
Coca, I, 112
Coca Cola, xv, 29, 31
Codes, 154–158, 207–208
Cohn, R., 82
Cold Case, 120
Collective memory, 176–177
Collins, J., 79–80
Colors, 62–63, 222
Comedy. *See* Situation comedies
Comic Visions (Marc), 110
Commander-in-Chief, 122
Commercials, 22, 24, 29–30, 58, 206.
    See also Advertising
Communication, 140, 143–144
Computers, xv, 169. *See also* Technologies
Context, 206–207

Conway, T., 12
Cops, 59, 127–128
Cosby Show, The, 8, 139, 144, 171, 174
Costas, B., 129
Costumes, 208
Couldry, N., 152
Couric, K., 115
Credits, 222, 225–226
Crime shows, 77, 97, 104 (table),
    120–121. *See also* specific
    crime shows
Criminal Minds, 121
Crichton, M., 171
Criticism. *See* Television criticism
Crosby, J., 4
CSI: Crime Scene Investigation, xvii, 37,
    40–41, 72, 81–82 154, 215–231
    actors, 40, 81–82, 224, 240
    criticism, 215–231
    career influence of, 216
    encoding/decoding, 154–155
    female characters, 154–155
    forensic science in, 11
    laboratory equipment, 121, 218
    spin-offs, 216
    staff, 37–38
    story ideas, 40–41
Cultivation studies, 7
*Cultural Contradictions of
    Capitalism, The* (Bell), 191
Cultural criticism, 137
Cultural norms, 97, 99
Cultural studies, 8, 149–159
Cultural Studies: The Basics (Lewis), 149
Culture, 149, 167, 191
Cunningham, S., 194
Cutting. *See* editing
CW channel, 129

Dae Kim, D., 170
*Daily Show With Jon Stewart,
    The*, 113, 187
Dancing with the Stars, 167
Dateline, 119

Dating Game, The, 17
David Letterman. See *Late Night With David Letterman*
Davies, M., 29
Davis, G., 12
Dawson's Creek, 129
Day After, The, 29
Daytime dramas. *See* Soap operas
Daytime talk shows, 102 (table), 113
de Certeau, M., 71
Decency, xvii. *See also* Censorship
Decoding, 154–156, 158–159, 166
DeGeneres, E., 46, 173
Della Femina, J., 26
Deming, C., 186
Democracy, 148
Demographics, 23, 36, 205–206
Denver Post, The, 98
Descartes, R., 183–184
Designated market areas (DMA), 24
Desperate Housewives, 87, 98
Detective stories, 104 (table).
    See also Crime shows
Diachronic sequence, 90–91
Dialog, 208
Digital insertion, 31
Digital video recorders (DVRs), 24, 188
Digital video, xv, 56–57, 188.
    See also Technologies
DiMaggio, M., 81
Directors, 41–42, 65–66
Disabilities, 174, 230
Discovery channel, 9
Disney channel, 9, 129
Diversity, 116, 120, 153–154,
    170–173, 230
Docudramas, 107 (table), 125
Dominant groups, 170
Donahue, A., 40, 224
Dourdan, G., 224, 230
Dramas, 54–55, 97, 119, 104–106
    (table), 123
Dr. Phil, 113
DVDs, xv. *See also* Technologies

E! Entertainment Television channel, 119
Early Show, The, 30, 118
Eco, U., 79–80
Economics. *See* Business
Editing, 59–61, 157
Elbows shot, 53
Electronic communications technologies.
    See Technologies
Elizabeth Smart Story, The, 125
Ellen, 173
Elvis, 125
E-mail, 182
Emmy awards, 34, 83, 95
Encoding, 154–156, 163, 166
Encyclopedia of Television, 5, 27
England. *See* British television
Enigma, 75–76, 226
Ensemble casts, 43, 100, 119, 122
Entertainment Tonight (ET), 119
ER, 10, 17, 33, 42–44, 55, 60–62, 72,
    78–79, 81, 122, 150, 170, 204
E-Ring, 12, 122–123
Ethnicity. *See* Race and
    ethnicity, *Diversity*
Ethnocentrism, 148
Ethos, 140
Everybody Loves Raymond, 39
Executives, xvii, 15, 33–35
Extras, 43
*Extreme Makeover: Home
    Edition,* 31, 128

Facial expressions, 55, 208,
    220, 223, 229
Family dramas, 106, 123
Family Ties, 42
Farhi, P., xiv, 172
Father Knows Best, 173
Federal Bureau of Investigation
    (FBI), 35, 120–121
Federal Communications
    Commission (FCC), xvii, 24
Fejes, F., 173
Felicity, 129

Female characters:
  changing roles of, 97, 173
  CSI, 154, 173
  ER, 150, 204
  idealized image of, 150, 154–155,
    173, 176, 229–330
  lead, 120
Female viewers, 22, 27, 44
Fenelon, F., 141
Film (celluloid), 56–57, 58
First Amendment, xvii
Firsthand experience, xv–xvi
Fisher, W., 71
Fiske, J., 155–159, 188
Flashbacks, 121, 219
Flintstones, The, 110
Flow, 32–33, 152
Focus groups, 36
For the Love of a Child, 125
Ford, G., 85
Formulas, 77–78, 96
Foster H., 192
Foucault, 191–192
Fox channel, xiv, xvii, 98, 117, 118
Fox, M. J., 42
France, 191
Franklin, N., 145
Franz, D., 29, 120
Frasier, 39, 56, 73, 77, 90–91, 148
Free speech, xvii
Friedlander, L., 189
Friends, xv, 25, 29, 35, 42, 72–73
FX channel, 9, 16

Gallagher, V., 153, 154, 158
Game shows, 109, 129
Gandolfini, J. 173
Gans, H. J., 148
Gaonkar, D., 138
Gays and lesbians, 8, 99, 173
General Electric, 30
Generation X, 23
Genres, 95–132, 101–109
  (table), 201, 203

George Lopez, 171
Gergen, K. J., 189
Gitlin, T., 36
Good Morning America, 30, 118
Gould, J., 4
Ghost Whisperer, 124
Golden Globes, 34
Good Morning America, 118
Grazer, B., 37
Greece, 140, 141. *See also* Aristotle
Grey's Anatomy, 122, 170, 175
Grammer, K., 186
Groening, M., 39–40
Gunsmoke, 63

Hail, 155
Hall, B., 37–38
Hall, R. D., 230
Hall, S., 152, 154–156, 164, 166, 167
Hallmark Hall of Fame, 40, 125
Hammock scheduling, 33
Handheld camera, 59
Hart, R., 71, 86
HBO, 16, 34, 58–59, 63–64, 70, 82, 125
HDTV. *See* High-definition digital
  television
Headline News, 117
Hearing-impaired character, 174
Heath, R., 144
Hegemony, 153, 210
Helgenberger, M., 82, 219
Henry, W., 93
Hermeneutics, 75, 203, 226
Heroes, 85, 87–88, 202
High-definition television (HDTV),
  xiv, 57–58, 67, 165
Hill, A., 71
Hill, P. 44
Hill Street Blues, 27, 78
Hilliard, R., 81
Hispanics, 154, 170, 171
History:
  collective memory of, 177
  television, 61, 63, 97, 112, 131

Homosexuality. 8, 99. *See also*
    Gays and lesbians
Honeymooners, The, 5
Horan, M., 39
Hospital dramas, 122. *See also* specific
    hospital dramas
House, 53, 56, 60, 62, 122
Households Using Television (HUT), 26
Human Communication as Narration
    (Fisher), 71
Hunt, D. M., 174
Hybrid:
    dramas, 106, 123–124
    genres, 186, 201
    pitch, 36
    shows, 95–96, 98
Hyperreality, 193

Identification, 143–144, 160, 211
Identity. 86, 92, 159, 160, 169
Ideology, 15, 153, 158, 160, 210, 229
Illusion, 168. *See also* Representation
I Love Lucy, 4–5, 63, 97
Images:
    in collective memory, 83–85, 177
    MTV, 188–190
    need for 169–170
    repeated, xvi, 193
    technologies, 169, 181
    as visual representation, 164–169,
        176–177
    of women, 154–155
Individualism, 148
Industrial Revolution, xv
Influence of television, 145–146, 194
Information talk shows, 102, 114
Intentionality, 142
Internal Affairs Bureau (IAB), 120
International viewers, 16–17
Internet, xv. *See also* Web sites
Interpretation, 7, 75, 158, 165–166,
        209, 212. *See also* Decoding
Intertextuality, 79, 111–112, 186–187

*Invasion of the Body
    Snatchers*, 98–99, 187
Invasion, 98, 124, 187
Investigative shows, 104, 118
Iraq, 115, 117

James, K., 173
Jameson, F., 184
Jencks, C., 185
Jeopardy!, 27, 28–29, 130
Jericho, 124, 174
Jerry Springer Show, The, 113
Joan of Arcadia, 27–28
Johnson, H., xiii
Journalistic critics, xvii
Jung, G. C., 83-84

Kanner, E., 42
Kaplan, A., 190–191
Karen Sisko, 88
Kennedy, J., 191
Kennedy, J. F., xvi, 85
Kellner, D., 183, 191,193
Kellogg, R., 86–87
Kelley, D., 37,38
*Key Concepts in Communication
    and Culture* (O'Sullivan), 99
King, L., 114
King of Queens, The, 173, 207
Kingston, A., 122
Kirschenbaum, A., 12
Kushner, T., 82

Lackawanna Blues, 125
Language, 146
Larry King Live, 114
Las Vegas, 122
Las Vegas, 216, 217, 218
Late night programming, 32, 64,
        101–102 (table), 112–113
Late Show with David Letterman,
        35, 64, 101 (table), 112, 190
Laugh tracks, 98

Laurie, H., 122
Law & Order:
  real-life references in, 13–14
  school shootings in, 10–11
  story ideas, 39, 79, 121, 139
Law & Order SVU, 11
Lead-ins, 220, 224–225
Leave it to Beaver, 173
Lee, D., 39
Leno, J., 64
Leonard, S., 110
Letterman, D., 190
Lévi-Strauss, C., 89–92
Lewis, J., 149, 152–153
Lieberman, D., 28
Lifetime channel, 9, 32
Lighting, 55–56, 157, 209
Line producer, 37
Lipsitz, G., 177
Littlefield, W., 42
Littman, J., 218–219
Live audience, 62, 64, 98, 112, 113
Lloyd, C., 39
Local news, 103, 115–116
Logos, 140, 141
Long shot, 52, 53
Look, program, 207
Look. *See* Style
Loory, S. H., 117
Los Angeles Times, 5
Los Angeles, 28, 45, 218
Lost, 32, *105,* 170, 187
Lyotard, J. F., 183, 192–193

MacNeil, R., 116
Made-for-television movies,
  61, 72, 125
MadTV, 112
Magazine shows, 103–104, 117–119
Makeup, 208
Malinowski, B., 86
Mannoni, O., 169
Marc, D., 110, 166, 178

Marcus, J., 8, 35
Market research, 36
*M*A*S*H,* 72, 158
Mass audience, xvii
MasterCard, 29–30
Masterpiece Theatre, 24, 72, 124
Maury Show, The, 113
May, R., 85
Meaning, 7, 14, 149–159, 166–167,
  211, 229. *See also* Codes
Mead, G. H., 170
Medical dramas. *See* Hospital dramas
Medium, 123–124
Medium shot, 52–53
Meet the Press, 116
Memory, collective, 176–177
Mendolsohn, C., 40, 218
Mercedes Benz, 29
Methodology, 18
Meyer, J., 12
Meyrowitz, J., xv, 85
Middle-aged characters, 174
Milch, D., 17
Miller, B., 43
Miniseries, 106, 119
Minority groups, 171
Minority viewers, 28
Mitchell, J. T., 164
Mittell, J., 131
Modernism, 183–184, 193
Monaco, P., 52, 70
Monk, 201–202
Monroe, M., 191
Moonves, Leslie, 31, 42
Morals, 147. *See also* Values
Morphology, 75
Morphology of the Folktale
  (Propp), 75
Movies, history, 54
Movies, 52, 54, 55, 56, 57,
  60, 61, 63, 64, 65
MSNBC, 117
MTV, 9, 129, 188–190

Multi-camera production/production, 54, 55, 58, 60, 65, 66
Multiple story lines, 78
Murder in a Small Town X, 98
Murphy Brown, 110
Museum of Television and Radio, 32, 111, 116, 217–218
Music, codes in, 157, 209
Music videos, 188–190
Mystery!, 72, 80, 124–125
Myth, 85–90

Narratives:
  analysis, 92
  characters, 80–83, 86
  definition, 73–74
  forms of, 71
  structure, 69–70, 77–78, 88–92
  television, 69–70, 72–73, 77–82, 87–89, 192, 202, 226-228
  theories, 74–77
  tradition of, 70–72
Narrowcasting, 31–32
National Association for the Advancement of Colored People (NAACP), 172
National Audience Demographics (NAD), 24
National news shows, 102, 115
Native Americans, 175
Nature of Narrative, The (Scholes), 86–87
Navarro, M., 171
NCIS, 121
Needs of viewers, 169
Negotiated meaning, 155
Nehamas, A., xvi
Nelson, C., 138
Nelson, R., 185–186
New media. *See* Technologies
New Technologies. *See* Technologies
Newcomb, H., 14, 37, 131
News anchors, 115, 116, 147
NewsHour with Jim Lehrer, The, 116

News in television stories.
    See Real-life references
News shows, 32, 59, 70, 102–103 (table), 114–117, 148
News-talk-entertainment shows, 102–103 (table), 114–118, 148
New Yorker, 145
New York Herald Tribune, 4
New York Times, The, 4, 5
Nichols, M., 63
Nickelodeon channel, 129, 187
Nielsen Homevideo Index (NHI), 24
Nielsen Media Research, 24, 28
Nielsen ratings system, 23, 28
Nielsen Station Index (NSI), 24
Nielsen Syndicated Service (NSS), 24
Nielsen Television Index (NTI), 24
Nighttime talk shows, 101–102 (table), 112–113
Nixon, A., 44–45, 126
Numb3rs, 12, 121
NYPD Blue, 17–18, 29, 59–60, 120

Obscenity, xvii. *See also* Censorship
OC, The, 123
Off-the-hour scheduling, 33
Once and Again, 99
Ontiveros, L., 171
Opening segment, 204, 226
Oppositions, 77, 90–91
Oprah, 113
Ostrow, J., 98
"Other", representation of, 170–171, 228–229

Pacino, A., 82–83
Packer, B., 129
Panavision, 58
Parachute journalism, 115
Parents, representation of, 174
Parody, 111, 187
Pastiche, 184
Pathos, 140
Pay-per-view, xv

PBS. *See* Public Broadcasting Service

Pecora, N., 129

Peoplemeter, 23, 28

Perception, viewer 6, 143, 146, 167

Persuasion. *See also* Rhetoric, 138–139, 140–141, 148, 160

Petersen, W., 81, 173, 218, 219

Piaget, J., 89

Picture Theory (Mitchell), 164

Pilots, 35, 36

Pitches, 35–36

Playhouse 90, 5

Pleasure:
    viewer, 145, 158–159, 187, 230

Plots, 74, 101–109

Poetics (Aristotle), 74

Poltrack, D., 27

Polysemy, 150–151, 160, 187

Pomerantz, E., 174

Popular language, 146

Porter, M, 92

Poster, M., 182

Postmodernism, 181–195

Postmodern television, 185–190

Postmodern theories, 191–195

Povich, M., 113

Power, 152–153, 170, 210, 228

Practice of Everyday Life, The (de Certeau), 71

Presidents:
    fictional, 122

Price is Right, The, 130

Prime time, 32

Prison Break, 122–123

Procter & Gamble, 44

Producers, 37–38, 44, 61, 69, 153, 166, 171, 218

Producer's Medium, The (Newcomb), 37

Product placement, xv, 30–31, 120–121, 218, 222

Production, 34–37, 43–45, 58–59, 97

Production design, 61–64

Program genres. *See* Genres

Program Web sites, 81, 200

Project for Excellence in Journalism, 30

Propp, V., 75

Public affairs shows, 118

Public Broadcasting Service (PBS), 25, 40, 124. *See also* British dramas

Public broadcasting sponsors 24–25

Race and ethnicity, 8, 144, 150–151, 170–172, 173. *See also* Diversity

Radio, 52–53

Radio Times, 122

Ratings, xvii, 22–28, 167

Reaction shots, 54–55

Reagan, R., 85

Realism. *See* Representation

Reality codes, 156–157

Reality shows, 108, 127–128

Real-life references, 9–12, 110, 122, 206–207

Reasoner, H., 118

Reed, J.S., 80

Reilly, K., 122

Reiner, C., 110

Representation, 157–158, 163–178, 229
    of age groups, 174
    business and, 176
    coding and, 156–158, 176.
        See also Codes
    definition, 164–165
    interpreting, 165–166
    of "other," 170, 174
    of racial groups. *See* Race and ethnicity
    of women. *See* Female characters
    of the world, 163–164

Representation: Cultural Representations and Signifying Practices (Hall), 164

Rhetoric (Aristotle), 140

Reverse angle shot, 54

Rhetoric, 138–144, 160–161
    television, 145–147

Rhetorical criticism, 137–145

Rich, L., 37

"Ripped from the headlines."
    See Real-life references

Rituals, 84–85
Roddenberry, G., 27, 36
Romeo and Juliet, 71
Rose, C., 114
Rosenberg, E., 82
Rosenberg, H., 5
Rosenthal, P., 39
Rosteck, T., 137–138, 160
Roth, P., 35

Satellite radio, 182
Satellite television, 22, 63, 187.
    See also Technologies
Satellites, in news reporting, 114, 115
Satire, 111
*Saturated Self: Dilemmas of Identity
    in Contemporary Life,
    The* (Gergen), 189
Saturday Night Live, 112
Sawyer, D., 118
Scanzoni, R., 46
Scheduling, 32–33
Schindel, B., 11
Scholes, R., 86–87
School shootings, 9–11
Schwarzenegger, A., 113
Science fiction, 108, 127
Scott, R., 26
Scripts, 43–44
Searle, J. R., 142
Seinfeld, 73
Senior citizen characters, 174
September 11, 2001. *See* World
    Trade Center attacks
Series television, 70, 72, 119
Sesame Street, 109 (table), 129, 147
Sets, 45, 62, 207–208, 222
Sex in the City, 110
Sexuality, 123, 129–130, 173
Shales, T., 5
Shalhoub, T., 200
Shares, 26–27
Shield, The, 120–121
Show runner, 37

Shots. *See* Camera shots
Showtime channel, 34
Siegler, S., 45–46
Silverstone, R., 92–93
Simon, R., 128
Singer, J., 176–177
Single-camera production, 58–59
Simpsons, The, 39, 79, 110–112, 186
Sitdown with the Sopranos, A
    (Barreca), 173
Situation comedies, 62–63, 97–98,
    100, 101 (table), 110–112
Slotkin, R., 85
Smarty Jones, 76
Smiley, T., 64
Smith, R. R., 84
Smith-Shomade, B., 171
Snap-zoom shots, 121, 222
Soap operas, 44, 97, 107
    (table), 125–126
Social class, 151, 174
Social codes, 156–158
Social comments, 110
Social issues, 126. *See also*
    real-life references
Social norms. *See* Cultural norms
Social positions, 155
Social types, 80
Solomon, J., 185, 189, 190
Solomon, K., 45
Sony, 58
Sopranos, The, 9–10, 31, 34, 44,
    55, 76–77, 123, 173, 187, 200
Sorkin, A., 38
Sound, 60, 65, 157, 209
South Africa, 144
Spielberg, S., 81
Spin-offs, 46, 73, 110, 216
Split screen, 64–65
Sponsors, 15, 24–25, 29–30, 44,
    190, 206, 225. *See also* Advertising
Sports, 30, 32, 59, 62, 65, 109, 128–129
Springer, J., 113
St. Augustine, 141

Stahl, L., 118
Star Trek, 27, 36, 127
Stark, S., 118, 126
Steadicam, 60–61
Stein, J., 218
Steinberg, H., 121
Stereotypes, 80, 170–171, 173
Stern, S., 174
Stevens, J., 39
Stewart, J., 113
Stories. *See* Narratives
Storytelling, 70–72, 93, 131
Streep, M., 82–83
Structure, program, 205
Structurist analysis, 89–92
Students, 3–4, 7
Studio One, 5
Style, 18, 51–67, 119, 181
Style, postmodern. *See* Postmodernism
Subgenres, 99, 101–109, 131
Subordinate groups, 170
Subtexts, 45, 83, 208, 223
Summer programming, 28
Super Bowl, 25–26
Supernatural powers, 87–88
Surfing, xiv
Survivor, 51, 128
Sweeps, 16, 23, 26, 45
Symbols, 142–144, 148, 168
Syntagmatic sequence, 90–91

Talk shows, 101–102 (table), 112–114
Tartikoff, B., 42
Tavis Smiley, 64
Technologies, 16, 57–58, 115,
    169, 181–182, 187–188
Telefilms. *See also* Miniseries, 106
Teleplays, 124
Teletubbies, 129
Television business. *See* Advertising,
    Business
Telecommunications Act, 57
Television compared to movies,
    52, 54, 55, 56, 61, 63, 65

Television critics, xvii, 4–6, 13–15
Television criticism:
    academic, xvi, xvii, 6, 14
    encoding and, 176
    genres and, 99
    guidelines, 199–212
    introduction to, 3–9, 17–19
    journalistic, 4–6
    process of 13–15, 17–18, 200–213
    purpose of, 3–4, 7, 213, 216
    questions for, 201–211
    representation and, 165, 175–176
    sample, 215–231
    writing of, 212
Television Critics Association, 36
Television Culture (Fiske), 156
Television genres. *See* Genres, 82
Television history, 61, 63,
    97, 112, 131
Television influence, xiii–xv,
    145–146, 194
Television technology.
    See Technologies
Television rhetoric, 145–147
*Television: The Critical
    View* (Newcomb), 14
Telos, 141
Tent-pole scheduling, 33
Terrorism, 12, 120
Text messaging, 182
Thaw, J., 80
Theme songs, 225, 226
Third Watch, 10, 170
Thompson, E., 82–83
Thompson, R., 11
Three-Hour Rule, 129
Timberg, B., 113
TiVo, 24, 188
Today, 30, 118
Tonight Show, The, 64, 112–113
Tragedies, 85
Treatment, 40–41
Trickster, 84
Turner, C., 31

Turner, T. *See also* Cable News
　　Network, 117
TV Barn Web site, 5

USA Today, 5, 23, 28

Values, 147–149, 210
van der Meer, G., 56
Variety comedy shows, 101, 112
VCRs, xv, 33
Viacom, 30
Viewers:
　　advertising and. *See* Demographics
　　age of. *See* Demographics
　　choices of, xiv,xv, xvi, 7, 188, 195
　　diversity of, 170–171
　　familiarity with TV conventions,
　　　　70, 73, 77, 80, 96
　　female, 22, 27, 44
　　genres and, 96
　　identity of, 160, 169
　　involvement of, 166–167, 155, 230
　　International, 16–17
　　keeping, 119, 126, 187–188, 225
　　meaning construction of, 14,
　　　　150–151, 154–155, 166
　　participation of, 167
　　perception of, 7, 143, 146, 167
　　pleasure of, 79, 145, 158–159,
　　　　187, 230
　　relationship with characters,
　　　　54, 81, 82
　　technologies and, 58
　　values of. *See* Values
Violence, 7–8
Villains, 75, 105, 109, 120, 202
Virtual reality, 182–183
Visual representation. *See*
　　Representation, Style
Visual style. *See* Style
Vivendi Universal, 30

Wagner, R., 56, 60
Wall Street Journal, 26

Wallace, K., 147
Walt Disney Company, 30, 35, 42
Wardrobe, 223
Warhol, A., 191
Warm Springs, 125
Warner Brothers, 34–35
Warren, A., 85
Washington Post, The, xiv, 5
Watson, J., 71, 78
Weather, 116
Web sites, 5, 81, 200
Webster, J.G., 23
Wellek, R., 85
Wells, J., 42, 122, 171
West Wing, The, 12, 122, 171
WGBH, 125
What is Post-Modernism
　　(Jencks), 185
Whitman, W., 9
Who, The 225
Who Wants to Be a Millionaire,
　　17, 29, 129–130
Wide-angle shot. *See* Long shot
Will & Grace, 8, 33, 171, 173
Williams, R., 33, 151–152, 169
Winfrey, O., 113
Without a Trace, 11, 33, 35–36,
　　55, 121
Wolf, D., 38, 39
Wollen, P., 188
Women in television. *See* Female
　　characters
Women viewers, 22, 27, 44
Wordsworth, W., 169
Working class characters. *See* Class,
　　social
Workplace dramas, 105 (table),
　　121–122
World news, 102 (table)
World Trade Center attacks,
　　xiii, xvi, 12, 85, 99, 177
World, representation of, 163–164
Writer's Guild of America, 40
Writers, 21, 35, 37, 38–40, 43

Writing process, 39–41, 43
Writing television criticism.
    See Television criticism

X-Files, The, 15–16, 87, 111, 186

Yes, Dear, 12
Young Americans, The, 31
Young & Rubicam, 29

Zuiker, A., 40, 218, 222, 219, 230

About the Author

Victoria O'Donnell is Professor Emeritus and former Director of the University Honors Program and Professor of Communication at Montana State University–Bozeman. Previously she was the Chair of the Department of Speech Communication at Oregon State University and Chair of the Department of Communication and Public Address at the University of North Texas. In 1988 she taught for the American Institute of Foreign Studies at the University of London. She received her Ph.D. from the Pennsylvania State University. She has published articles and chapters in a wide range of journals and books on topics concerning persuasion, the social effects of media, women in film and television, British politics, Nazi propaganda, collective memory, cultural studies theory, and science fiction films of the 1950s. She is also the author (with June Kable) of *Persuasion: An Interactive-Dependency Approach, Propaganda and Persuasion* (with Garth Jowett), *Readings in Propaganda and Persuasion: New and Classic Essays* (co-edited with Garth Jowett) and *Speech Communication*. She made a film, *Women, War, and Work: Shaping Space for Productivity in the Shipyards During World War II,* for PBS through KUSM Public Television at Montana State University. She has also written television scripts for environmental films and has done voice-overs for several PBS films. She has served on the editorial boards of several journals. The recipient of numerous research grants, honors, and teaching awards, including being awarded the Honor Professorship at North Texas State University and the Montana State University Alumni Association and Bozeman Chamber of Commerce Award of Excellence, she has been a Danforth Foundation Associate and a Summer Scholar of the National Endowment for the Humanities. She has taught in Germany and has been a visiting lecturer at universities in Denmark, Norway, Sweden, and Wales. She has also served as a private consultant to the U.S. government, a state senator, the tobacco litigation plaintiffs, and many American corporations.